BROWN BEAR
SUMMER

BROWN

Line drawings and maps by Elizabeth Mills

BEAR SUMMER

Life Among Alaska's Giants

Thomas Bledsoe

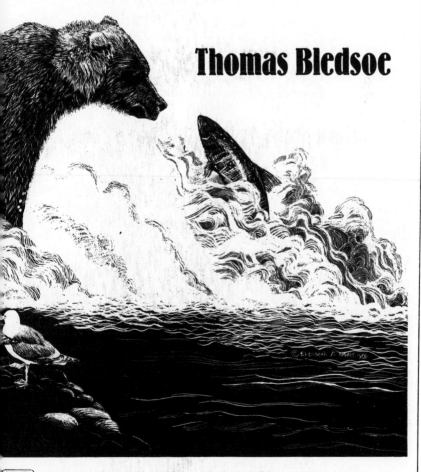

TRUMAN TALLEY BOOKS / E. P. DUTTON / NEW YORK

Published in the United States by
Truman Talley Books • E. P. Dutton,
a division of NAL Penguin Inc.,
2 Park Avenue, New York, N.Y. 10016.
Published simultaneously in Canada by
Fitzhenry & Whiteside Limited, Toronto.

Library of Congress Cataloging-in-Publication Data
Bledsoe, Thomas.
Brown bear summer.
"Truman Talley Books"
Bibliography: p.
Includes index.
1. Brown bear—Alaska—McNeil River State Game Sanctuary.
2. McNeil River State Game Sanctuary
(Alaska) I. Title.
QL737.C27B49 1987   599.74'446   86-27207
ISBN 0-525-24530-8

DESIGNED BY MARK O'CONNOR

10 9 8 7 6 5 4 3 2 1

First Edition

Contents

CONTENTS

Twenty-four pages of photographs follow page 120.

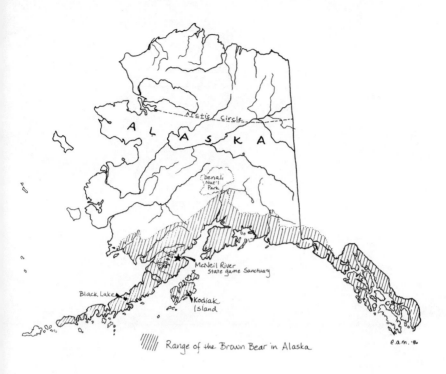

*The State of Alaska showing the range of Alaskan brown bears and
grizzly bears, the location of the McNeil River Sanctuary, Black Lake,
and Kodiak Island.*

Preface

McNeil River, Alaska, is the most incredible place on Earth to me. Where else can one observe thirty or more Alaskan brown bears on a beautiful white-water river going about their summer fishing activities without disturbance? At McNeil Falls, near the mouth of the river, the bears fish, interact, fight, mate, and play, with little or no regard for their human observers. Single bears, sows with cubs, and even large boars wander casually past people at distances as close as ten feet. Place this ursine spectacle in the wilderness splendor of the Alaska Peninsula and you have a wildlife experience unparalleled in the world.

I had the good fortune to spend three summers (1973–1975) studying the McNeil bears as part of a research project with Utah State University. This was indeed a dream come true for a wildlife biologist. In May 1973 I had never even seen a brown bear nor had I been to Alaska. That first summer I got a crash course in brown bear behavior and wilderness living, but it was the beginning of the best three summers of my life.

I first began work on this book in 1976. The first full-length draft was not completed until 1978, and was reorganized in 1984. Return visits to McNeil (summers of 1976, 1977, 1980, and 1984) continued to give me new insight into these remarkable and often puzzling creatures, so long-term study has provided a more accurate and comprehensive text.

It has been my intention from the beginning to make this a book about bear behavior and ecology and little else. I describe the summer of 1975, but I also refer to past and future events further to illustrate the bears' natural history. I made an effort to keep the involvement of people to a minimum. I felt that the McNeil bears could tell their own comprehensive life history without the interference of human problems, government bureaucracy, or details of how the study was conducted. Also, there is no mention of "bear tales," legend, or myth. I long ago discovered that all "tall bear tales" are about 99.9 percent fiction. On the other hand, in some of the events that I describe we appear rather cavalier in our attitude toward the bears, but I warn the reader that the McNeil bears are very "humanized." That is, they have become habituated to people and generally ignore their observers. The bear-human relations that I describe should not be taken as any sort of general rule in dealing with any bear. The McNeil bears are very special animals and my confidence around them was due to their uniqueness and to knowing each individual bear's personality well enough to know what he or she was likely to do in a given situation.

The documented history of McNeil River dates back to the early 1950s, when the U.S. Fish and Wildlife Service conducted some research on the bears, including predator control experiments. The Alaska Department of Fish and Game began tagging bears at McNeil for population studies in 1963; this work ended in 1972. The Utah State University project began in 1970 and ended with my last summer in 1975. Larry and Mo Aumiller became the Alaska Department of Fish and Game representatives at McNeil in 1976, and Larry remains at that post at this writing. Larry has diligently recorded data on all the bears for the past ten years, which, together with our study, provide comprehensive data on some bears from 1970 to the present, and some population data dating back to 1963. The result is over twenty years of information on some bears.

Many of the older bears have witnessed changes over the years at McNeil Falls. As late as 1970, very few people knew about the summer concentration of bears at McNeil, but by 1974 it had become so famous that many regulations were implemented by the Alaska Department of Fish and Game to limit and control the human impact on the bears. A maximum of ten people per day are allowed to visit the falls, and since demand today is often ten times that number, visitor permits are awarded by lottery each year.

The Alaska Department of Fish and Game has probably struck the best possible compromise between tourism and protecting the bears at the falls. This was reflected in the summer of 1985, when Larry Aumiller reported sighting a record ninety-seven different bears and cubs during the summer, including a record sixty-six present at the falls at one time. What a sight! It is my hope that they will remain protected on unspoiled land.

October 1986
Seattle, Washington

BROWN BEAR
SUMMER

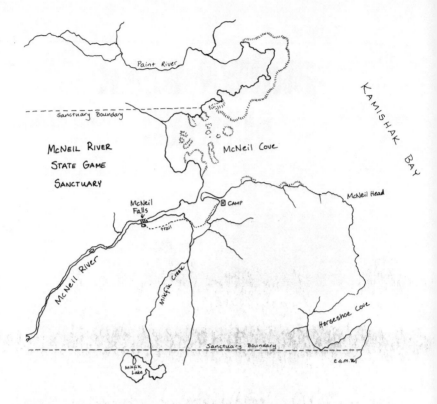

A detailed view of the McNeil River drainage area showing the McNeil River Sanctuary, camp, McNeil Falls, trails, Mikfik flats, Kamishak Bay, McNeil Head, and McNeil Cove.

1

Late Spring

McNeil Falls thundered in the distance for a moment and then the roar faded softly on the sea breeze until all was quiet and still. This simple sound, perhaps the most vivid in my mind, brought memories of the two previous summers rushing back to me. I stood alone on the beach of McNeil Cove and scanned the vast wilderness scene around me. The country was immense, quiet, and empty.

It was June 1, 1975, and I had one day to be completely alone at McNeil. Tomorrow, Jim Taggart, my co-worker, would arrive on the high tide with our second and final load of summer supplies. I had spent enough time here and I loved it so much that I felt a closeness with the country that was intensified by being alone. The familiar hum of Bill deCreeft's

"Beaver" float plane had already vanished out over Kamishak Bay, having deposited me and a planeload of gear on the beach near our camp. In the deep silence of early evening, I slowly began to perceive the subtle sights and sounds of McNeil.

I decided to put off setting up camp so that I could have a first look at the country in the evening light. I grabbed a chair from the tiny cabin and climbed a ladder to the flat roof and sat down, with the panorama of McNeil before me in a misty gold sunset (see plate 1). The sun shot between the mountains and clouds northwest of camp and poured down over McNeil Cove with the kind of deep intensity that can appear only at sunset from beneath dark clouds. The jagged peaks of the Aleutian Range lay buried in late spring snow and formed a steep frozen wall to the south and west. Patterns of deep purple and gold undulated across the slopes as the clouds formed and rolled, then disappeared beyond the pinnacles.

The source of the McNeil River plunged from one of the many small glaciers that lay hidden in protected bowls in these mountains. From its icy beginning, the McNeil flows north and then east until it emerges from the steep bluffs, winds across the tidal flats, and slips into the sea through a deep channel near our camp (see map on p. vii). The long days of early June were rapidly melting the snow and filling the river with a racing, foaming torrent of icy blue water. Again, the roar of McNeil Falls 1½ miles from camp drifted in and out on the sea breeze and alternated with the plaintive cry of the glaucous-winged gulls.

The lower mountain slopes were streaked with snowdrifts and greening alder brush all the way down to the tidal flats, where 20- and 30-foot drifts remained in the lee of the bluffs. East of camp the massive cliffs of McNeil Head jutted out into the sea and ended abruptly with sheer 700-foot cliffs plunging directly into the surf. The cool ocean breeze rose over the cliffs and formed soft wisps of fog that curled and billowed like giant breakers as it flowed softly down the slopes toward camp.

These were the sights and sounds that I remembered most from McNeil. It was a good welcome back for the summer. I felt a belonging, as though McNeil were a part of me and I had become a part of it.

The last streaks of sunlight were slanting across the tidal flats when I noticed two bears out on the flats about a half mile south of camp. They appeared to be together and one was quite large, so I assumed that it was an estrous sow with a large boar in mating consort. June is the most common month for mating so it was not unusual to see boars and sows in consort at this time. I was curious to know their identities, so I grabbed my binoculars and headed down to inspect them.

I followed the well-used trail that led down the beach, across the tidal flats, and eventually on to the falls. Six-foot snowdrifts remained on the beach, but they were rapidly melting, and already pale yellow shoots of wild celery and beach grass were reaching around the edges of the crusted snow. The plants had no patience with this late spring. Out on the tidal flats sharp points of sprouting sedge peppered the slimy mud on the scattered areas that were not still covered by a thick mantle of muddy ice. Soon I reached Mikfik Creek where it joins the McNeil (see map on p. xiv) and then I hiked along its banks until I had a clear view of the bears.

While en route I had noticed a few familiar characteristics of these bears and so I was almost certain I knew the pair. They undoubtedly were both McNeil residents because neither was concerned with my presence. This is because the resident McNeil bears have been habituated to the presence of humans, whereas nonresidents are usually frightened of people and will run when they encounter them. Now that I had a good close look, I could verify that they were Patches, a twenty-one-year-old boar, and White, a seven-year-old sow. Patches and White were both familiar to me and vice versa, so I moved closer to observe the pair.

White still wore her thick, creamy blond winter coat that made her look larger than her 300 pounds (all weights are estimates). She had a full "teddy bear" face and a fat, rounded belly that gave her the typical look of a sow. Patches' blond coat was marred by a large black bald spot that saddled across his hips and gave him his name. He weighed about 750 pounds, which is not particularly large for a twenty-one-year-old boar.

I was never quite sure if Patches had noticed me observing him that day. His apparent senility had grown worse each year and I was certain he also had very poor vision. I doubt if if he would have acknowledged my presence, even if he had noticed me, because, of all the McNeil bears, he was the most nonchalant toward people.

I had never noticed any evidence that White had been in estrous in previous years and her behavior now suggested that this might be one of her first estrous cycles. Patches obviously frightened her, for she moved away from him constantly while cautiously glancing back at him. Her ears were laid back against her neck and she cowered slightly, which were signs that she was either under stress or, in this case, just plain afraid. White's reaction to Patches was typical, because any young bear is afraid of an older or larger bear. When she was older, White would be less afraid of a boar consort.

White was moving fast and soon the pair disappeared in the alders on the edge of the flats. Patches would have to pursue her for at least a day or two and probably longer before White would begin to become habituated to his presence.

While walking back to camp, I reflected a bit on White's estrous condition. She was one of the six McNeil sows I had counted the summer before that potentially could have cubs this year, although realistically I hoped that two or three would show up with young. Several litters of cubs would make the summer very exciting, so I was especially interested when I noticed the tracks of a sow and two spring cubs on the beach near my trail. The smooth wet beach sand, freshly washed by tidal waters, was broken in a wandering line by the unequal tracks of the family. The large determined prints of the sow were braided unevenly by the tiny marks of two inquisitive cubs. Their tangled line of travel continued across the slick tidal mud flats toward the river and disappeared in the glare of the lingering sunset. Little did I know that those tracks were just the beginning of yet another summer filled with unbelievable observations of maternal behavior, some of which were previously undocumented.

The next morning I made a quick tour of the five structures in camp and found that everything, including the gear we had left in storage, had made it through the winter in good condition. I untied the nylon lines that had held the roofs on the two small corrugated steel cabins during the 80-knot winter storms, and then I swept out the dust and debris that had accumulated in the cabins during the past nine months. The two canvas wall tents that Jim and I would live in for the next three months were clean and dry inside the thick-walled cedar-shake sauna, which was located beside a pond 200 feet south of the two cabins. An elevated food cache and a cedar-shake outhouse were situated closer to the cabins.

Our little camp was literally on the beach of McNeil Cove. During high tides, the waves lapped within 10 feet of my wall tent. The location of the camp was a discreet 1½ miles from McNeil Falls, but its position was primarily a practical necessity, as it was the only protected beach area where float planes could land and unload people and supplies. The camp dated back over twenty years to the early 1950s, when the U.S. Fish and Wildlife Service first began research on the bears. The area was closed to hunting in 1955, and in 1967 the Alaska state legislature provided permanent protection by making approximately 72 square miles around the river a state sanctuary (see map on p. vii). Near the mouth of the river we found the ruins of a small native village from an unknown era and also a few broken-down cabins of a small mining town that had a brief history in the 1920s (see map on p. xiv). No one knows how these early inhabitants affected the bears, but today the McNeil brownies use the immediate area during the summer with very little disturbance.

The bears congregate each summer on McNeil Falls to fish for chum salmon. The falls is not a true falls in the usual sense; rather it is a 300-foot stretch of violent white water located a mile from the mouth of the river (plate 2). This falls is created by a descending series of conglomerate rock slabs in the riverbed, which also create many excellent fishing spots for the bears along the riverbank. The chum salmon are not powerful swimmers, so they are easy prey for the bears. I have seen as many as thirty-five bears fishing on the falls at one time, and sixty to seventy different bears will fish during July and August.

This concentration of fishing bears makes McNeil Falls an

ideal outdoor laboratory for the study of brown bear behavior. Each summer these solitary, asocial animals are brought together into an intensely competitive situation and forced to deal with one another in a social context. Aggression runs high and bears interact constantly with one another. Every day it is possible to observe and document behaviors at the falls that would never be seen among solitary bears in open country. Furthermore, the same bears return every year, which makes it possible to follow the behavioral development of many individuals.

We had the perfect location for a behavioral study that was also a very timely undertaking. There was a total lack of field studies on brown bear behavior. There had been ecological field studies that dealt with home range, seasonal movements, denning, reproduction, and food habits, but their behavior in the wild remained essentially unexplored. The importance of behavioral study was apparent in newspaper headlines of the bear-human conflicts in national parks and elsewhere. Clearly there was an urgent need for more understanding of the behavior of wild brown bears.

The coastal brownies at McNeil are the same species (*Ursus arctos*) as the interior grizzly bear. In fact, this single species includes all North American, European, and Asian brown bears, as well as all North American grizzlies. There are subtle morphological differences between the grizzly and brown bear, but size is the most obvious variable. Brown bears attain a size easily twice as large as the interior grizzlies because of their habitat and diet. The longer growing season, lush vegetation, and, most important, the abundant salmon of the coastal areas are all factors that contributed to the evolution of the large size of brown bears. In contrast, the short growing season and leaner diet of the interior grizzlies mandate a smaller body size.

The range of brown bears in Alaska follows roughly the coastal areas where salmon runs are plentiful in the summer. Grizzlies range over most other interior areas. The famous Kodiak Island brown bears are often thought to be the largest of all brown bears, but this reputation is partly due to the well-established trophy hunting on the island. Bears on the Alaska Peninsula, which includes McNeil River, reach sizes equal to those on Kodiak Island.

The beautiful weather on my first day added to my excitement about the summer. It was difficult to keep my mind on setting up and organizing camp when I could have been beachcombing or hiking on the alpine tundra of McNeil Head. I was thankful to hear Bill deCreeft's plane in the distance the next afternoon with Jim and the rest of our gear onboard. The plane was unloaded quickly, and when Bill took off he was our last contact with the outside world for the next five weeks. We had no radio equipment, and no planes were due until after the first of July, when an Alaska Department of Fish and Game technician would arrive in advance of the first tourists. These visitors would begin arriving the first or second week in July, when the bears began fishing on the falls. The number of both tourists and fishing bears peaks in late July and then dwindles by mid-August. Jim and I always relished our June isolation because all the subtle activities of McNeil carried on more naturally when few people were around.

The final leg of our annual trip from Logan, Utah, to McNeil was finally completed. We had flown from Salt Lake City to Anchorage with most of our essential gear. I'm sure the airline agents hated to see us approach with thirty-five odd-shaped boxes and packs. In Anchorage we rented a van and spent three days assembling food and more supplies before driving 220 miles down the Kenai Peninsula to Homer, a small, picturesque fishing village that would be our final stop. The only access to McNeil from Homer was by chartered float plane. We always used Bill deCreeft's Kachemak Air Service for the 140-mile flight across Cook Inlet. Bill's "Beaver" float plane could carry about one-half of our summer gear, so two trips timed on the high tide were necessary. Much of our life at McNeil was timed by the tides, which could rise and fall as much as 28 feet.

I couldn't have found a better man than Jim Taggart to work with me. He was a mountain climber, rock climber, runner, hiker, wilderness skier, naturalist, and a real adventurer. Jim explored the McNeil country more than anyone had ever done and was responsible for finding trails and routes into previously unexplored areas. Hikes and climbs with Jim gave me much more insight into the country than I would have had without him. Sometimes, while trying to keep up with him, I felt like 5 feet of his blond 6-foot frame was all leg.

It was sunny and calm, so we wasted no time in unpacking and putting up our wall tents and cook tent. Only the occasional hammering of a nail or stake broke the silence and resounded off the bluffs. Now and then we were startled by a cracking explosion as the ice and snow covering the flats began to break up. Twice each day the warm tide advanced on the icy mantle and slowly tore small black icebergs from its edges. These rafts of ice, which were often 20 feet across and 2 feet thick, floated about on the currents of the tide and rammed into other ice formations and massive cornices of snow and accelerated the breakup of the ice-clogged cove. As the tide receded, the crashing and splintering of ice ended and the floating pieces silently rode the tide out to sea.

Early evening found us finished and sitting on top of our cabin with spotting scopes to observe the flats and bluffs. We saw no bears, but this was expected as very few bears arrive on the flats until mid- to late June. An occasional young bear or estrous sow with a boar consort might stop briefly on the flats, but generally we saw foxes, bald eagles, and very rarely moose, wolves, and wolverines.

The summertime concentration of salmon-fishing bears around McNeil gives the impression that there is an enormous permanent population of bears in the immediate area, but this is not the case. For most of the bears, McNeil is only one stop in their annual range, which may extend over 60 miles of country. From late August until late June of each year most of the bears are in other areas and very few are found around McNeil.

The annual activities of the McNeil bears center primarily on feeding on salmon, berries, and, to a lesser degree, the sedge that grows on the tidal flats. Their year usually begins in

April when most bears emerge from their dens with the first signs of spring. This is the leanest time for the bears because no reliable food is available from the snow-covered land. They wander in search of the carcasses of animals that died during the long winter, and sometimes they prey on animals weakened by the winter and the old, sick, or newborn animals. Some beachcomb for beached whales, walrus, seals, and sea lions, and for clams and even seaweed. The sprouting grasses, forbs, and particularly the protein-rich sedges in June provide the first dependable food for the hungry bears. Then the vital salmon runs begin in late June, peak in July and August, and continue sporadically through the fall. Finally, a variety of berries are very important in late summer and fall until the bears den in November.

2

New Beginnings

During the first two weeks of June the McNeil bears were still in the springtime wandering and searching stage of their annual schedule, so we rarely spotted any of our ursine friends. This was our time to relax and enjoy all aspects of McNeil from beachcombing and hiking to digging for clams and fishing for king salmon. Late evening always found us sitting on top of our cabin to take in the spectacular scenery and to watch for arriving bears.

I remember one evening in mid-June 1973 that was unusually enjoyable. A strong west wind had blown afternoon showers over the area, and straight curtains of rain had fallen in the dead calm that followed the wind. Heavy wetness hung in the air long after the rain had stopped and the drenched landscape was clean and crisp. The tide shimmered like a glowing mirror with sharp reflections of snow-covered mountains. The higher peaks held wispy remnants of the showers in protected bowls as streams of setting sun shot randomly through the clouds and set the lush green flats ablaze with color. McNeil was good to us and we were glad to be there.

The day was just fading into twilight when I noticed three bears ambling along the beach toward the sedge flats. A quick glance with my spotting scope revealed them to be a sow and a pair of two-year-old cubs. They were too far away for identification, so we scrambled off the cabin roof and headed down the beach for a closer look. We stopped at the end of the beach behind a sandbar to avoid being seen. From this closer vantage point, I could identify Goldie, a familiar McNeil sow of unknown age, and her two cubs. The two cubs lagged behind and played while Goldie strolled along toward the flats. Goldie was a shy sow who usually avoided people, so I decided we should remain hidden to avoid spooking her.

Goldie's cubs were average size for their age. They were great golden balls of fur with large puffs of shimmering hair obscuring their facial features and giving them teddy bear faces. The nose of one was a bit longer than the other, so they were temporarily dubbed Long Nose and Short Nose, but they were later named Clara and Rama. Early in the summer all cubs the age of Clara and Rama have dense fluffy coats, which make them appear larger than they really are. From a distance, they may appear almost as large as their mother, though she may weigh three or four times as much. (Many of the names of McNeil bears dated back to the early 1960s when personnel of the Alaska Department of Fish and Game chose names for various reasons. The majority of names originated in the first years of the Utah State University study [1970–1972] and were derived from names of friends, relatives, celebrities, and by what just seemed to fit a bear's personality. I continued this naming tradition that had no rhyme or reason.)

Goldie and her cubs grazed alone on the green sedge that rippled and swirled as the sea breeze danced patterns around them. Clara and Rama ate the protein-rich sedge voraciously, since they were no longer nursing from Goldie. As spring cubs (first year, newborn cubs) they depended mostly on milk but also ate sedge, fish, and other solid foods. The next summer, as yearlings, they utilized more solid foods and nursed much less. If Goldie now came into estrous, this would mean that she had not nursed the cubs recently, because lactation inhibits the onset of estrous in bears. When cubs have been weaned, the sow ceases to lactate and comes into estrous, thereby allowing a sow to leave her cubs only after they have become independent of her as a food source.

A sow retains her cubs until coming into estrous, but when a boar first approaches her, the cubs must leave immediately, because the boar may possibly kill them if given the chance. The sow will initially attempt to avoid the boar, but his persistent following soon forces her frightened cubs to flee, and even though they may rejoin their mother briefly, this forced separation is soon complete.

Occasionally a sow does not wean her cubs on schedule and retains them for a third summer. Because two sows who did this during my study had large litters of three or more cubs,

I concluded that the cubs, with less milk and fish to go around, had remained dependent on their mother's milk and thus inhibited her estrous cycle and their weaning. However, this occurs sometimes even with single cubs, so perhaps other factors are involved.

Goldie's cubs would soon leave her, as a large dark boar appeared on the flats and approached the trio, which was conclusive evidence that Goldie was in estrous. Jim and I froze and crouched below the sandbar in excitement. I had never observed a sow leaving her cubs before, so we wanted to be careful and not let the boar detect our presence. Goldie became uneasy and began to move away after realizing that the boar was approaching, but she was no longer the excessively aggressive mother who had protected Clara and Rama for the previous two years. Before coming into estrous she would have run frantically or fought fiercely when confronted with a mature boar, but now she only halfheartedly avoided the boar and let her cubs run and fend for themselves. Goldie undoubtedly would have chased her cubs away from the danger of the dark boar had they not fled on their own.

Clara and Rama headed straight for the cliffs that overlook

Goldie walks along the beach of McNeil Cove while her two cubs, Clara and Rama, lag behind and play rather than staying close to their mother.

the sedge flats, running as only young bears can run: hind paws placed in unison in front of and on either side of where the front paws had landed together, rocking back and forth, a blur of flying paws and legs, a jolt and shimmer of fur with each planting of the paws. Once to the cliffs, they ran up one of the many bear trails that crisscross every slope in the area and settled on a spot with a good view and watched as Goldie meandered about the sedge flats with the boar in tow.

Goldie's behavior was typical of a mature sow's reaction to a boar consort. She was tolerant of his presence, but moved constantly as if attempting to escape. Her erratic movements eventually led them into the alders and out of sight. The cubs, alone for perhaps the first time, held their position on the bluff and eagerly surveyed the scene for their mother, as though not sure of a course of action without her direction.

The late-night sunset had given way to midnight twilight when Goldie returned without the boar and searched around for a few minutes before locating her cubs' outpost. Unlike younger cubs who can seldom recognize their mother from a distance, Clara and Rama identified Goldie and descended to her. After some smells of recognition, all three grazed undisturbed in the gathering darkness.

The cubs were on their own when I next sighted them two days later. Even though I did not witness their final separation, the temporary split two days earlier proved to me that the process had been gradual. I had no idea how many times the cubs left and rejoined Goldie before making a permanent break, but based on other observations, I suspect that eventually a boar became persistent and separated Goldie from her cubs for a long enough period of time to affect a permanent separation. Whenever a sow and cubs of any age are separated, there is a possibility that they may simply fail to find one another again. This hypothesis is certainly a plausible explanation for the final separation and it is supported by the fact that Goldie had no active role in the temporary separation I witnessed. Nonetheless, there is a point at which a sow will have nothing more to do with her cubs. For instance, approximately three weeks after their departure, Goldie ran into her cubs at the falls and aggressively chased them away from the fishing area just as she would have done with any young bears. At no time during my study did I observe any familial attachments between a sow and her cubs after their final separation.

After two and a half years of consummate maternal protection, the sudden reality of being alone is a drastic change in a cub's life. During the years it spent with its mother, it became more and more confident as every new element in its environment was discovered, investigated, and, with the influence of the sow, most likely dominated. The loss of the sow's support destroys most of a cub's confidence in dealing with other bears. Years of learning by trial and error will be needed to rebuild the confidence it had had only one day before that final separation.

Goldie's cubs retained a little confidence by staying together after being weaned. Siblings, like Clara and Rama, invariably remain together for their first summer and sometimes a second summer, and in extreme cases for a third and fourth summer. This sort of sibling relationship is advantageous to the young cubs, who can present a common front and thus dominate single bears their own age or older. This is particularly important at the falls, where dominance can control fishing success.

Clara and Rama remained on and around the flats for several days. One afternoon, while surveying the sedge flats with my spotting scope, I noticed the golden pair roaming around the bluffs overlooking Mikfik Creek, where sockeye salmon were still running. I suspected that they were fishing the many shallow areas along the creek, so we gathered up our gear and set out in hopes of observing their first attempts at catching fish.

Mikfik Creek has a number of small waterfalls where the sockeye are vulnerable to eagles and bears. The shallow waters of the creek are ideal for eagle and bear predation, but the run is too small and sporadic to provide a reliable food source, so the brownies fish the creek only in passing. However, the eagles fish intensively for two or three weeks and often as many as twenty of the majestic birds can be seen on the bluffs over-looking the creek.

We spooked several eagles on the trail leading to our over-look at the first waterfall, where we settled down in an opening and waited for some action to develop. The deep pool below the falls was plugged with salmon that surged in schools every few seconds and jumped from the pool, flip-flopping about in the thin veil of rushing water. Hearing all this commotion, Clara and Rama came splashing upstream toward the falls with salmon splashing in every direction as they approached. Both cubs jumped around sporadically, then stood on hind legs to better view the concentrations of schooling salmon that swirled all around them, then they continued splashing and jumping here and there in total confusion. Clara stood with her head jerking wildly around not knowing which direction to go, for every frantic chase ended with the salmon escaping to deep water. Soon the shallow rapids were so full of fish that experience and technique were less important, and Clara pinned a fish with her paws and grabbed at its back several times before securing it. Rama became aware of the success and ran to share the catch, but Clara had something else in mind and headed for the creek bank with her sister in pursuit.

It was a close race to dry ground with Rama alongside Clara, snapping incessantly at her catch. Once ashore, Clara crouched closely over her fish, pushing her back to her new adversary, who began the low guttural growl or deep-pitched infantile bawling that characterizes fish stealing in all young bears. It is similar to the insistent cry of hunger or begging that spring cubs emit when ready to nurse. Rama's method of steal-ing from her sister was considerably more brazen than it would have been with any other bear, as she did not fear her sister and made few of the appeasing gestures that accompany steal-ing from a higher ranking or less familiar bear. Clara held her fish to the ground and pivoted around it, while Rama clawed and snapped at the salmon. The grunting and roaring con-tinued for several seconds before Clara tried to escape up a steep bluff with her salmon flopping so unguarded in her mouth that Rama easily grabbed the tail and began a short tug of war, which split the salmon and provided both cubs with a portion.

The cubs acted out this same stealing episode after catching two more salmon, but as they returned for a fourth try, both cubs suddenly lifted their noses to the wind and scanned the bluffs. They had detected our scent or that of an approaching bear. In order to keep from being seen, we froze in our places and moved only our eyes, knowing that the cubs could spot moving objects from great distances but their vision made it difficult for them to discern stationary forms. The cubs were unable to spot the source of an apparently strange scent and so they set out to find it. I was fairly certain that we were the objects of their curiosity, as the cubs would have run away in fear had they smelled another bear approaching. Their interest in us was not surprising because young cubs are often curious about humans, particularly cubs like Clara and Rama, who had had little previous contact with people. Their mother, Goldie, was a shy, retiring sow who kept her distance from people.

We were downwind from the cubs, but the breeze had apparently swirled around in the gorge and reached their super-sensitive noses. They began to circle around us and disappeared into the alders and were gone for several minutes as they moved downwind to locate our position. I had almost decided that they had become frightened and left, when suddenly the pair appeared on our right scarcely 15 feet away with their mouths frothing heavily as they held their noses high, sniffing and chewing the air closely, while meandering around and observing us for several seconds. This brief inspection apparently satisfied their curiosity, for they left quickly. While sauntering away, Clara stopped to roll around on a low-growing alder bush as though scent marking it or herself. The purpose of this behavior was not clear, but perhaps it was somehow connected with our meeting.

Jim and I were somewhat surprised at the boldness of the newly weaned cubs, because such behavior is more typical of yearlings and two-year-olds that still have their sows to back them up. Although a sow has enough experience to steer clear of people, yearlings and two-year-olds, who are accustomed to their mother's protective shield, are confident and very inquisitive about people. Occasionally, they may approach in a playful romp or even a menacing stalk, while smelling the air and sizing up the strange beings. This daring behavior by cubs can force a sow into protective action and cause her to be more aggressive than she would be in other situations with humans.

After returning to the creek, neither cub fished with the same wild abandon that had characterized their hungry attempts before detecting the two of us. Our presence made them so uneasy that frequent glances in our direction interrupted their efforts and reduced their success. Before another fish was caught, both cubs once again lifted their black noses to the wind and deciphered the breeze. Almost immediately they climbed the bluff on the far side of the creek and stopped on the summit long enough to survey the drainage below and to take another whiff of breeze before continuing their retreat. Their fearful behavior almost certainly meant that another bear was approaching. A moment later, Big Ears, a five-year-old male, came lumbering downstream with a spray of salmon parting in his wake. Big Ears smelled the cubs and, pointing his nose to the wind, he set out to find them. Clara and Rama had already traversed two small hills in their retreat, while stopping frequently and standing on their hind legs for a better view. Meanwhile, Big Ears loped up the drainage below them and made an unseen approach. The cubs obviously were afraid that the intruder would attempt to track them down but, unfortunately, by the time they had detected his presence, the pair had unwittingly cornered themselves on a dangerous precipice overlooking the creek 60 feet below. Suddenly looming out of the alders directly in front of them, Big Ears stood and casually scrutinized the pair, who were beside themselves with terror as they backed to the edge and scrambled to maintain their footing on the rocky cliff. Loose rocks broke free and showered into the water below as their hind feet slipped from the edge and scratched frantically for a new hold on the crumbling ledge. Then, just as one or both cubs seemed certain to fall, their antagonist turned and slowly retreated to the salmon stream and began to fish eagerly as the frightened cubs cautiously withdrew into the brush.

Big Ears had interrupted what was certain to be a successful fishing bout just to investigate two young cubs. This is a typical reaction, for despite their asocial nature, most bears are immensely curious about other bears. I inferred from his swift, undaunted approach to the cubs that Big Ears was capable of discerning from smell alone that they were young bears, for he certainly would not have approached a mature boar or sow with such confidence. In fact, he most likely would have avoided such bears in the same way Clara and Rama had avoided him. Critical perception of this sort may be hard to appreciate until one realizes that bears depend on their sense of smell for their very livelihood and can detect strong odors from miles away. Discriminating young bears from sows or boars by smell alone may well be routine.

Following their traumatic encounter with Big Ears, Clara and Rama disappeared and were not seen around the flats for several days. During their absence other newly weaned cubs appeared around the flats and provided us with continuing insights into the activities of weaned cubs. Two new arrivals were M.J. and Miss Kitty. Their mother was a sow named Leeland P., who never returned to McNeil during my study and was killed in the fall hunt of 1976. Her two-year-old cubs were incredibly beautiful. The light female cub, Miss Kitty, was a dazzling platinum blond with a small black bald spot that resembled a beauty mark below her right eye. The dark male cub, M.J., wore a deep auburn coat that parted in deep creases as the breeze whipped around him. They were not playful cubs and seemed quite businesslike as they grazed methodically on the lush sedge.

When these cubs spent long afternoons foraging on the flats, I often sat on the beach very near the pair and watched them for hours. Two summers at the falls with their mother had so habituated them to people that they totally ignored me. I tossed stones into a nearby stream to see if they might venture after the splashes, hoping for fish, but quick glances toward the splashes were their only reactions.

M.J. and Miss Kitty remained on and around the flats until late July. They preferred to stay on the coastal areas where mature bears seldom venture and where visibility is excellent, making it possible effectively to isolate themselves from their greatest danger—other bears. The proximity of our camp to the sedge flats created an atmosphere of potential conflict between people and young bears like M.J. and Miss Kitty, because the latter have no fear of humans and will venture boldly into camp if they smell food.

One day in late July several persons were roasting several fresh chum salmon on an open fire in the middle of camp, when M.J. and Miss Kitty came sauntering up the beach. As it happened, I had just climbed on top of the cabin to scan the flats, so I noticed the pair as they approached on the beach with their noses high in the air. Suddenly the smell of salmon hit Miss Kitty and she broke into a dead run and headed straight for the roasting salmon. Fortunately Jim was talking to campers near the fire, so I yelled at him and pointed out the approaching cubs. He ran at them waving his arms wildly in the air in an aggressive display that surprised the cubs, ended their foray, and sent them running in the opposite direction. Had Jim not been there the cubs might have run head-on into the midst of the campers and plunged into the roasting salmon to create a scene that would have been unbelievable, though I doubt if anyone would have been hurt.

That was the last time I saw M.J. and Miss Kitty in 1973, and as they did not return the next year, I was both surprised and glad to see them arrive on the flats two summers later in 1975. They grazed near each other but stayed apart and had nothing to do with each other. Close observation soon revealed that Miss Kitty was more ill-tempered and asocial than her brother and was probably responsible for the dissolution of their sibling bond. After playfully approaching Miss Kitty several times and being aggressively rebuffed each time, M.J. soon found more playful bears on the flats and abandoned all attempts to join his sister.

When a play partner was unavailable, M.J. often found inventive ways of entertaining himself. He was particularly fond of body sledding on the 30-foot snowbanks that remained under the bluffs surrounding the flats. After climbing to the top of a large drift, he usually flipped over onto his back and slid down feet first to the bottom, but later he contrived several different methods of sledding: feet first, head first, on his back, on his stomach, tumbling, rolling, and combinations of these. After several runs he took a short break to straddle the peak of the snowdrift and scratch his belly for several seconds.

M.J. found several suitable play partners on the flats, but most often he played with Flashman, a four-year-old male. They were the same age, about the same size, and very playful. While on the flats, the pair normally stayed apart except for prolonged play bouts, but later in the summer they became closer when they entered the competitive situation at the falls. They usually arrived at the falls together and would remain together and watch the fishing action from a distance if the falls was crowded with bears. M.J. and Flashman closely resembled brothers in a sibling bond, but unlike siblings, they did not cooperate with each other at the falls in fishing, stealing, or in agonistic encounters with other bears. They were primarily amiable play partners.

The history of M.J. and Miss Kitty leads me to believe that the temperament of siblings largely controls the length of time they remain together after being weaned. This is supported by the history of Red, White, and Blue, who were weaned in 1970. White, who was more asocial, left her siblings by 1971. In contrast, Red and Blue were amiable and playful and remained together in 1971, and rejoined in 1972 and again in 1973. White's early independence from her sisters was not made possible by greater dominance, because Red was more dominant than either White or Blue. White was simply a very solitary animal who preferred to be alone.

The difference in dominance and the temperaments of these sisters illustrates that there is no clear-cut similarity between a sow and her cubs. It is logical to assume that a sow might transmit, either genetically or through learning, some aspects of her disposition to her offspring, but such transference is not apparent. I was never able to detect any familial similarities. Instead, the observable aspects of dispositions are extremely variable in different bears and become more so after weaning.

3

The Bears Arrive

The Mikfik sedge flats south of camp were created by the constant intertidal action at the mouth of the McNeil. At each high tide the ocean water advances into the cove and dams up the river, filling the entire area with fresh river water. The flats are alternately dry and flooded twice daily by up to 28-foot tides. This constant intertidal action creates tidal flats covered with deep, slimy sediments deposited during high tide. Dense growths of sedge *(Carex langlii)* cover the tidal flats on all areas protected from the pounding surf by sandspits or gravel bars. The sedge is a grasslike plant that is often called *sedge grass,* even though it is not a member of the grass family. It is a perennial that sprouts from rootstock as soon as the ice and snow melt in the spring. The thin pointed blades grow thick and luxuriant and cover the flats in a rippling green sea of vegetation that reaches a depth of 3 or 4 feet before maturing and turning brown in late July or August.

The sedge is important to the bears because in its early stage of growth this plant contains up to 26 percent protein (as percentage of dry weight). It is also the first vegetation that sprouts in the spring, which makes it the first abundant, reliable food source in the bears' meager springtime diet. The Mikfik flats produce an enormous crop of sedge in close proximity to McNeil Falls, so this area is important in the early summer activities of many McNeil bears.

Young resident McNeil bears, such as Clara, Rama, M.J., and Miss Kitty, are often the first bears to arrive on the flats in June. They are invariably the offspring of McNeil sows that spend each summer fishing on McNeil Falls. This annual exposure to people habituates the young bears to humans and allows them to continue utilizing the area as adults without fear. However, there are wary bears at McNeil. Boars, many mature sows, particularly those with cubs, and many other cautious bears are rarely seen on the wide-open exposed tidal flats. Their avoidance of the coastal areas, which is where most bears are killed by hunters, enables them to survive to maturity. They are big and old because they fear man.

What causes a bear to become so wary of man? There are several arguments that could be proposed to explain this phenomenon. First, the bears learn that man is dangerous and that he can be avoided. Second, intense trophy hunting eliminates all the fearless individuals at a young age and leaves only those that are shy to survive to maturity. Third, bears are initially afraid of man on first encountering him because he is a strange being they have not encountered previously in their natural world. Later, this wary behavior may be reinforced in unprotected areas or, in parks and protected areas, repeated uneventful encounters with man may teach bears to overcome their initial fear of man. I suspect that the wariness of bears may result from a combination of all these factors.

Whatever combination of these factors produces wary behavior, the result is that in general younger bears are less wary than older bears. However, the younger bears occupy the coastal areas for reasons other than their fearless attitude toward man. Since adult bears have historically been the only enemies of young bears, the latter avoid adults as if they were predators. Therefore, younger bears remain near the coast where they are less likely to encounter adult bears and where good visibility helps them avoid the few adults who do venture near the coast.

Of course the coastal area is prime brown bear habitat that is obviously very desirable for any bear, and so it is not as though young bears are driven into marginal habitat, as is the case with many animals in which the young disperse after weaning. It is possible that the only reason the young bears occupy the coastal area is to utilize the bountiful food sources found there. Nonetheless, I believe they receive these benefits by default, since historically this segregation pattern was probably reversed. That is, before man arrived on the Alaska Peninsula, mature bears probably roamed the coastal areas without fear of any living thing, whereas today they are relegated to inferior, remote habitat in order to survive.

This sort of regional segregation by bears might appear to be simply an efficient division of habitat and food for optimum use of available resources, but even though the habitat is effectively divided by this segregation, the latter does not occur because of necessity. For instance, bears do not divide up their use of sedge flats because there is not enough sedge to go around. On the contrary, only a small fraction of the sedge is eaten on the flats each summer. It is obvious that the Mikfik flats and other sedge flats could easily support many more bears in early summer, but the reluctance of most bears to risk the exposure of grazing on the flats reduces the utilization of sedge.

Because the sedge is the first major stand of vegetation that sprouts from the thawing landscape, one would expect the bears to eagerly welcome this abundant, nutritious addition to their meager springtime diets. Historically, however, they wait until one or two weeks before the start of the fishing season at the falls before grazing heavily on the sedge. By this time the protein content of the sedge has declined considerably because the percentage of crude fiber increases, which makes the plants' texture much ranker and presumably more difficult to digest. Why they wait for two weeks or more before grazing on the sedge, where they are located, and what they are doing during this time was a mystery I intended to explore.

It is common knowledge that brown bears eat very little in the spring, but they have no choice, as very little food is available. McNeil brownies probably wander around in the springtime and pursue a variety of scarce and unreliable foods. Since there are no abundant staple foods, such as the sedge, salmon, and berries, which appear later in the season, I suspect that they literally follow their noses and pursue any smells that might lead to potential food. These rare foods include carrion, beached whales and other marine animals, seaweed, clams, roots, tubers, and perhaps sick or weakened moose or moose calves.

Why do the bears continue to seek these unreliable food resources long after the rich sedge has sprouted on the flats? In order to discover some clues to this intriguing puzzle I needed to observe bear activities in early spring, while the land was still frozen and snow covered. Fortunately the late spring of 1975 provided me with this opportunity.

Each night in mid-June we sat on top of the cabin in the midnight twilight and surveyed the powder-white highlands and wondered where the bears were and what they were doing. We decided to wait until the flats had a good stand of sedge and then ski up into the McNeil drainage in hopes of discovering something about the bears' activities. What were they doing while the sedge grew rapidly and ungrazed on the flats?

By June 20 the sedge was several inches high and covered most of the flats. This was our signal. We planned and prepared for a seven-day ski trip and left camp that morning. The land above 400 feet elevation was still covered with snow, so we carried our cross-country skis strapped to our packs. Our early morning trail led to the falls where the McNeil, swollen by melting snow, thundered over the rocks. As the country upstream was entirely unexplored and unknown to us, we stopped at this familiar place and studied our topographic maps. We knew that picking a route would be tricky because most of the terrain from sea level to an elevation of 600 to 1,000 feet was almost entirely covered with dense alder thickets. Wherever these alders grow in uninterrupted stands they make travel on foot impossible. Even though the region ahead of us appeared to be impenetrable, we found that careful use of the detailed maps allowed us to pick an easy trail along streams and through clearings in the alders.

This first day of sloshing along streams and soggy meadows led us about 8 miles up the drainage before we were stopped by an incredibly dense thicket of willows and alders. There appeared to be no direct routes ahead so we scrambled up a nearby ravine that was filled with snow and finally reached the top of a 400-foot ridge. From this vantage point we inspected the lay of the land and planned a route to the snow-covered alpine tundra on the mountains ahead.

The next day we skied up ravines, along ridges, through tiny valleys of snow, and eventually reached the tundra at the 1,000-foot level on the mountains to the south of the river. The sun was beating down directly on the snow and the radiating heat warmed and dried our cold, wet clothes, so we made use of the good conditions and skied another 5 miles over the alpine tundra and stopped in late evening to establish a base camp at 1,500 feet on the mountain slopes (plate 3). We planned to make several day trips from this camp in search of bear activities.

The sun was setting through white jagged peaks to the northwest as we finished anchoring our tent with heavy rocks to guard against the 80-mile-per-hour winds that can rake the area when strong Pacific storms move over the Peninsula.

Clean snowy peaks rose all around us, appearing distinct and somewhat unnatural against a contrasting backdrop of threatening blue-gray clouds made dark by the sunset. McNeil Cove was dwarfed at the base of the drainage by surrounding peaks and massive Kamishak Bay. Forty miles out in the Pacific the icy white cone of Augustine Volcano rose from the sea in solemn isolation (plate 4).

The next day got off to an exciting start when a wolverine wandered into camp while we were eating breakfast. He made an unseen approach and then suddenly appeared from behind a scrubby alder about 10 feet from us and was calmly inspecting me when I first looked up and met his gaze. He so startled me that I jumped and yelled at Jim and caused the wolverine to spook and run. While we watched, he loped away at a smooth, easy pace, stopping every 50 feet or so to turn and inspect us again. He looked very much like a lanky yearling bear cub with a shaggy summer coat. He continued this intermittent retreat and disappeared over a ridge into the river valley below.

I hoped that this encounter with the wolverine was a good omen for our ursine quest, which had been unenlightening for the first two days. Our destination on the third day was the source of the McNeil, which was now only 5 miles southwest of our camp. As we set out across the slopes, the evidence of bear activity became increasingly apparent as tracks crisscrossed the snow in many places. The divides of several river drainages were in close proximity in this area and it was obvious that bears were traveling over these divides from one drainage to another.

Three miles from camp, while ascending the divide between the drainages of the McNeil and Little Kamishak rivers, we came upon a frozen alpine lake that was beginning to break up. From beneath its thawing ice a blue-green tributary of the McNeil surged to the surface and roared over smooth slabs of blue ice before disappearing again under a mantle of snow as it raced to the valley below. Despite the precarious state of the lake's ice, distinct tracks in the slushy snow revealed that a bear had just negotiated its way directly across the center of the lake. These fresh tracks continued up and over the divide ahead, so we hurried to reach the summit in hopes of spotting the bear.

The beautiful panorama from the crest of the ridge made

us immediately forget about the tracks that vanished into the valley below. From this lofty outpost we looked at a succession of river valleys and mountain ranges that gradually faded toward the horizon in the hazy June air. Directly in front of us rose a group of 5,000-foot mountains that held numerous river-spawning glaciers on their steep slopes. The beginnings of the Little Kamishak River tumbled from a snow-covered glacier that extended up the mountain two miles to our right, and smaller glaciers filled the spaces between the many jagged peaks surrounding it. Our maps revealed that the McNeil originated from its glacial source on the opposite side of these peaks, so we skied toward a low saddle in the mountains ahead.

Big, black bumblebees zoomed overhead as we eagerly skied up the slushy melting snow to our final destination. Then, as we edged our way over the summit, the vertical slopes of the mountains plummeted before us and the deep, rugged drainage of the McNeil loomed suddenly into view. The headwaters of the river sprang from a large glacier that clung to the northwest face of a nameless mountain, and splashing white and lively the young McNeil fell from this lofty source and disappeared into the valley below.

We stopped and ate lunch on this spot and considered the bear sign we had observed that morning. It was obvious that many bears were moving from one river drainage to another through this high country. The snow-covered high country was used only for travel, as there was no sign of life, no reason that the brownies would be here. The bumblebees continued to zoom along overhead, but nothing else moved.

The mountains we sat on divided the Peninsula into two regions: the Aleutian Range on the east and the lowland lake country on the west. Most of the bears appeared to be traveling over these mountains from the lake country to the rugged river valleys that pour off the Aleutian Range on the eastern coast (for example, the McNeil). As the Aleutian Range covers only the extreme eastern coast of the Peninsula, it is quite probable that some McNeil bears seasonally occupy the more expansive lowland lake country in the spring and fall and move over the mountains into the McNeil drainage during July and

August to fish the salmon run. The many migration routes in the mountains around us supported this hypothesis.

The wooded lake country is more protected from winter storms by the mountains, so the area receives less snow and spring arrives earlier than at McNeil. Some of our bears could find the early spring food prospects more rewarding along the many streams and lakes in that region. Such movements would be possible because the McNeil area and the lake country are only 25 miles apart, and travels of such length would be routine for the bears. Glenn (1975, see Bibliography) found that bears in the Black Lake region of the Peninsula 300 miles southwest of McNeil made similar migrations. In Glenn's study male bears ranged as far as 60 miles, though they averaged 26 miles between points of capture and recapture. Females traveled only half as far, but made movements as great as 36 miles. Considering this evidence, some bears could easily move from the lake country to McNeil and back again each year.

If many bears do make extensive migrations from other areas to fish McNeil Falls, then it is obvious why they do not forage on the new growth of sedge. That is, they have food sources in other areas that they utilize until moving to McNeil to fish. And in the meantime the valuable sedge goes untapped. The bears obviously cannot use every available food source, but they would be expected to go after the most nutritious items. What foods are better than sedge in early June is not known.

We awoke the next morning and found that the unusually nice weather had deteriorated. Low, wet clouds slid silently over the alpine slopes and reduced visibility to 30 feet or less. Two previous summers had left me very wary of McNeil weather, which can be stormy for a week or longer, so with this possibility in mind we cut the trip short and headed for home. Our old ski tracks were faintly visible at times in the wet snow, so we used these to decipher our original route through the dense fog that occasionally reduced visibility to near zero. The ceiling of low clouds rose above us as we skied down the slushy mountain slopes and reached the valley floor below.

We saw no bears during the two-day trip back to camp, and even the sedge flats were completely vacant when we arrived there in late evening. The sedge was growing rapidly, so the next day I collected samples for protein analysis from shoots that were 8 to 10 inches high. I checked around the flats and found no evidence of grazing by bears, which intensified my curiosity about their failure to utilize this food during its most nutritious stage of growth. They were ignoring a very valuable food source during a time of food scarcity. Even though we had just discovered evidence that bears had recently begun to move into the area from other regions, I was certain that some bears occupied the McNeil coastal area year round. Where were these permanent residents? What were they doing? What were they eating?

A number of bears prey on the red salmon during brief runs that begin during mid-June on two or three tiny streams in the area. Red salmon are lake-system spawners, so they are not found on river systems, like the McNeil, that do not flow from lakes. Some McNeil bears fish for reds on Mikfik Creek, but this unreliable run does not represent a significant food source for them. The Mikfik salmon run is very small most years, and the sockeye often run the 3 miles of stream to Mikfik Lake quickly after each high tide. These sockeye salmon are at best morning and evening hors d'oeuvres for a few bears.

The Mikfik red salmon run approximately coincides with the early stages of sedge growth, but even though the bears fish on the creek within a mile of the sedge flats, most of them never utilize the sedge at this time. In contrast, they often alternate fishing with grazing after the fishing season begins at McNeil Falls, but for now the sedge grew and swayed silently with the sea breeze and was disturbed only by shore birds and an occasional flock of brant geese.

There were so few bears around that I suspected we could smoke some sockeyes without attracting any of them. Catching and filleting the reds on Mikfik Creek was the most dangerous part of the project for us, but the only close call came one afternoon when Patch Butt, a five-year-old male, came loping down the creek and surprised us just as we were preparing to leave. Moments before we were filleting reds beside the creek, but fortunately the fish were packed away in plastic bags by the time Patch Butt arrived, so we made a hasty exit and left him sniffing some bloody grass and rocks.

The next day we kept our reds on a string in the creek until we were ready to leave and then carried them intact onto the flats to fillet them. We watched carefully for bears until we left the brush and blind corners on the creek and reached the open flats where we felt safe with our salmon. We dropped our guard a bit too soon, however, and it was just by chance that I happened to catch some movement behind us out of the corner of my eye and whirled around to see Blue, a seven-year-old female, about 20 feet away and approaching fast, with her eyes and nose glued to our salmon. Jim held her at bay by yelling and waving his arms at her, while I hurried across the creek and down the trail. Blue decided to circle around Jim, so he retreated across the creek and held her back by throwing big rocks in the water around her. Jim knew that warning shots would never even faze our old friend Blue, so he continued to yell and bombard her with rocks until I was halfway back to camp and out of sight.

Our salmon-smoking procedure was fairly simple. The fillets were cut into strips and soaked in a strong brine for about one hour. The strips were then skewered on green alder twigs and hung from wire racks in our smoker, which was nothing more than an old canvas wall tent with a wood stove inside. A few green alder twigs placed on top of the slow-burning stove provided just the right amount of delicate smoke flavor that we preferred.

The smoker was placed on a gravel spit away from camp so that if a bear got into the salmon it would not associate the fish with our camp proper. Fortunately we never had a single bear problem while smoking salmon four times in two summers. This vividly illustrates that few bears are in the McNeil area early in the summer, or we certainly would have lost some salmon.

When the flats continued to remain vacant, we decided to hike over to Akumwarvik Bay to see if any of our bears were

grazing the massive sedge flats in that area. A trip to Akumwarvik along the beach was a difficult 15-mile hike that had to be
timed between the tides, so we chose to survey the bay with
spotting scopes from on top of McNeil Head. Jim had earlier
discovered an easy route to the top of the mammoth headland
that juts into the sea between McNeil Cove and Akumwarvik
Bay. Alpine tundra covered about 3 square miles of this headland, which allowed us to move freely on top and use it as a
fantastic observation post for surveying the McNeil landscape
in every direction.

Our trail to McNeil Head left the gravel-covered beach
north of camp and snaked up a deep, wide crack in the 50-foot
conglomerate rock cliffs that border the sea and battle the
breakers at every high tide. Wave erosion had sculptured
smooth, rounded chambers and columns in the face of the
cliffs. Above these vaulted formations and the breaking sea,
our trail wound through waist-deep fields of fireweed, where
the ground was soft and wet with the peaty remains of the lush
vegetation. The tall fireweed and grasses gave way to varied
tundra flora as we climbed higher along the cliffs, for here the
Pacific gales roar up the sheer cliffs and cut across the headland
to eliminate all but the low-growing tundra plants. Any stems
protruding higher than 1 or 2 inches in winter are exposed
above the thin crust of wind-swept snow, and ice crystals propelled by the wind quickly gnaw through these exposed stems
and kill the plants. Wherever a slight ridge, slope, or depres-
sion provided a place for snow to drift or accumulate, scrubby,
low-growing plants clung to the rocky soil with their stunted
stems clipped and frayed evenly at snow level.

The trails that we followed were the well-defined bear
trails that meander all over the McNeil landscape and form a
network of travel routes that the bears maintain through habit-
ual use. Most of the paths were worn down in a smooth continuous trail, but a few routes that were rarely used were nothing
more than a series of round bald spots in the grass where bears
had walked so uniformly that only their paw prints marked the
trail. Even the trails on the barren tundra of McNeil Head
were clearly visible through the lichens and crowberries.

While walking across the highest section of the headland, we spotted a large area of upturned earth where a bear had dug for roots or for an arctic ground squirrel (plate 5). The ground was dug deeply on the slope in an area 8 by 3 to 4 feet. Even though it was extensive, the dig had probably taken the bear only a short time to accomplish.

The most interesting observation about this dig was the fact that it was so rare. Jim and I had thoroughly explored this headland, and this was only the second dig by a bear that we had discovered during three summers of extensive hiking. This was a puzzling observation because brown bears supposedly utilize roots and ground squirrels when other foods are scarce, particularly in the spring. The paucity of bear activity was further demonstrated by the fact that we very rarely found a scat on this tundra and we never saw a bear grazing on the vast areas of crowberries found here. Later that summer, when we climbed the mountain that rises to the north of the falls, we were unable to locate any bear sign whatever on the berry fields found there. These observations emphasized the seasonal use of the area by McNeil bears and suggest that the permanent population may be small. The berries, sedge, ground squirrels, roots, and other vegetation appear to be significant food sources, but apparently they are not sufficient to maintain many bears the year around.

Further down the trail we passed beside the 700-foot cliffs where thousands of double-crested cormorants nest each summer. Hundreds of adults were soaring, landing, and then taking off again from their precariously placed nests on narrow ledges overlooking the sea. Hundreds of their broken eggs littered the top of the cliff—victims of predation by ravens and glaucous-winged gulls.

Behind us, camp was barely visible on the edge of McNeil Cove. The McNeil River drainage extended south and west into the Aleutian Range (plate 6). We reached the southern edge of the headland and set up our spotting scopes on a smooth knoll overlooking the bays and flats 900 feet below. Akumwarvik Bay dominated the scene, and the several square miles of sedge flats around it were clearly visible past two smaller coves in the foreground. Ravines and ridges on the dark, barren mountains beyond the bay were still streaked with snowdrifts in surreal patterns of black and white that gave the country a most unusual appearance. Beyond this the glaciated mountains of Cape Douglas rose like great mounds of whipped cream through delicate wisps of ocean fog (plate 7).

The sedge flats were 3 or more miles away, but our scopes zoomed in and clearly revealed that even these important flats had no grazing bears. We spent over an hour scanning the entire area, but we never located a single bear. Clearly our bears had not begun their annual pilgrimage to the McNeil area.

The initial arrival and congregation of bears on coastal sedge flats represents the first close contact of the year for most bears. In fact, the last time many of them rubbed shoulders may well have been on salmon streams the summer and fall of the previous year. They are so used to being alone after this long period of isolation that they must rehabituate to one another's presence. This annual process of habituation is dramatic. Initially, an older bear may not tolerate a younger bear on the flats, even though it may be as much as a half mile away. Later the same two bears may graze closely, and still later they may fish almost shoulder to shoulder at the falls.

One of the best examples of their early-season intolerance occurred on the flats in 1973 during my first summer at McNeil. A five-year-old female, named Red, had been grazing on sedge alone for two days when Big Ears, a five-year-old male, first arrived on the flats. Big Ears quickly spotted Red about one-half mile away and immediately began pursuit. The instant that Red started to retreat Big Ears broke into an easy lope, which spurred Red into a frightened run. The running pair traversed the flats and headed up the beach toward camp with Red about 100 yards in the lead. As soon as she passed camp, Red darted into the alders and disappeared. Big Ears then broke off his chase and ambled back toward the flats, apparently satisfied that he had driven Red away.

This was an extreme example, but it vividly illustrated

how intolerant brownies are of one another early in the summer. Most bears will simply avoid others by spreading out widely on the flats to graze. However, at this early date Big Ears apparently preferred to have the entire area to himself and it was a simple task to remove Red.

Big Ears remained on the flats and grazed intensely, so we decided to hike down and inspect him at close range. I suspected that he would be a bit spooky on his first day back at McNeil, so we edged our way along the beach and hid behind sandbars to keep out of sight. We managed to sneak within about 150 feet of Big Ears before we entered his field of vision. He was grazing with his back to us, so we crept along slowly, being careful to freeze if he lifted his head or looked around. It was not long before he smelled us and started to look around carefully. We crouched behind clumps of beach grass so that Big Ears could not quite spot us. We were visible but as long as we did not move a muscle he was unable to locate us. After a thorough look around, he hesitantly returned to grazing, but the next puff of breeze brought more evidence of our intrusion and once again he stopped to look around. It seemed incredible that he was unable to perceive our stationary forms, but he smelled us and knew we were there, so he cautiously began moving away. He continued to look around while retreating to the alders on the edge of the flats, but we remained still and he never succeeded in locating us that day. This was further evidence that the bears' vision does not discern stationary forms very well.

Big Ears' solitary reign of the flats was broken the next day by the arrival of a thirteen-year-old sow named Hardass, who had received her unusual name the year before when two successive immobilizing darts failed to penetrate her rump. Hardass was a power to be reckoned with, but Big Ears either was unaware of this or else was just confident enough to attempt to push the old girl around. At any rate, he grazed slowly in her direction and then approached in a menacing stalk with his head down and ears back. Hardass had initially ignored him, but when he came closer she suddenly stopped grazing and lunged after him in an outright charge. Big Ears' bullying act fell apart on the spot and he turned tail and ran for his life. Needless to say, Hardass had no further trouble with Big Ears.

The aggression and intolerance that the first bears on the flats displayed began to diminish as more bears arrived in the area. It generally took only a day or two for most bears to become accustomed to sharing their grazing area with others. This process of habituation proceeded more rapidly as the number of bears increased. When new arrivals found several other bears already grazing on the flats, they generally joined the others without an extended period of adjustment. By the third week of July, it was common to see ten bears grazing calmly on the flats. Most often they were widely spaced over the area, but occasionally they would all be clumped on a 3- or 4-acre section. Aggression was minimal because any bear that felt crowded could simply graze in the opposite direction and avoid the others.

All of the action was taking place on the flats, but soon the fishing season would begin at the falls. It was time for the earliest chum salmon to begin running the McNeil, so Jim and I set out one afternoon for a preliminary check of the falls. The trail to the falls crossed Mikfik Creek at its mouth in a spot where our hip boots were just high enough to keep us dry as we inched across on tiptoes. The well-used path then left the flats and crossed over an area of alpine tundra before descending to the falls.

An elevated vantage point on the bluff above the river provided us with a complete view of the falls. Just upstream from us the blue-green McNeil came racing and foaming around a bend and roared inexorably toward the falls. Just below us a series of conglomerate slabs breached the riverbed and turned a 100-yard stretch of the McNeil into a thundering white-water spectacle (plate 8).

The upper falls was the main fishing area for the bears because here the water cascaded over and around large slabs of conglomerate rock and created numerous good fishing spots where the salmon were highly vulnerable (map, p. 38). The number-one fishing spot, the best spot on the falls, was on the

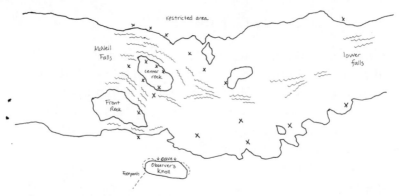

A drawing of McNeil Falls showing our "cave" and observer's knoll, the upper falls, lower falls, major rocks, fishing locations, restricted areas, and trails. The Xs indicate fishing locations.

opposite bank directly across from us. The far side of the river was a restricted area that was off limits for people because the more wary bears, particularly the large boars, used the area exclusively. There was a large rock outcropping, which we called the center rock, in the center of the upper falls. There were numerous fishing spots around this rock and it was a center of fishing activities on the falls. The middle and lower falls areas had fewer fishing locations and the bears did not utilize these areas as intensely.

Our summer-long observation spot, or the "cave" as it is often called, was parallel to the upper falls about 30 feet from the riverbank. It was not a cave at all, but rather a small eroded spot on a knoll beside the falls (plate 9). However, it did provide us with protection from the rear and shielded us from the stormy east wind and rain. We always moved on top of this knoll in good weather for a commanding view of the falls. Several bear trails passed beside the cave en route to the fishing spots on the upper falls. The more casual bears routinely sauntered past us on these trails at distances as close as 10 feet and often did not even glance in our direction.

We pulled our small handmade chairs out of the cave and sat down on top of the knoll to watch the falls for a while. Careful observation of the white water and deep pools on the upper falls revealed that the chum salmon had not begun their summer run. Any bears that might stop by the falls to check for salmon would not stay long.

The sedge flats would continue to be the center of activity until the salmon run began. The adult bears always grazed alone in their asocial, solitary existence. However, some young bears preferred to be with other young bears at times. As I mentioned before, newly weaned siblings remain together, but other unrelated juveniles of similar age will also stay together in loose association on the flats. It was not unusual to see a group of three, four, or five of these young bears grazing and playing together for days at a time. Other juveniles, like Big Ears, were more aggressive and preferred a solitary existence. This difference in bears seems to be simply a matter of individual temperament.

Most of the young bears at McNeil who have grown up around people can be downright brazen when it comes to dealing with them. A classic example of this involved the three siblings that were appropriately named the Marx Brothers. This fearless, mischievous trio were together from 1974 to 1979. They were the three survivors of a group of five (yes five) spring cubs that Red Collar, a large and dominant McNeil sow, had brought to the falls in 1974. Red Collar did not wean them on schedule and kept them with her for a third summer. This gave the cubs one extra summer of experience and confidence building with their powerful mother.

The Marx Brothers began their most outrageous exploits in June 1977 when they appeared on the flats as newly weaned three-year-olds in close sibling bonds. I was able to observe them that year during a two-week visit in June and again for a week in July. (As it turned out, my visits in the years following my study resulted in some of the best information on sibling relationships. This was simply the result of greater numbers of cubs being produced and weaned.) Red Collar had never brought her cubs close to camp, but the proximity of the latter to the flats combined with their sensitive noses and tremendous curiosity soon brought them around camp.

One evening they were grazing on the flats, so I hiked down with my camera and photographed them at close range in the soft evening light. They ignored me and grazed undisturbed until a distant splash in the river sent all three racing

through the shallows after an early running salmon. It was a wild race that could not be won, as all three were soon fighting over the single fish in a chorus of roars, growls, and grunts. Moments later they were grazing and playing again with the setting sun casting halos around their fluffy coats. They seemed not to notice me.

Later that evening they came ambling up the beach toward camp in the midnight twilight, romping and playing as they walked. Then, instead of continuing down the beach, they walked right into camp and proceeded to engage in an extended play bout in our front yard. We tried to discourage any bear from entering camp, so I yelled and clapped my hands and waved my arms at them, only to have them stop and casually look up as though they were saying, "Yes, can we help you?" I summoned the assistance of five tourists in camp and together we managed to shoo them away and down the beach.

The next day was unusually warm and late morning found

Four young brown bears grazing on the Mikfik sedge flats in early June with a scenic background of the Aleutian Range.

me sitting in front of the cabin basking in the sun and reading. Harpo, who was the most audacious of the brothers, had spotted or smelled my tent while sauntering by the edge of camp and decided it was worthy of further inspection. Fortunately, I looked up just as he started tugging on the rain cover, and so my screaming charge down the path came in time to save my tent. However, the next day while I was out on a hike, another young bear chewed on my rain cover, broke two tent poles, tore out the mosquito netting, and dragged out my sleeping bag before a hesitant tourist could scare him away. They apparently singled out my tent as it was the first item they encountered on the edge of camp.

Harpo was capable of considerable finesse during his forays into camp. Not long after my tent had undergone alterations, Larry and Mo Aumiller, the Alaska Department of Fish and Game employees who administered the McNeil Sanctuary, arrived for the summer with lots of fresh food, which they stored in a *cool box* in the ground beside their cabin. Two days later, while everyone was out of camp, Harpo lifted the lid of their cool box and neatly dined on a 5-pound brick of cheese, luncheon meats, and some moose burger. He did not eat or disturb the remaining food and even the plastic package of lunch meat had been opened, the meat removed, and the package left behind. When Larry and Mo returned after a brief absence, they unknowingly found Harpo licking his lips on the beach in front of camp.

I first met Larry and Mo Aumiller in July 1976. McNeil couldn't have been blessed with a nicer pair. Soon, I learned that Larry was a quiet, easygoing, and sensitive man of slight stature with curly black hair and beard and dark, expressive eyes that perhaps revealed some of his deep love for Alaska and the McNeil bears. Mo was a delightful, jovial, blond Australian lady with a no-nonsense practicality that seemed perfect in every situation. I remember asking her how in the world an Aussie found her way to McNeil River, Alaska. Without a moment's hesitation she said, "the same way a Texan does I expect." (I was born and raised in Texas.) Whenever I planned a visit back to McNeil, I looked forward to seeing Larry and Mo as much as the bears and the country.

During my visits, I tried to help Larry and Mo learn the identities of the resident bears. It was their diligent observations and data collection beginning in 1976 that helped me to keep in touch with events at McNeil. The Marx Brothers were early favorites of Mo and Larry, and so they kept me updated on their activities.

Before I left in 1977, Groucho, Chico, and Harpo had their greatest adventure at the expense of some commercial fishermen. These innocent visitors anchored their boat in the river at high tide, then left it moored beside a sandbar at low tide and hiked upstream to go sport fishing. While they were gone, the Marx Brothers all boarded the boat and proceeded to rummage around, perusing every section of the vessel. The crew returned and caught them red-handed before any damage was done, but imagine their surprise on finding three fair-size brown bears on board!

Despite all this early summer mischief, the Marx Brothers did not become real problem bears that summer or in later years. Unfortunately this was not always the case with young bears around camp. White started out much the same way the Marx Brothers did, but she went on to become a problem.

Most bear problems begin with human error and White was no exception. Her trouble began when she was four. She found and ate some salami that a careless tourist had left just outside the door of his tent. This treat prompted her to return to camp, and it was not long before she was peering in cabin windows and trying to enter tents. Twice she was shot in the rump with bird shot from a 20-gauge shotgun, but this failed to deter her, so the third time larger shot was used. This caused some injury and she rested without moving for two days on a nearby bluff. Soon she was back to normal, but she never again entered camp.

White undoubtedly associated people with the pain of being shot, but this did not cause her to be afraid of us. In fact, she continued to be one of the more fearless McNeil bears. She had the unusual habit of following people around with a rather menacing look and approaching to very close range to inspect them. She stopped this curious behavior for three summers, but it appeared once again in 1976 when she had spring cubs at age eight. Unsuspecting tourists were particularly unnerved when she approached with her cubs to within 40 feet and stood on hind legs to look at them.

Not all young McNeil bears were as fearless as White and the Marx Brothers. Each summer there would be two or three juveniles who would invariably run from us on the flats in the early summer. Every year these bears had to habituate themselves to the presence of people in the same way that they had to get used to other bears.

4

Of Dens
and Hibernation

Most of the bears in the area were now grazing primarily on sedge, which would be their staple diet until the chum salmon began running at the falls. Only a few late-running red salmon could be found in Mikfik Creek, so the bears had abandoned their fishing efforts there. I thought it might be possible to get some idea of how much bears had preyed on Mikfik sockeye salmon by checking out the bear sign along the creek and around Mikfik Lake, which is the source of the creek, so we planned a day hike to these areas.

I got up early the next morning and was putting on a pot of coffee when I noticed old Patches ambling up the trail toward camp with his nose almost touching the ground and his hind legs swinging out stiffly in a labored waddle that is typical

44

of mature boars. I was not concerned about Patches coming this close to camp, but since he had never approached so closely before, I stopped to watch what he was doing. His progress was slow but soon he was almost in camp and yet he did not seem to notice where he was. I was just about to yell at him when he suddenly looked up and noticed for the first time the group of tents 20 feet ahead. He stopped and studied the closest tent for about thirty seconds, as though puzzled, and then angled off the trail to circle around camp. He only progressed about 50 feet before he stopped again and casually began grazing on grass while ignoring the proximity of camp. He continued to graze undisturbed on the edge of camp.

My assessment of the strange behavior of Patches may seem rather subjective, but as I had observed him each year he slipped further and further into very obvious senility. He again displayed his infamous nonchalance toward people as we set out on our hike up Mikfik Creek. While crossing the flats we came upon a large mound of mud where the old fellow was lounging, fast asleep on his stomach with all four legs spread-eagled. We passed within 50 feet without arousing him and I whistled to awaken him. He slowly looked around through half-open eyes and took a couple sniffs of breeze, but he was unconcerned and quickly dropped his head heavily and continued his nap. We marveled at how he had survived so many hunting seasons without being shot.

The bear trail that we followed wound along the creek through thickets of willows and alders where we whistled and shouted to make our presence known to any bears that might be nearby. There were many rapids and waterfalls on the lower part of the creek where the sockeye are vulnerable to eagle and bear predation. The eagles used this white-water area a great deal, but the bears were only occasional predators here. The bear trails did not show heavy use, and we had seldom seen bears while fishing here ourselves.

Further up the creek the alder brush became dense on the banks, and we had to walk in the stream the rest of the way. There was no further evidence of bear activity until we reached the lake. The bear trails were wide and heavily used along the lakeshore and along the tributaries that fed the lake. Salmon carcasses and remnants littered many areas. It was obvious that the bears had fed on the Mikfik salmon much more than I had anticipated.

We decided to take a different route back to camp and headed up another drainage from the lake that led us to the alpine headlands to the east of camp. While exploring this new country, we found large patches of salmonberries that would be a tasty treat in August, but the most exciting find came when Jim spotted what appeared to be a bear den on the east slope above our trail.

We scrambled up the steep slope and found that it was indeed a bear den. There was freshly dug dirt outside the entrance with conspicuous bear tracks. The entrance was not quite 3 feet wide as was the tunnel, which curved slightly down and to the right a short 3 feet to the den chamber. We had no flashlight or matches, but from inside the chamber we determined it was round and about 5 feet long, 4 feet wide, and 4 feet high. Their was no bedding material found in the chamber. The bear may have dug this den during October or November the year before. They seldom use the same den twice, since dens dug in soft rocky soil like this often collapse after the spring thaw. This chamber appeared to be firm and sturdy and could easily be reused. Natural caves are often used repeatedly by the same or different bears (Reynolds et al., 1976).

There has been considerable controversy concerning whether bears are "true" hibernators. Perhaps the real controversy concerns the definition of hibernation. Many rodents have always been considered true hibernators. For instance, the thirteen-lined ground squirrel reaches a chilly body temperature of 5°C. (41°F.) during dormancy, but becomes active on the average of every four days to eat, urinate, and defecate. In contrast, the body temperature of a hibernating grizzly does not drop more than 5°C. (less than 10°F.), while its heartbeats may drop from forty to eight beats per minute during its winter sleep (Folk et al., 1976). Even though their metabolic rate does not slow down as completely as the ground squirrel, the grizzly will not eat, drink, defecate, or urinate during its entire hibernation period, which may last for six months or longer. Metabolic water is produced from fat and the bear does not produce products of protein metabolism that require urinary excretion (Folk et al., 1976). Considering the above evidence, bears may be considered to be better hibernators in a functional sense than the rodents.

I was surprised to find this den at such a low elevation and so near the coast. Brown bear dens are usually found at higher elevations where a constant insulating layer of snow will cover the den through the winter. Dens on Kodiak Island are found at an average elevation of 1,800 feet, while dens on the Alaska Peninsula average 1,300 feet elevation (Lentfer et al., 1972). On the other hand, McNeil receives a very heavy snowfall, and this den at 300 feet was in the lee of the wind where snow would drift to great depths.

We returned to camp down a previously unexplored drainage that turned out to be most rewarding. The icy stream grew quickly as we descended and on the lower stretch it cut through a deep gorge of smooth rock that was filled with delicate ferns, mosses, devil's club, and tall, thin alders. Every new trail in this rugged country was an adventure. The stream abruptly left the gorge and split out upon the flats within a half mile of camp. Further out on the flats four bears, including a sow and a boar consort, were grazing undisturbed. Slowly but surely the bears were arriving for another summer of fishing on the falls.

5

Social Life at the Falls

The third week of July brought the arrival of the first chum salmon to the falls, but the bears were not there to fish. Patch Butt first searched the falls for salmon on July 17, but he had poor success because the fish were not yet running in large numbers. During the next five days he returned daily to fish and on July 19 White also appeared. Both bears had good fishing and they had no competition from other bears until July 23 when seven bears arrived and began the fishing season in earnest.

The first bears to arrive at the falls were always regular McNeil residents, all of whom had most likely come to the falls as cubs with their mothers. It was most unusual for a nonresident bear to arrive at the falls and establish itself as a regular fishing bear. When strange bears did appear, they normally did not stay longer than an afternoon before vanishing.

This suggests that in order to deal with the aggressive, competitive situation at the falls, a bear must be introduced to it early in life. Spring cubs and yearlings learn from their mothers and their own experiences how to handle the falls situation and this enables them later to become McNeil regulars. In addition, bears are traditional animals, so it follows that cubs who are reared at the falls will return to the falls in later years. Likewise, bears who are raised in other areas and learn other summertime feeding activities should not be expected at the falls. Thus, when nonresident bears happen on the falls, it is expected that they would return to their regular summer areas rather than trying to cope with the falls, even though the latter must be very enticing.

This tradition of McNeil cubs returning every summer to the falls is contrary to the findings of other studies. Glenn (1976) found that young females in the Black Lake region of the Alaska Peninsula generally remained on their maternal home range, whereas young males made long movements that indicate changes in home range. Pearson (1976) found the reverse was true among young male and female grizzlies in the Yukon Territories. It is possible that the strong reinforcement of successful fishing at the falls is sufficient to entice most young McNeil bears to return to the McNeil portion of their maternal home range. On the other hand, the salmon streams in other areas of the Peninsula may be more or less equivalent, and thus young bears would have little to lose by emigrating.

Why should any young bear emigrate from its maternal home range? Dispersal of weaned young from their parental home range is very common among animals, so it might be expected that weaned bears would also disperse. Generally, the adults of a given species occupy the prime habitat and their weaned young are necessarily driven into marginal habitats to eliminate competition. This sort of dispersal is usually necessary because the parental home range is limited in resources and could not support additional individuals. In contrast, brown bears have very large, flexible home ranges that are shared by many other bears. For instance, as many as sixty or seventy bears may utilize the falls during July and August, so the McNeil area is common ground in the ranges of all these bears. This does not mean that all sixty bears have the same home range, because the McNeil area may be the only overlap in the ranges of many bears. In other words, bears from the north, west, and south probably converge on the falls for the salmon run and then disperse into more widely spaced ranges during the remainder of the year. This is obvious at McNeil before and after the salmon run when the area seems devoid of bears. This ability to congregate at concentrated food sources and then disperse over wide areas to utilize other foods is characteristic of brown and grizzly bears.

Considering these frequent seasonal movements within a large home range, it is difficult to understand why a young male would disperse and settle in a distant home range. The most common proximal cause of *dispersal* (that is, the young being driven from prime habitat into marginal habitat) does not seem applicable to brown bears, as each home range has concentrated prime habitat—sedge flats, salmon streams, dense berry fields—scattered within vast areas of marginal habitat. Any subordinate young bear could easily avoid competition on its maternal home range by remaining on the marginal habitat. Furthermore, as the bear population on the Alaska Peninsula is considered to be as productive and viable as ever (Glenn, 1975), there is little reason to believe the degree of competition or the availability of prime habitat would be any different in surrounding areas.

Many early arriving bears alternated between grazing on the sedge flats and fishing at the falls until the fishing season really got under way. Whenever we made trips to the falls to check for early fishing, we often met bears on their way to and from the falls, where they also were checking for early salmon. Young bears who often grazed and played together on the flats would sometimes go as a group to check on the falls. These young bears were usually some of the first bears to fish.

Some bears were consistently early arrivers and others

were always late, but generally there was considerable variation each year in the time a specific bear would arrive. Sows with cubs and mature boars were often late arrivers and young bears and single sows were among the earliest arrivers.

The early bears were much more intolerant of one another in the beginning than they would be later in the fishing season because they once again had to go through a process of habituation, just as they had done earlier on the flats. Further habituation at the falls is necessary because the latter is a much more competitive situation than the flats. While the bears were grazing on sedge, they could spread out over a wide area and avoid close contact, but at the falls they must actively compete for choice fishing spots within a relatively small area.

The actual level of aggression was lower early in the season than later because fewer bears were present and they were so intolerant that they generally avoided one another altogether. Younger bears usually withdrew from their fishing spots or even from the falls when they sighted a larger bear as far away as 200 to 300 feet. This sort of extreme caution in early season was warranted because dominant bears often interrupted their fishing to chase away subordinate bears.

It may seem a contradiction, but as more bears arrived and became accustomed to fishing with others, then aggression increased. The reason for this was that as they became more tolerant they moved closer to one another and the situations that led to aggression increased. Closely ranked bears began vying for good fishing spots, and younger bears became more bold and often pushed their luck too far with higher ranking bears, which elicited some aggression.

Patches would not share the same side of the river with Reggie during the first few days of the season, but only a week later he allowed her to fish within 30 feet and perhaps closer. Reggie did not boldly walk into such close quarters with Patches; instead she might fish progressively closer and closer until she reached a desired spot, or she might approach slowly and in stages, testing Patches and giving him time to get used to her presence.

Young bears, such as Light, a five-year-old male, were so

apprehensive during the first days that they could hardly fish
at all. Light lurked for several minutes around the edge of the
river to check out the situation and perhaps to get up the nerve
to venture out on the falls proper. When he did begin to fish,
Light spent most of his time looking all around for approaching
bears and occasionally standing for a better view.

As soon as he got wet, Light looked like a drowned rat with
the shaggy remnants of his winter coat draped thinly over his
lean, gaunt frame. Three weeks later every hair of his old coat
would be shed, leaving the deep, plush, dark-brown velvet of
his new coat shining and rippling over 150 pounds of new fat
that smoothed and rounded his frame and transformed him
into a handsome bear.

Light's behavior was also transformed during the season
because he adapted expertly to the fishing situation. Each day
he became more bold because he quickly learned where he
could most effectively fish and where and how he could avoid
others and also whom he should avoid. He learned each day
that other bears were becoming more tolerant of him and that
he could move closer and closer to them and even fish alongside some individuals. He learned that most adolescent males
and one or two young females were friendly, and later, when
fishing was really good and they were satiated, he played frequently with these bears. He learned he could attain and hold
a fishing spot by returning the threats of his peers and also the
threats of some higher ranking bears. He no longer ran from
the falls at the approach of a dominant bear, because he soon
learned that he could effectively avoid it by walking downstream or by simply changing his fishing location. Light
learned to use the falls.

All young McNeil bears go through behavioral changes similar
to Light's, although some of them do not adapt as successfully
as Light did. Mature bears also go through changes but not as
dramatically as do the younger bears. Their dominance plus
their experience from previous years allows them to move in
confidently and utilize the falls from the outset. Nonetheless,
the increase in their tolerance of one another as the season
progresses is striking.

The resident bears were rarely concerned with our presence when they arrived at the falls for the first time each summer. This is not surprising since people have been present at the falls every summer for thirty years. However, I did find it interesting that the bears' attitude toward people did not change significantly after the procedure of immobilizing and tagging them. The immobilizing drugs used were Sernylan (phencyclidine hydrochloride) or Etorphine (m-99) injected with Palmer Cap-Chur darts. I have no clear idea just how conscious the bears were while under these drugs, but they appeared somewhat alert, particularly when coming off the drug. However, after recovering from the effects, bears would return to the falls undeterred. They were cautious at first and gave us suspicious glances, but it was not long before they behaved as though nothing had happened.

Visible ear tags of various colors were attached to the ears so that individual bears could be identified by different people for many years. This made it possible for someone who had never seen the bears to identify them from color-coded tags. This was especially important for young bears because their appearance changes from year to year. Adult bears change very little and so after my first summer I knew all the McNeil adults on sight. Each bear is distinctive in both appearance and behavior. It was impossible to confuse the identity of the regular McNeil adults.

Bears were normally darted on Mikfik flats and occasionally at the falls. The primary concern—beyond the correct dose of drug—was to keep track of the bear until it went down. This was not easy as they usually headed straight for the dense alder brush after being hit by a dart. We stationed as many people as possible on the highest vantage points in the area so the bear could be visually tracked. If the dose of drug was correct, a bear would go down before losing us in the alders.

One of the most interesting darting episodes in 1973 involved Zubin, a playful 800-pound boar. He did not venture onto the flats, so we had to dart Zubin at the falls as he approached to fish during July. I was one of three lookouts scattered over the area to track Zubin as he fled the falls. When he was hit by the dart, he jumped and whirled around and then ran from the falls. However, as he ran up the riverbank Zubin was met by Spooky, a sow with three spring cubs. Spooky mistook Zubin's escape for an aggressive charge and she immediately attacked him in a rage of maternal protection. By the time Spooky had retreated and fled with her cubs, Zubin had apparently forgotten about being darted and he conveniently fell within 20 feet of our observer's knoll.

We began work on Zubin as soon as we were sure he was completely immobilized. The permanent identification of a tattoo on the upper gum in his mouth revealed that Zubin had been tagged at McNeil in the 1960s, but since that time he had lost all of his ear tags. He had been absent for several summers, so he was a new bear to us. We retagged him and took a small premolar tooth for age determination (bear teeth have annual rings much like tree trunks). While we were taking his body measurements, Zubin's temperature began to rise, which indicated a possible adverse reaction to the drug. Fortunately he was near the river so we could easily supply plenty of cold water to cool him. The most effective cooling was to pour water over his panting tongue. Zubin soon stabilized and we completed work on him without further incident. None of the other bears present seemed to take notice of our work on Zubin.

Most darting episodes were not as easy as our effort with Zubin and some failed altogether. One particularly difficult bear was Romeo, a ten-year-old boar. It was very important that we immobilize Romeo, for he wore a nylon rope collar that he was quickly outgrowing. It had to be removed.

Romeo appeared only at the falls where he was moderately wary of people. We waited patiently for him to fish on our side of the river, but he stayed on the restricted side safe from the dart gun. Finally we put together a plan to cross the river and ambush Romeo from the rear. We hiked upriver and crossed at a shallow spot about one-half mile above the falls and then followed a bear trail back to where Romeo was fishing. Unfortunately, by the time we reached the falls, Romeo had sensed something unusual—probably our scent from upriver where it did not belong—and retreated into hiding. Romeo managed to remove the tight collar himself before the next summer, but it left a lifetime scar around his neck.

The last bears were tagged in 1973. The Alaska Department of Fish and Game decided that the McNeil Sanctuary was best utilized for tourism rather than research and the use of unsightly ear tags was discontinued.

The rate of aggression among the bears at the falls is influenced by many factors. These include the dominance, sex, age, reproductive status, and disposition of the bears present at the falls, also the number of bears, their fishing success, their fishing locations, the number of salmon, the water level of the falls, and the time of season. All these factors are constantly changing and working together to produce the prevailing social climate at the falls. Seldom are any of these variables mutually exclusive and it is rare to pinpoint a single variable that significantly changes the rate of aggression among the bears.

The water level of the falls can have complex effects on aggression by changing many variables. As water level increases, many fishing spots are submerged and the salmon are less accessible. This reduces fishing success, which usually increases aggression (hungry bears are generally more irritable). However, many bears leave the falls when the water rises, and a reduction in bear numbers usually causes a decrease in aggression. Each variable must be viewed in the overall context in which it occurs.

In contrast, a significant drop in water level can also cause changes in aggression. My data showed that there was a significant increase in aggression late in the season of 1974, despite declining bear numbers and increasing fishing success—factors that usually reduce aggression. The only factor that correlated with this increase in was a sudden drop in the water level of the falls. The water was so low that fishing spots became scarce and the few bears present were forced to fish closer and closer together as they competed for fewer choice locations. This increased the rate of aggression, even though the other factors indicated conditions that usually reduced aggression.

The overall rate of aggression was expressed as the number of encounters per bear hour. A *bear hour* was one hour that one bear was present at the falls. If ten bears were present for five hours, this was fifty bear hours. If there were seventy-five aggressive encounters during this five-hour period, then the rate of aggression was 1.5 encounters per bear hour. As many encounters were simple passive deferrals of a subordinate bear to a dominant bear, a more meaningful measure of aggression was the percentage of encounters that included the major forms of intense aggression (challenge threat, bite threat, charge, and attack). The percentage occurrence of these four forms of aggression were more positively correlated with the variables of fishing success, bear numbers, water level, and time of season. I refer the interested reader to the Appendix for more in-depth presentation of quantitative research data and discussion of aggression.

The bears had arrived to fish the falls later than normal, but this was expected in this year of delayed season; historically the timing of their summer activities had been influenced by climatic variation. That is, when spring arrived early, the bears also appeared early and the opposite occurred when spring was late. This raises the question of how the bears know when to begin fishing at McNeil Falls—or do they know? The salmon run, being more influenced by photoperiods than by seasonal variations, begins at approximately the same time each year. In contrast, the bears have varied the start of the fishing season by as much as four weeks, and sometimes their initiation of fishing did not coincide with the arrival of the first salmon. For instance, in 1971, a late summer, the salmon ran the falls in enormous numbers for two weeks before the first bears fished on July 27. In contrast, during the very early summer of 1974, the first bear arrived to fish on June 30, a week before many salmon appeared at the falls.

What draws the bears to the falls for their annual fishing? It is doubtful that the first salmon entering the river have sufficient odor to attract the bears. In addition, they may misjudge the actual start of the run at the falls. The two-week error by the bears in 1971 suggested that the initiation of fishing is perhaps controlled by something in the environment that is tuned to annual climatic variations. It is conceivable that brown bears, who presumably are much larger than their inland grizzly counterparts because of a richer protein diet, could develop a hunger for this essential protein. I presume that any bear is always hungry for salmon, but as these staple fish are not available until summer, they rely on their traditional springtime foods until salmon time. Then when these springtime foods no longer satiate them, the bears become hungry for salmon and seek out McNeil Falls.

Because the sedge is the only important, reliable protein food in the bears' diet just prior to salmon fishing, this plant was first believed to be a possible factor controlling the initiation of fishing. As mentioned earlier, the high percentage of protein in sedge declines as the plant matures, and because protein is important in the bears' diet, we hoped we could correlate a specific protein level in the sedge (as a percentage) with the initiation of fishing. That is, we hoped to find a critical point in the declining protein of sedge that will no longer satiate the bears' need for protein, and once this critical level is reached the bears become hungry and search for the salmon at McNeil Falls.

This sedge-protein hypothesis seemed plausible, so sedge samples were collected each summer for protein analysis. The best test of this hypothesis would come from comparing a late summer with an early summer. Fortunately 1974 and 1975 provided the sort of contrasting summers I needed. The results of the protein analyses from sedge samples are presented in Table 1.

These analyses reveal that in both summers the bears first fished when the protein of the sedge dropped to 12 percent (11.91 and 12.29). This 12 percent level was reached in 1974 before the salmon run began, and bears fished the falls before the salmon were present, but in 1975 the run began before the protein declined to 12 percent and fishing was delayed until July 20, which coincided with the 12 percent protein content of the sedge.

These results support the hypothesis that the bears fish

TABLE 1

Protein analysis of the sedge (*Carex langlii*) growing on the Mikfik sedge flats near the mouth of McNeil River. Bears began fishing on McNeil Falls when the protein content of the sedge dropped below 12.0 percent.

1974			1975		
Collection Date	% Crude Protein	% Neutral Fiber	Collection Date	% Crude Protein	% Neutral Fiber
6-20	14.50	52.41	6-22	25.77	52.08
6-25	15.51	51.72	6-24	22.21	53.98
6-30	11.91[1]	58.20	6-29	22.71	53.79
7-5	11.63	50.16	7-2	20.46	50.69
7-10	10.19	56.80	7-4	19.23	52.67
7-15	13.21	61.25	7-7	16.11	55.79
7-20	10.88	55.93	7-10	14.48	58.70
7-25	12.92	55.86	7-13	15.55	60.63
7-30	11.05	56.39	7-16	13.64	58.75
8-4	10.90	52.81	7-19	12.29[2]	60.01
			7-22	10.74	58.75

[1]1974 fishing began 7-2
[2]1975 fishing began 7-20
 Both dates correlate with a 12.0 percent level in the declining protein of the sedge.

only after their early summer diet of vegetation becomes deficient in protein, but despite the evidence, I cannot accept this hypothesis for a number of reasons. First, the data are certainly lacking, as more than two summers would be needed to thoroughly test this hypothesis. Second, I have no proof that sedge is really so important in the diet of bears. It is possible that their digestion is incapable of fully utilizing the protein in sedge. I only assume that it is an important protein food because many bears graze on it intensely before fishing. Finally, there remains the mystery of why few bears utilize the Mikfik sedge. It is obvious that wary bears avoid the exposed coastal flats and remain secluded in the backcountry until salmon time, but many unwary McNeil residents who are undaunted by people at the falls also fail to appear on the Mikfik flats. Because the bears who initiate salmon fishing each year are often those who make no apparent use of sedge, I find the sedge-protein hypothesis doubtful.

I think it is more logical to look for a very simple explanation for the fishing initiation puzzle. I suggest that the McNeil bears have an annual routine of activities that they learn to follow early in life and then continue to follow as a matter of tradition. It is reasonable to assume that bears are capable of learning to respond to cues in their environment that lead to each of their food-getting activities. They simply know when to search for sedge, salmon, and then berries. Their very lives depend on these perceptions. They have learned through experience that specific foods are not available until specific times and as a result they arrive at the falls at approximately the same time that the salmon begin to run. Very early or very late seasons would naturally offset their sequence of activities accordingly. For instance, in years with very late springs, the bears emerge from their dens late, move to sedge or other vegetation late, and then arrive at the falls late; whereas the opposite would occur in early seasons. This explains why the bears occasionally misjudge the start of the salmon run. The 12 percent level of protein in the sedge may just happen to coincide with the average arrival time of the bears at the falls.

On Kodiak Island the brown bears heavily utilize the sedge species *Carex marochaeta* in July and early August on alpine slopes between 2,000 and 3,000 feet. They feed almost exclusively on this sedge until they move to salmon streams in late August. The departure of bears from the alpine slopes coincides both with the arrival of salmon and the time when new shoots of sedge are no longer being produced (Atwell et al., 1980). At the time Kodiak bears are feeding on alpine sedge, the McNeil bears are fishing the falls for salmon. I have no evidence that McNeil bears utilize alpine sedges before or after the fishing season. This is a good example of the opportunistic flexibility of brown bears.

Once the fishing season was in full swing, the bears made use of several behavioral strategies that enabled them to utilize the falls more efficiently. These involved dividing up the fishing area in time and space so that maximum use could be made of the fish resource. Of course the bears are not cognizant of these adaptations, rather they are simply a result of each bear's effort to attain the greatest possible fishing success.

Temporal division results from fishing at different times of the day. The most obvious example of this is the almost exclusive use of the falls by large, mature boars and wary sows during the hours of darkness. They fish at night because darkness provides them with concealment and because people are not present at night. These wary bears will never fish when people are present and they run into hiding the instant they sight people approaching.

Twilight during July lasts until after 10:00 P.M., and Jim and I often stayed until that time to watch the arrival and activities of the wary night bears. If we sat in the deepest section of our cave and remained still, then most of the night bears would come down to the falls and fish undisturbed. Mature boars, such as Nails, Arlo, Nathan, Bones, Boxer, Shades, and Charlie Brown, would dominate the falls after 10:00 P.M. It was a rare occasion when more than three or four of these big fellows were present at one time, and so there was always room for other bears. Mature sows, adolescent males, and sows with cubs were often present as the twilight dimmed.

There was a diurnal cycle of activity at the falls that was consistent from day to day and from year to year. Just after dawn the falls were often vacant for several hours. Two or three large boars usually fished through the predawn hours, but they disappeared into the alders with the first light of day. From dawn to 2:00 P.M. it was rare to see more than two or three bears fishing at one time. These isolated fishers might be from any age or sex class, but most often they were young bears.

Red Collar coming ashore with a salmon catch for five hungry cubs.

It seems logical that young, low-ranking bears would take advantage of this morning lull and fish intensely while there was no competition, but there was no concerted fishing effort by young bears as a group. Most often there were more young bears present at the falls during the evening hours of peak activity than during the morning lull. There were no more salmon running during the evening than during the morning, and the bears that fished early had good fishing success. The unexpected conclusion from these observations is that the bears' diurnal activity patterns are so rigid that they will endure greater competition in the evening hours rather than adjust their activities. This is a surprising conclusion considering that brown bear behavior is usually very flexible as they adapt to varying conditions and circumstances.

Activity at the falls began to pick up after 2:00 P.M. and it steadily increased until 8:00 P.M. when twenty to thirty-five bears might be fishing at one time (plate 10). Mature sows, adolescent bears, and sows with cubs were predominant from 4:00 P.M. until 8:00 P.M., then the mature boars arrived and heightened the activity until dark. The number of bears fishing would begin to dwindle as darkness progressed, and by midnight or perhaps a bit later only a few boars and maybe a sow or two would be left fishing.

A night vision device, which magnified the available light thousands of times, allowed us to observe these night bears while they fished. Just how they managed to continue fishing in darkness was never really a mystery. Even on the darkest of nights the movement of a dark salmon is visible against a background of foaming white water. In addition, many bears fish even in daylight by standing in the river and pouncing on a salmon when they feel it run into their legs. The night bears did rather well under their cover of darkness.

We stayed through the hours of darkness huddled into our little cave, peering out with the night vision device to spy on the shy night bears. In retrospect, this seems like a rather stupid thing to have done, but it did not seem so at the time. We had shotguns, but they would have been of little use in the dark at close range. As usual, we depended on the good sense of the bears to avoid us. And they did.

Most of the regular daytime bears were gone by 10:00 P.M. and by midnight only a few seldom-seen boars remained. We never experienced any close calls in the dark and the aggression between bears was low. However, on many calm nights in camp the sounds from the falls drifting in on a slight breeze indicated that things were not always peaceful in the darkness. Perhaps my most vivid memory of night sounds at McNeil is the distant roaring of fishing bears accompanied by rushing water and cries of gulls.

The falls are also partitioned in terms of space. The success rates of the various fishing spots largely determine this spatial division, as the more dominant bears retain the best spots, while the subordinate bears are relegated to more inferior or isolated spots.

The physical structure of the rocks, which create the falls, determines the location of fishing spots and also the success rates of the spots by the way the water is directed around them (see map, p. 38). Some areas have a concentration of many good spots, while other areas have isolated or inferior spots.

This spatial division is not static; two major variables influence it during the season. First, as I have explained before, the bears habituate to one another's presence through the season, so the number of spots utilized increases as they fish closer together. This obviously changes the distribution of bears on the falls. Second, the water level of the river drops through the summer as the snowpack melts, and as it drops new fishing spots emerge and old ones are eliminated. These factors make spatial partitioning of the falls a very dynamic process.

Techniques that McNeil bears used to catch salmon were as interesting and varied as all other aspects of their behavior. In addition to a number of basic techniques that were used by most bears, there were several unique methods that some bears specialized in.

The basic fishing techniques consisted of several components that the bears put together in a variety of ways to produce their individual techniques. The basic components were orientation, pursuit, and capture. The bears oriented themselves to their prey by standing or sitting on rocks beside the water and scanning the river for salmon, or they might stand in the rushing water at various depths and watch or feel for salmon swimming by. The method of pursuit depended on the location of the salmon and its distance from the bear when it was sighted. A bear would simply pounce on a fish that swam close by, but an active chase was necessary when a fish was sighted at a distance in shallow water. If the prey was spotted out in deep water some bears would dive headlong from a rock to attempt a capture. The actual capture of a fish was made with mouth and forepaw(s) together, with forepaw(s) alone, or with mouth alone.

Many bears expanded on these basic techniques and produced unique fishing methods, which were beautiful examples of the opportunistic ecology of bears.

Both Goldie and Lady Bird, two large, mature sows, used a wild plunging technique, but it was Lady Bird who made it famous at the falls. She would appear on the bluff directly above the number-one fishing spot with a wild, excited stare in her eyes while her lower lip hung loose from her jaw and flopped around, exposing her teeth as she scanned the falls. Then without further delay she launched herself down the bluff, racing at breakneck speed toward the river, and without hesitation threw herself into the rushing water with a tremendous belly flop. This wild technique was often successful because she dove into a certain area that was consistently plugged with salmon. When she landed suddenly in the midst of a school of salmon, it was a simple matter to grab one with her forepaws and mouth.

The two juvenile males, Dark and Patch Butt, frequently performed a complete dive into deep water from the center rock in the falls (plate 11). This usually occurred after they became jaded with poor fishing at other spots and started to prowl around the edge of the center rock to scan for fish in deep water. Dark most often stopped at the end of the rock and stood calmly, watching the deep currents for the movements of fish. Several times he crouched with weight on his hind legs as though ready to spring into the water, but then decided against an attempt and returned to a relaxed stance to await a better opportunity. The actual dive often came very suddenly without any noticeable preparation. Dark lunged instantly into the air, soared spread-eagled over the water, and landed in the deep current with a resounding belly flop. This diving method was rarely successful, but these two playful bears seemed to enjoy diving, and I suspect that they continued to use the technique partially because the simple enjoyment of it was reinforcing.

Once Patch Butt and Dark had completed their dive from the center rock, they usually continued to fish in the deep water by employing the *swim-and-lunge technique* (plate 12). Romeo and Zubin also used this technique but Romeo was by far the star performer. Instead of diving into the water from the rocks, Romeo would simply walk out into the current and stand on his hind legs when the water got too deep to continue on all fours. From a standing position he waded around in 4 or 5 feet of water, with his head down, searching for the movements of salmon. Whenever he spotted a fish, he lunged forward into the water with his forepaws extended in an effort to grab the fish. This technique was also generally unsuccessful, but the bears did not appear to grow tired of it quickly for they would continue to wade, swim, and lunge about in the deep water for several minutes.

Red, Zubin, Light, and Dark all used a snorkel technique to spot and snag dead fish in the deep pool below the upper falls. Zubin especially seemed to have a taste for the decaying salmon carcasses that accumulated in the pool. He waded out into deep water until only his head bobbed above the surface and then he stuck his face into the water and scanned beneath the surface for salmon carcasses. His ears seemed to be sensitive to the water because he was very careful to keep them above the surface, and if his ears did submerge, he immediately threw his head up and shook it violently until his ears were dry. While bobbing around with his eyes submerged, he appeared to be grappling for fish with both forepaws and hind paws as though it required a bit of juggling to get the carcasses to the surface. Once he secured a carcass, he held it in his forepaws and nibbled on it while remaining submerged to the neck in the pool.

One would assume that Zubin and other bears resorted to scavenging dead salmon because they could not catch fresh fish, but this is not the case. In fact, whenever Zubin went scavenging for dead fish he normally left a spot at which he enjoyed phenomenal fishing success, as though he had grown tired of fresh fish and desired a taste of putrid flesh. If the wind was blowing in my direction, I usually got several strong whiffs of his tasty treat though he was 100 feet away.

Light and Siedelman were the only McNeil bears who carried the snorkel method one step further by diving completely underwater to get dead salmon. Siedelman would snorkel around just as Zubin did, but then he would suddenly pull his hindquarters up and plunge underwater in a complete dive. Occasionally he remained submerged as long as twenty to thirty seconds before surfacing with a salmon carcass in his jaws. The first thing he did was shake the water from his ears (plate 13).

Siedelman, an adolescent male, was the only bear that developed an unusual technique and used it extensively and with considerable success. He learned the method apparently by accident one summer and then refined it greatly. The next summer he used it every day for long periods and with good success. The inventive Siedelman sat completely submerged in the lee of the center rock of the falls and waited for salmon to be swept down the main current and into the calm water behind the rock, where he sat in ambush and simply chomped them with his mouth. He often remained underwater for one to two minutes before coming up for air.

Siedelman's unique method brought about another interesting behavior. Groucho, a six-year-old male, began observing Siedelman's success and gradually took more interest in the underwater technique. Soon Groucho was sitting beside Siedelman in the water, and occasionally he looked underwater to see what was going on (plate 14). However, he never fully developed this method and never caught salmon because he would not completely submerge his head, which was possibly because of the normal reluctance to wetting the ears. Nonetheless, the series of events involving Siedelman and Groucho's learning this new behavior is of great interest. It is rare for any animal to develop an entirely new, complex behavior. The cultural transfer of the new behavior via learning to other members of the population is especially fascinating. Such learning implies to me that Siedelman and Groucho were well above average in intelligence.

One of Patch Butt's favorite techniques involved sitting and waiting for a fish to become stranded on a particular section of the falls. The section he watched was something of a trough where water accumulated after flowing in a thin veil over an expanse of rock. Salmon would swim into this trough and then could go no further because the water was too shallow. Patch Butt simply sat and waited for a fish to enter the trough and then he ran up and blocked its exit and pounced on it with forepaws and mouth.

Charlie Brown's fishing technique was not unusual but it is noteworthy because he executed his moves with incredible speed and agility, which was unexpected from such an enormous animal. He stood at the number-one spot and constantly scanned the water, back and forth, with a very even metronomelike motion of his head. When he spotted a fish he brought his entire 1,200-plus-pound bulk down with nearly invisible speed and grasped his prey in his jaws. He very rarely missed. No other bear came close to achieving Charlie's speed, agility, and accuracy. This points out that the qualities that make a bear the alpha boar in a population are not limited to size and strength alone.

The eating habits of bears change dramatically with the season and with their fishing success. During the first days of the season, bears are very hungry and they almost totally consume every fish that is caught. Usually the liver and always the testes of male fish are left uneaten, even on the first day of the season.

The bears become more selective in their eating as fishing success increases. Selective eating on male fish usually includes the skin, nose, the top of the head, viscera, and usually some flesh. Bears may select the same parts on female fish, but in addition, they go after the oil-rich eggs. Later in the season, when the bears are satiated on salmon and their fishing success is really good, some bears may eat only the eggs of female fish and leave the rest behind to be eaten by other bears or gulls. A few successful bears may even become selective to the extent of catching only female fish for their eggs. These bears apparently can detect the fullness of the egg-stuffed abdomens of female fish while holding the salmon in their mouths. Males are dropped immediately without even biting into them, whereas the females are kept and stripped of their eggs.

I have witnessed a few occasions at the falls when fishing success was so phenomenal that the bears lost interest and became lethargic in their fishing. They caught and ate all the salmon they could possibly consume and yet the prey-catching stimulus was so great that they continued to fish. They simply could not resist the swarms of salmon before them, and they would continue catching and letting fish go without killing them as if they were in a trance.

6

Bear Growls and Body Language

Encounters between bears are controlled largely by the social status, or dominance, of those involved, and this in turn is determined by the size, age, sex, reproductive status, and disposition of each bear. Although all of these variables contribute to the structure of the McNeil dominance hierarchy, the resulting structure is not always linear or stable. Generally a large bear ranks higher than a smaller bear; an older bear ranks over a younger bear; a mature boar ranks over a mature sow; and a sow with cubs ranks over single sows, and on rare occasions over mature boars.

Individual exceptions exist in the hierarchy, and other factors can temporarily change a bear's rank. For instance, when a bear has not caught salmon and is hungry, it is more likely to defend a fishing spot and thus maintain its dominance at the highest possible level, but after it has eaten several salmon it may allow a bear of equal or even lower rank to take over its spot. The result is that a bear's rank in the dominance hierarchy is not always static.

I determined the dominance of each bear entirely from its win-loss record in encounters with other bears. A bear lost an encounter if it deferred in any way when another bear approached. Likewise, a bear won an encounter if it displaced another. The season's cumulative record of wins and losses revealed a definite rank order despite the temporary changes that occurred.

I was able to observe the rise in dominance of young bears and the gradual decline in dominance of a few older bears during the years of my study. The increase in dominance of young bears as they grew older and more experienced was expected, and because all young bears were going through the same gradual changes, this process was not very obvious. In contrast, the decline in dominance of older bears from year to year was striking and most fascinating.

The decline of Patches was the most amazing case I observed. During my first summer at McNeil, Patches was nineteen years old and weighed about 800 pounds, not very large for a mature boar. There were several larger boars who were dominant to Patches, but he ranked higher than all other bears.

Patches always seemed to be living in slow motion. He walked, fished, ate, and reacted to almost everything at half speed; but this did not prevent him from maintaining his rank, for other bears knew he could burst into action with a fast charge when necessary. As I described earlier, Patches demonstrated that he was still forceful at age nineteen when he detected Reggie fishing over 300 feet downstream and chased her away from the falls.

Patches slipped faster and faster into very obvious senility during the next four years. He would often stand for hours at the number-one fishing spot and stare blankly at the water without making even one fishing attempt as though totally mesmerized by the flowing water. When he left this spot, a younger bear would move in and catch a salmon within seconds. When he caught a fish on our side of the river, he often carried it straight toward our cave. Only some loud yells and arm waving would stop him about 15 feet in front of us, where he would stand staring straight ahead and blink slowly for several seconds before backing away a few feet to eat the fish where he stood.

I was reasonably certain that Patches was quite forgetful by the time he was twenty-three years old. For example, one afternoon on my way to the falls I met a group of four McNeil tourists standing beside Mikfik Creek watching Patches graze calmly in deep sedge about 50 feet away. I passed in plain view of Patches, but he never looked up at me, and after I joined the others to watch him for a while, I felt sure that he was unaware of his observers. When some of the tourists left in a skiff, the sound of the motor startled Patches and he looked up in wide-eyed alarm and turned to run away, but he ran only about 20 feet before he stopped, stared ahead blankly for a few seconds, and then slowly dropped his head and began grazing again as calmly as before. He never looked around to check on what had definitely alarmed him only seconds before. This was perhaps just the ultimate in nonchalance, but why did he suddenly ignore what had alarmed him three seconds earlier?

I concluded from this that he had simply forgotten what had originally scared him. This is a subjective evaluation of Patches' behavior, but he displayed similar forgetfulness on a number of occasions in ways that precluded other interpretation.

The other bears were also aware of Patches' senility, and this resulted in a gradual decline in his social status. All boars and many sows with cubs began displacing him at prime fishing spots and eventually he was relegated to fishing with younger bears around the center rock. His fishing success was miserable and he spent increasing amounts of time sleeping on the center rocks in the falls (plate 15). Young bears continued to give him wide clearance, but most mature bears gradually began to ignore him. At the falls Patches was an aging fixture that was slowly fading from the scene. Patches was never seen after the summer of 1981. During his last summer, at age twenty-seven, he was more senile than ever, and on a couple of occasions he almost walked into a crowd of people at the falls.

Other bears in their twenties did not age so obviously, which suggests that perhaps Patches was an extreme case brought on by unknown causes. For instance, Red Collar had a spring cub at age twenty-three and appeared to be as strong, healthy, and alert as ever. Charlie Brown still maintained his position as the alpha boar at McNeil at an estimated age well in excess of twenty.

Charlie was firmly entrenched as the dominant boar at McNeil when Derek Stonorov first began his study in 1970. A film that Derek produced in 1971 reveals that Charlie was an enormous 1,000-plus-pound boar at that early date, which would put his age at a minimum of ten, and probably twelve or older, in 1971. Almost ten years later, in 1979, Charlie still held his position at an age certainly in excess of twenty.

Charlie Brown was such an awesome sight to behold in his prime that it would be difficult to imagine a more powerful-looking animal (plate 16). Muscles bulged and rolled in great slabs on every part of him as he emerged confidently on the edge of the bluff overlooking the falls and surveyed the scene for several seconds before descending to fish. As he headed straight for the number-one spot, it was obvious that Charlie was in absolute control at McNeil. He did not hesitate or look from side to side as he approached and he showed no concern whatever for any of the fishing bears. He knew that no bear was a threat to his dominance and he ignored them all and moved quickly to his fishing spot.

Charlie often approached from the rear and caught some unlucky bear unaware at his spot, but he never charged or attacked these individuals. Instead, he walked up calmly and ignored them when they ran or fell backward into the falls to escape him. All of the bears within 100 feet or more scattered like scared rabbits when Charlie first appeared and few of them would return closer than 75 feet while he fished.

There were only three or four boars that were large

enough to be of any concern to Charlie Brown. These large males never challenged him and as long as they deferred to him and kept a safe distance away, he ignored them as well. Even though Charlie seemed to ignore the bears around the falls, he actually monitored most of the activities rather closely. He demonstrated this one evening during an exciting incident after the arrival of a large boar who was a stranger at the falls. I had never seen the 900-pound male, and his behavior indicated that it was perhaps his first visit to the falls. He was unfamiliar with the fishing spots, so he ran around fishing recklessly and paid no heed to other bears. Charlie glanced at the brazen stranger a couple of times and then left his number-one spot and began approaching the boar with increasing speed. It was obvious that this boar did not know Charlie, because he only glanced at him approaching and continued his wild fishing. Charlie was in a full charge when he plowed into the strange boar, who barely had time to turn and brace himself for Charlie's assault.

Their struggle was so fast and furious, with such quickness and agility, that it appeared to be a blur of jaws and paws. Suddenly they were on hind legs with forelegs locked around each other's shoulders. Charlie seized a big hunk of the stranger's neck in his jaws and began twisting it, pushing him slowly but inexorably to the ground. The strength in this standoff was so intense, so overwhelming, that it seemed to go on forever. As Charlie twisted and pushed harder it appeared as though the entire side of the stranger's face and neck surely would be ripped off. Still harder he twisted and finally their balance was broken and the stranger fell to the ground, broke free of Charlie's grip, scrambled from under his blows, and fled the scene. He did not return to the falls, but if he had returned I suspect he would have respected Charlie's dominance.

Charlie firmly held his position as McNeil's alpha boar through 1979, but physical signs of aging became more apparent each year. When I first saw him in 1973 he was one solid mass of muscle from head to toe and his coat was not blemished by a single scar. By 1975 he had a few minor scars on his neck and sides and in 1977 he arrived severely battle-scarred with a large open wound across his left shoulder. His once-sleek physique was rounded by an enormous pot belly that almost dragged the ground. It was obvious that he was growing old and that he was having greater difficulty defending his position against the challenges of other boars. It was sad to observe the aging of Charlie Brown because he was a symbol at McNeil. I always hoped that he would simply fail to show up at the falls one summer, rather than age as Patches had done. Fortunately, he was never seen after the summer of 1979. He never lost his dominance at McNeil.

While Charlie Brown and Patches were in their decline, several young boars were rising to take their place. I had strong expectations for Patch Butt, who was four years old during my first summer at McNeil. Big Mamma, the largest sow at McNeil, was his mother, so he certainly had great potential. Patch Butt was large for his age and he already had features more typical of mature boars. His head appeared broad and too large for his young frame and his haunches already had the massive rounded musculature of large boars. His growth during the next two years was phenomenal. I knew Patch Butt could be the next alpha boar at McNeil when he reached a weight of over 500 pounds at age six.

One key factor that could prevent Patch Butt from attaining the highest dominance was his easygoing nature. During his adolescence, Patch Butt was one of the most amiable of all McNeil bears. He was often playful and was rarely aggressive with his peers. Most bears will fight to protect their fish catch, but in his youth Patch Butt routinely allowed others to stand beside him and share his catch. It was this gentle nature that might prevent him from replacing Charlie Brown.

I thought that Patch Butt might mature into a playful "falls hound" similar to Zubin, but he became a more typical boar. I observed him in 1980 when he was eleven years old and weighed close to 1,000 pounds. He had a massive frame but still lacked the bulging musculature of top boars. His lower jaw hung loose and crooked, indicating a serious fighting injury. He fished irregularly and usually did not arrive until evening—a

pattern typical of boars. Patch Butt chose to fish at the number-
one spot, but he was not overtly aggressive in defending it.
Only once did I see him charge a subordinate bear that fished
too close to his spot. He was businesslike and rather ignored
the bears around him.

Patch Butt would continue to grow and he might become
more aggressive in asserting his dominance, but he had a long
way to go to overtake the boar that unexpectedly rose to replace Charlie Brown. Dismay equaled Patch Butt in size, but
he had the massive, bulging musculature reminiscent of
Charlie's prime. He was also aggressive and made a point of
maintaining his position. Patch Butt and Dismay had played
together as adolescents, but now they were direct competitors.
The fine line of difference between them was of size and temperament.

Once again a major aspect of social behavior is influenced
by the temperament of those involved. Because Larry Aumiller had observed Patch Butt and Dismay through their
adult lives, I asked him to comment on their dominance relationship. Larry related that "Patch Butt in reality has more
[potential] dominance than he is either aware of or chooses to
push. He's a pussycat." This coincides precisely with my impression of Patch Butt. How well I remember him as an over-
grown six-year-old fishing on the falls. He routinely allowed his
peers to sneak up and steal his salmon catches without any
protest whatsoever. As a thief slinked away with his salmon,
Patch Butt would calmly watch him retreat, lick his lips, and
then return to his fishing spot.

The stealing of a salmon catch is one of the most flagrant
violations of a bear's individual space, and yet Patch Butt usually did not object. It was hard to imagine in 1975 that this
"pussycat" would ever rise to become McNeil's alpha boar, and
indeed he did not.

The social status of bears determines the types of encounters
and the patterns of communication that occur during such
encounters when bears are at the falls. This suggests that it
would be possible to predict some of the behavior of bears

during encounters if one was familiar with their rank and temperament, but it is commonly believed that bear behavior is "unpredictable." Any visitor to wilderness parks in the western United States, Canada, or Alaska will know this after being bombarded with literature and signs warning them about bears. Is this reputation of unpredictability entirely accurate? Well, yes and no. *No?*

I must say no because individual bears are indeed predictable. I think I have made clear that I can predict with considerable accuracy what any of the most familiar McNeil bears will do when confronted with another bear or even a human. For example, sows with cubs are reputed to be the most unpredictable of all bears, but I know (as the reader will soon know) that Red, Lanky, Jeanne, Big Mamma, Reggie, Red Collar, and White will pay very little attention to me and will go about their business undisturbed when I am in the area. Other sows such as Lady Bird, Goldie, Reagan, and Buella will turn and run in fear while huffing alarms at their cubs, and Jezebel will most likely give me a bluff charge or two before running away in a frenzy.

The obvious conclusion from these observations is that there exists a tremendous range of temperaments in individual bears, and it is this individuality that is responsible for bears having the reputation of being unpredictable. I may know how the familiar McNeil brownies will react to me, but if I hiked into Glacier National Park in Montana I would have no idea at all what a given grizzly would do during an encounter. The same holds true for any hiker in bear country.

If the individuality of bear behavior is considered, it is easy to understand why all bears are believed to be unpredictable. For example, a group of hikers enter bear country and encounter three bears during a week of hiking. Bear A ignores them and continues to graze in a meadow undisturbed. Later, bear B, a sow with cubs, huffs alarms at her cubs on sighting the hikers and runs away into hiding. The last day they encounter bear C, another sow with cubs, who bluff charges them before running away huffing and puffing wildly.

The hikers conclude from their experiences that bears are

unpredictable. They decide that a given bear may ignore them or attack them depending on what strikes its fancy at the time. The fact is that bears A, B, and C would "probably" react again and again in the same way under the same circumstances. Unfortunately, in practical field experiences, the reputation of unpredictability holds true, for very few people have the opportunity to get personally acquainted with the bears in a particular area. (Of course, a sow with cubs, regardless of her temperament, may react violently if she feels that her cubs are threatened. The classic example occurs when someone gets between a sow and her cubs. The previous discussion refers to encounters at greater distances or in open country.)

Perhaps the main reason that bears have gained their reputation for unpredictability is that their reactions to humans can result in severe injury or death. The behavior of many other animals is also unpredictable, yet they have no such reputation. For instance, when a person goes door to door in a strange neighborhood he will have no idea what each dog sitting on a doorstep is likely to do. Will the dog wag its tail and lick a hand, or will it bark and attack the stranger? The postman knows, and the situation is exactly the same with bears. Bears vary just as dogs vary.

Why do bears have such a wide range of temperaments? A very simple answer is Why not? Genetic diversity gives rise to a *behavioral continuum* (a range of temperaments) with upper and lower limits within which bears can successfully survive and reproduce. A bear's position on the continuum (such as its level of aggressiveness) may be largely a result of its lifetime learning experiences. However, I have a hard time believing that the differences between the very aggressive sows and the mellow sows at McNeil were due entirely to learning experiences. I think it is conceivable that such extreme differences in temperaments may have a genetic basis. The differences in the temperaments of various breeds of dogs is well known and obviously were selected for by the dog breeders. I see no reason why complex traits such as behavioral temperaments cannot have a genetic basis.

How predictable is brown bear behavior in general? To answer this question I conducted a quantitative analysis of the communication system of the McNeil bears. Encounters between two bears were filmed and later analyzed in detail. Twenty-one discrete behaviors (signals) were catalogued in terms of their sequence within each encounter (see Appendix, Table A-13). In other words, when bear A approached bear B, I began recording the numbered behaviors as they occurred. The result was a sequence of behaviors on an action-reaction basis (for example, behavior of bear A, behavior of bear B, A-B-A-B-A-B-A-B, and so on). A total of 12,460 behaviors in 1,696 encounters were quantified.

The resulting sequences of behavior were analyzed in terms of their probabilities of occurrence. The resulting measures, which are referred to as *uncertainty,* can be determined for single behavioral events, as well as for groups of two, three, four, or more events. The decrease in uncertainty observed as the sequence lengthens tell us how much the bears are basing their behavior on preceding behaviors. That is, how much bear A is affecting the behavior of bear B through his actions, or how much A is communicating to B about his intentions.

These measures of uncertainty are most meaningful when they are compared to similar findings from other species. Because bears are distinctly asocial, I shall contrast my findings with Stuart Altmann's study on social rhesus monkeys (Altmann, 1965).

Figure 1 illustrates the decrease in uncertainty of behavior as sequence length increases. That is, a behavior is more predictable if the preceding behavior is known, and it becomes increasingly predictable if the preceding two and three behaviors are known.

The uncertainty of rhesus monkey behavior is initially higher than that of brown bears because of the larger number of behaviors that are considered (120 vs. 21). However, the uncertainty drops at a much faster rate and is finally lower than that of brown bears. The greater predictability of rhesus behavior is presumably due to their rigid social organization, which precludes much freedom of action for subordinate members.

Even though my data show that brown bear behavior is less predictable than rhesus behavior, the data also reveal that behaviors of the McNeil bears are influenced by preceding behaviors. This is not surprising, because it must be assumed that the social behavior of any animal can be influenced in some way by members of the same species. The most important information in the bear-rhesus comparison is the relative difference in the data concerning the structure of their communication systems and the possible insights into the evolution of the systems.

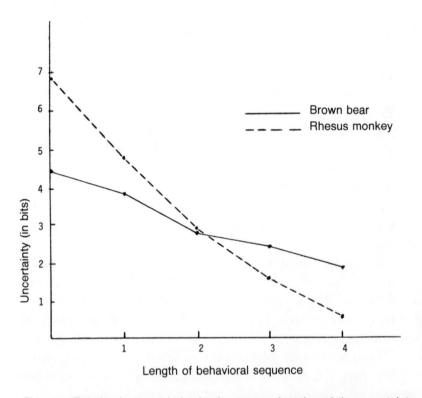

Figure 1. Relation between behavioral sequence length and the uncertainty of behavioral events. Behaviors become more predictable (less uncertainty) as more preceding behaviors are considered. The rigid social organization of rhesus monkeys presumably makes their behavior more predictable than that of brown bears.

Why is the behavior of the social rhesus more predictable than the behavior of an asocial brown bear? The rhesus monkeys use exaggerated submissive and dominant signals *(behaviors)* in their interactions that serve to stabilize or bring order to their social organization. The young or low-ranking rhesus use submissive signals to acknowledge the dominance of higher ranking animals. For example: everyone is familiar with the cowering, groveling (submissive) behavior of a young dog when it is approached by a large adult dog (dominant). This is a simplistic example, but similar submissive signals are used by subordinate rhesus monkeys. They must be submissive in order to remain within the group and survive to reproduce later. The dominant animals in turn must assert their dominance in order to maintain their rank and the reproductive privileges that rank provides.

Ritualized dominance and submission signals have not evolved in brown bear communication because bears have no elaborate social organization that could result in the selection or evolution of such behaviors. A young bear does not gain any privileges by appeasing an adult, and the adults do not have to maintain their dominance over younger bears for purposes of social organization. Bears do not depend on associations with other bears in order to survive and therefore sociality and social organization have not evolved.

After a young bear has been weaned and has left its siblings, it has only itself to look after. Every other bear represents potential competition for food and reproductive success. It is little wonder that bears are aggressive toward one another. In fact, what keeps them from killing each other? Indeed, the death of a competitor certainly reduces competition! Fights to the death are most unusual among larger animals because there is a selective disadvantage in being too aggressive. That is, a bear who initiates violent battles for trivial reasons may suffer severe injury and reduce its chances of survival and future reproductive success.

Brown bears have little need of communicative abilities during most of the year. After emerging from their winter sleep, they wander in search of carrion that winter has left behind. The vast frozen alpine areas, meandering river valleys, and desolate shorelines are all patrolled in solitude. When summer arrives they graze on sedge flats alone, and finally autumn finds them scooping up berries on alpine slopes in quiet isolation. During these times the brownies easily avoid one another by smell or by distant sightings. It is only during the summer and fall salmon runs that the bears must rub shoulders.

The McNeil bears are forced to associate with other bears to an unusual extent because of the crowded conditions at the falls. The resulting interaction between bears is an amplified version of what happens on any Alaska Peninsula salmon stream. The interactions are not atypical, although their frequency and intensity may be.

The McNeil bears deal with one another quite effectively with their imprecise system of communication. The vast majority of potential aggressive interactions are avoided when younger animals detect the approach of larger bears and leave the scene long before any aggression can take place. However, when ten or twenty bears are competing for fishing spots around the falls, aggressive encounters are inevitable. Even in these close quarters the lower ranking bears are usually successful in avoiding higher ranking bears, but occasionally they have aggressive encounters.

The most spectacular encounters involve what I call a *challenge threat,* which occurs when one bear fails to yield to another or when two bears of similar social status compete for a preferred fishing spot. The aggression erupts very suddenly into the challenge threat that seems to be on the verge of violent combat. There is no submission or dominance "signaling" during the early part of a challenge threat, because both bears give the most threatening displays possible. It is all a big bluff, particularly on the part of the lower ranking bear, and the reality of possible injury makes it an effective bluff.

A typical challenge threat develops in the following manner: A large, mature sow, Jeanne, approaches her favorite fishing spot and passes near Patch Butt, a 400-pound adolescent male. When Patch Butt fails to defer to her, Jeanne charges him with ears back, head level or down, and mouth open with teeth exposed. Patch Butt immediately turns to meet her charge with ears back, head down, mouth open, and hindquarters lowered in a crouch. Jeanne usually stops directly in front of Patch Butt and assumes his identical threat posture (plate 17), and then with mouths open in mock biting threats, both heads are thrown upward briefly before being lowered again (plate 18). This latter action of throwing the heads high with mouths open is an aggressive eruption of an intense challenge threat, which I call *bite threat*. This does not always follow a challenge threat, especially not those of lesser intensity.

Up to this point both bears have used identical threat behaviors, but after this initial aggression some submission signals appear. Patch Butt does not use the stereotyped submission signals that are typical of more social animals. There is no cowering or groveling because Patch Butt must keep his guard up at all times, always prepared to defend his life. If Patch Butt were to roll over and grovel like a dog, there would be nothing to prevent Jeanne from attacking and perhaps killing the defenseless bear. There does not seem to be much inhibition against such low-risk violence among bears.

The most submissive signal Patch Butt can afford is merely to make himself as inoffensive as possible, while remaining prepared to defend himself. Immediately after the intense aggression at the beginning of the encounter Jeanne may

A challenge threat between a sow and a young male showing the postures and signals of this stereotyped threat.

begin to back away, but Patch Butt avoids any sudden movements that might be construed by Jeanne as aggressive. He
remains still with head down, ears back, while staring at the
ground (see a similar encounter in plate 19). These are not used
in exactly the same context as classic submissive signals, but
they do not elicit further aggression. If Patch Butt does not
maintain his low profile, Jeanne may renew her aggression and
possibly attack him. Jeanne, however, is free to raise her head,
look around, lick her lips, shake all over, turn away, or even
leave the scene. I say "free" to do these things because she
knows that Patch Butt is a subordinate and will not initiate an
attack. The latter has no such assurances and thus remains still
and ready to defend himself. If Patch Butt took the liberty of
ending the encounter by walking away, Jeanne would attack
him from behind, as she must win the encounter in order to
maintain her dominance over Patch Butt. The benefits of her
dominance over Patch Butt will be reaped the next time she
approaches her fishing spot and finds him fishing. Patch Butt
will leave quickly and allow her access and uninterrupted
fishing time.

When I first began my bear studies, I was confused by the
apparent lack of dominant and submissive behaviors in aggressive encounters. I was puzzled by my observation that during
encounters, both bears, regardless of rank, performed identi-

*A bite threat between a sow and a young male showing the postures and
signals of this stereotyped threat.*

cal challenge threats. Then one afternoon I watched a yearling cub approach its mother, who was fishing near Goldie at the number-one spot. Goldie saw the cub and charged it. The yearling ran at first, but turned and displayed a classic challenge threat when Goldie caught up. Then, to my surprise, Goldie displayed a classic challenge threat and bite threat complete with low crouching, head high, ears back, and mouth gaping. There was obviously nothing submissive in her actions. It was all threat behavior. The cub put forth its only defense: an intense challenge threat of its own. In addition, the cub stood on hind legs and placed its open mouth directly in front of Goldie's face. It was obvious that this standing, which is sometimes used by young bears when confronted in an encounter with a much larger bear, served to intensify the threat by making the cub appear larger and by placing the cub in a stance for immediate combat.

This encounter made everything fall into place for me. Challenge threats are all bluffs followed by simple appeasing actions by subordinate bears. These threats are quite stereotyped and therefore predictable. The less complex encounters (for example, dominant bear approaches and subordinate bear defers) are extremely predictable. The final result is that most brown bear behavior is predictable.

Why then is it less predictable than rhesus behavior? It is primarily the long contesting encounters between equally ranked bears over fishing spots that cause this. The bluffing and testing may end quickly or it may go on for a very long time. For instance, when two closely ranked bears compete for a fishing spot they may bluff and test each other for ten or fifteen minutes or longer. These indecisive encounters reduced the predictability of the quantitative data.

The absence of effective submissive behavior is also obvious when fights erupt during encounters. For example, if Jeanne actually attacked Patch Butt during their encounter, the latter would fight as if he were fighting for his life, and indeed he would be, for there is no possibility of submission after combat ensues. Even when Jeanne ends her attack, Patch Butt will continue to snap at her face to indicate that he is prepared to defend himself. Submissive behavior is not used, only threats. Jeanne knows that Patch Butt can and will defend himself and this keeps her violence in check.

Sometimes a dominant bear will turn its head and expose its neck to an opponent during an encounter. This behavior appears to be submissive, but its function is appeasement. Neck exposure is always used by a bear of high dominance, usually a boar. For example, when Charlie Brown approaches Lady Bird and her cubs at the falls, she will inevitably charge at Charlie and violently threaten him by snapping and striking at his face and neck. Charlie offers no resistance at all and turns his head to expose his neck to Lady Bird's assault. In doing so, he appeases her by indicating that he has no aggressive intentions. He does not need to assert himself over Lady Bird, for she is not a threat to his dominance. Charlie's dominance was so great that he used this behavior in encounters with other boars (plate 20).

It seems logical to suspect that any behavior that exposes a vital part of the body to attack would be self-destructive and would be selected against in evolution. However, in this case Lady Bird does not actually dare to attack Charlie's neck with force, because to do so might be fatal for her. It appears to be a dangerous action, but there is really no danger for Charlie in the social context in which it is used.

Encounters were complex and often very long when bears of similar social status competed for preferred fishing spots. These encounters always involved a lot of bluffing and testing between bears and the outcome often depended on motivational factors such as hunger. For instance, when Reggie arrived at the falls in a state of hunger to begin fishing, she might be able to displace Romeo, a ten-year-old male, if he was satiated, but if he too had just arrived and was hungry, then Romeo most likely would defend his spot against Reggie's approach.

Romeo and Reggie had many classic bluffing encounters at the number-one spot that often lasted for ten to fifteen minutes. A typical example developed in the following manner: Reggie arrived at the lower falls in midafternoon and fished at her favorite spot for over an hour, but she had no success and soon she was working her way toward the upper falls. Reggie could see that Romeo occupied the number-one spot, so she approached slowly and stopped here and there to make halfhearted fishing attempts. In doing so, she gave Romeo advance notice of her approach and also allowed herself time to judge Romeo's mood. Would he allow her to fish close by? Would he charge her or perhaps defer to her? As she approached, Reggie was undoubtedly picking up from Romeo subtle clues that influenced her maneuvers.

Reggie continued her intermittent approach until she was about 50 feet downstream from Romeo and then she stopped and fished for several minutes. This fishing bout was mostly a ploy of Reggie's designed to assess Romeo's intentions further and also to allow him more time to become habituated to her presence. Soon Reggie began her final move by circling up and behind Romeo in an approach that resembled a stealthy stalk. Tension was apparent in the slow, stiff movements of her legs, depressed ears, lowered head, and cautious glances at Romeo. Each time that Romeo turned his head to check on Reggie's approach, she would instantly depress her ears further back, glance down and away to avoid eye contact, and hesitate a step until Romeo turned his head.

Just why Reggie chose to circle around Romeo and approach him from the opposite side was not clear, but this maneuver was commonly used by many bears, and I suspect it was another stalking tactic. After Reggie had circled around Romeo, she began a very cautious direct approach. A brief glance from Romeo stopped her cold and she lowered her head, depressed her ears, and gave an *open-mouth threat* (slow opening and closing of the mouth) (see a similar encounter in plate 21). Romeo would usually allow Reggie one or perhaps two of these hesitant advances and then the next time he would turn suddenly and bluff charge her. Reggie expected the charge and was prepared for it because she had been through this routine many times before.

Reggie was 20 feet away when Romeo whirled around and

charged with ears back, mouth gaping with a roar, and head lowered. Reggie stopped instantly to meet his charge with ears back, mouth open, and head low, but as Romeo closed in she crouched her hindquarters, raised her head, and displayed her most intense open-mouth threat. Romeo's head went up in unison with Reggie's as he stopped just short of plowing into her (plate 22). These bite threats appeared to be mock biting as though each bear were on the verge of chomping the other's face. The heads were thrown high for only an instant before being dropped so low that their noses almost touched the ground. At this low level the open-mouth threats and guttural growling continued the standoff as both bears faced each other with heads slightly sideways and only inches apart. This was the quintessential intense challenge threat (plate 23). Their standoff normally did not last more than ten or fifteen seconds before Romeo slowly turned and moved back to his fishing spot. He left in stages and turned to give Reggie open-mouth threats if she moved or glanced around too suddenly.

Reggie remained motionless with her head down and ears back until Romeo returned to fish, and then she yawned and glanced around while licking her lips and shaking her coat vigorously. These last acts, which often appear after an intense encounter, apparently helped to relieve the tension that resulted from such aggression. Reggie waited about thirty seconds before beginning her approach once again, and this time she crept along slowly a step at a time and paused after each advance to glance at Romeo. He rarely charged her a second time, but every few seconds he turned his head and gave Reggie an open-mouth threat, to which she always responded with her own threat, although she glanced away to avoid eye contact. This went on repeatedly until Reggie had worked her way down to the river's edge within 6 to 10 feet of Romeo. Both bears then fished in an atmosphere of high tension with open-mouth threats continuing, particularly when one made a fishing attempt or when they happened to look toward each other (plate 24). Early in the fishing season either Reggie or Romeo would soon leave as they were not accustomed to fishing so close to another bear, but later in the summer they might fish together for hours at the number-one spot.

Romeo and Reggie dealt with this complex confrontation quite effectively, utilizing their complex but imprecise ability to communicate with each other. Some of the signaling apparatus that is used in animal communication is lacking or reduced in brown bears. They have no tail; their ears are small and covered with dense hair; their facial musculature is not developed to produce complex facial expressions; and their entire body is covered with a thick coat of hair. They must use vocalizations, body posture and orientations, eye contact, head positions, and mouth displays. Of course these last mechanisms are more developed or more complex than those among many mammals, most birds, fishes, amphibians, and reptiles, but they are less developed than those of the primates, canids, and felids.

Romeo and Reggie used all of the above elements to produce the threats in their bluffing and testing of one another that resulted in a stalemate at the number-one fishing spot. There was no single element that produced the displays and determined the outcome of their interaction. Instead, all the elements combined to produce ritualized threats that controlled the interactions.

One of the most important factors influencing encounters at the falls is individual recognition and learning from previous encounters how each bear is likely to interact with others. Experience guides the bluffing and testing of complex encounters and is probably the most important factor influencing the outcome of such encounters. This is particularly true of brief encounters between a bear of high dominance and a subordinate. In these simple interactions a low-ranking bear recognizes a higher ranking bear approaching (or at least its large size) and immediately runs away or defers. The only signaling in these interactions is individual recognition. This is especially true of encounters involving a very high-ranking boar, such as Charlie Brown. The latter rarely utilized discrete signals, because his presence alone was sufficient to intimidate all bears at the falls.

Brown bear communication is an enigma in some respects. For instance, it is strongly influenced by individual

recognition, habituation, and hunger, and it is characterized
by threats, bluffing, and testing between bears. We are so used
to thinking in terms of communication in social animals (for
example, primates and canids) that asocial bears are perplexing. The classic encounters, like those between Romeo and
Reggie, initially appear much more complex than they really
are.

7

The Mating Game

The communication that occurs between a boar and a sow when they are in a mating consort is much more subtle than the ritualized threats of aggressive encounters. Occasionally a sow would be in estrous at the falls in July, but most often I spotted consort pairs earlier in the summer on the sedge flats, because June is the peak of the mating season for brown bears. Soon after a sow comes into estrous, a boar joins her for varying periods of time in a consort bond that may be sporadic, lasting for only brief periods of time, or it may be prolonged, lasting in some cases for the duration of estrous. How long a boar remains in consort with a sow may depend on his ability to fend off other boars, but the availability of other estrous sows and the stage of estrous of those present may also influence the duration of the bond.

I was interested in boar-sow consort bonds because they involved rare amicable interactions between adult bears. I always kept a keen eye out for pairs of bears whenever I scanned the sedge flats with my spotting scope. Late one evening in mid-June I spotted White and a boar from our observation spot on top of the cabin. I had not seen her since my first day in camp when she appeared briefly with Patches. The pair were moving in our direction quickly and soon I was certain that her consort was Arlo, an enormous boar of unknown age whom I knew from previous summers.

Arlo was an awesome sight as he roamed around the flats. His dense coat was light brown to blond and marred by large scars in many places. A massive dark-colored scar ran the length of his neck on the left side. His shoulders, neck, back, and legs bulged with muscle as if hundred-pound sacks of grain lay just beneath the skin. The right ear was badly torn and bent to one side, unable to stand erect. Every claw was brilliant flashing white, like polished ivory piled at his feet. Frothing heavily at the mouth and gasping quickly for each sustaining breath, his 1,000 pounds totally dominated the scene.

White, in stark contrast, skulked around and cowered in fear, obviously not overly at ease with this behemoth so close at hand. Her fluffy white coat was now wet and stringy and appeared very ragged as she meandered erratically with Arlo in tow. As she attempted to elude Arlo, her maneuvers soon brought the pair onto the trail that leads from the flats to camp. Her pace quickened to a slow jog as she headed straight for camp, but Arlo was undeterred. This was a rare appearance for Arlo, as mature boars are normally too wary to venture onto exposed areas near the coast, although they occasionally come out of hiding to seek out estrous females. Even so, I was surprised at Arlo's lack of discretion as he came closer and closer, seemingly unaware of camp and our presence.

White was constantly glancing back to check on old Arlo as she scurried along. Jim and I froze, hoping for a close look at Arlo as they passed near camp, but we got more than a close look, for White seemed bent on walking right in the front door of the cabin. Arlo was audible at 100 yards with his heavy, labored breathing resounding in the calm evening silence much like an old steam locomotive starting up, while his jaws dripped with foaming saliva that fluttered in and out with each breath. Dwarfing little White, his immense bulk loomed larger with every step.

When it became obvious that Arlo was about to come waddling among our tents, it suddenly occurred to me that this giant could easily level a tent or two in an attempt to escape, so I stood up yelling on the rooftop and waved my arms in the air. Both bears suddenly turned and bolted down the trail toward the sauna. Arlo was now unconcerned with White and thrashed his own path through the fireweed and wild geraniums and headed right between the sauna and pond. The sudden appearance of this structure so startled him that he swerved and went bounding through the alder thicket beside the pond. These alders, which are impenetrable for humans, were leveled like matches in a crackling, splintering explosion. The pair plowed through an expanse of muskeg and vanished into the alder-covered hills beyond camp.

The next afternoon I spotted a curious sight while scanning the flats with my scope. I was obviously looking at a bear, but the unusual shape and size of the form strongly resembled a small haystack. The sedge rippled all around the stationary object and then it began to move a bit. As I focused my scope I saw that the ursine mass was Arlo mounting little White.

She sat grazing on sedge with Arlo hunched over her from behind with his massive forelegs wrapped about her middle. Occasionally he lifted her hindquarters into a standing position only to have her sit again and continue grazing. At times, when she persisted in being unreceptive, Arlo would bite her nape, shake it viciously, and then lay his head back along her ribs and continue attempting to lift her into a copulatory position. This is strikingly similar to the "play mounts" that often occur during extended play bouts between adolescent bears. This play behavior is obviously a learning process.

White grazed calmly but displayed the visible signs of stress that all low-ranking bears exhibit when confronted with a more dominant animal. She crouched with her head lowered

A typical "play mount" that often occurs during extended play bouts between adolescent bears.

and ears pressed back against her head as she glanced cautiously back at him. Whenever Arlo dismounted for a moment or turned away, she moved away and attempted to elude him, for she was not yet as receptive to boars as older, more dominant sows in estrous. However Arlo's persistent following had gradually habituated her to his presence, so he approached her with greater ease and she was less frantic in avoiding him than she had been the previous day.

Their cat-and-mouse game continued for several minutes before Arlo mounted her again, but White sat down immediately. Then for seven minutes he remained mounted and spent most of this time lifting her from a sitting position. There was one series of slow pelvic thrusts in this sequence, and later, during a thirty-eight-minute mounting, Arlo exhibited the same slow thrusts, as well as rapid, quivering thrusts. The latter were apparently indicative of intromission and actual copulation, while the slower thrusts were precursory. Despite these frequent matings, White failed to have young the following year.

A sow, particularly a young sow like White, gains status from her boar consort, because the mere presence of a large boar will deter most bears. This new-found "dominance by association" is sometimes flaunted by estrous sows. I once observed White flagrantly abuse this sort of power while in consort with Patches. She was fishing on the upper falls early in the fishing season with Patches sitting behind a discreet distance and watching her out of the corner of his eye, while Jeanne, a mature sow, was fishing alone 100 yards downriver. Had White been alone she would have avoided the more dominant Jeanne at all cost, but with Patches on hand to back her up, she left her fishing spot and approached the older sow with Patches in tow, apparently intent on routing Jeanne from her fishing spot. Jeanne eyed Patches approaching and slowly began to retreat from the river. This retreat, which is always an obvious sign of submission, was the only signal that White needed before starting to throw her weight around. She charged Jeanne, while glancing over her shoulder to make sure Patches was following to back her up, and chased the old girl about 100 yards downstream before giving up and returning to fish.

Each summer I tried to document the length of the consort bonds between boars and sows, but I was not able to do this with White, Arlo, and Patches. A few days after our encounter in camp with Arlo and White, I again observed Patches in consort with White. Arlo had probably displaced Patches as White's consort for an unknown period, but the spotty observations told me very little. Unfortunately this was the case with most of the sows that were in estrous during June, since they only made one or two appearances on the flats.

Sows that were in estrous during the fishing season at the falls provided much more information. Most of these sows made extended daily visits to the falls, and so I was able to record some information on the duration of their estrous and make lengthy observations on a variety of reproductive behaviors at close range.

The summer of 1973 had been particularly informative because five mature sows were in estrous during the fishing season. Nathan's interest in Goldie on July 10 was interesting, since I had first observed her in consort on the flats on June 20, twenty-one days earlier. Whether this represented one long cycle or two shorter ones separated by an anestrous period is not known. Two other sows, Jeanne and Lady Bird, were in estrous for extended periods in mid- to late July. Jeanne was in estrous on July 16 and was sexually active until July 26, a span of eleven days. Lady Bird was in consort when we first spotted her on July 9 and was sexually active until July 21, which confirmed thirteen days of estrous.

Lady Bird was variously in consort with Charlie Brown, Nathan, and Patches, and demonstrated that female bears are promiscuous by mating with two of these boars on the same day. She may have mated with several boars during her estrous. The consort bonds between Lady Bird and these boars at the falls were often disrupted by fishing activities and by the presence of humans at the falls. One exception was her consort with Patches, our 750-pound friend who routinely sauntered past us at the falls seemingly oblivious to our presence. This relaxed attitude provided Patches with greater access to estrous sows at the falls and allowed him to follow the same sow throughout the day as she fished. This also made it possible for us to observe mating activities at very close range.

Patches spent a great deal of time with Lady Bird in mid-July. Even a large dominant sow like Lady Bird is somewhat apprehensive at the approach of a large boar. Even though she was more receptive to boars because of her estrous condition, there obviously remained considerable motivational conflict, for as Patches approached she seemed on the verge of running away. He approached without any signs of aggression and playfully nudged and smelled all around her face, ears, and neck, and then down her back and sniffed her genital area. Following this friendly greeting, Lady Bird allowed Patches to remain in consort with her, but he sat quietly behind her while she fished and maintained a low profile by cowering a bit. He kept his ears depressed and glanced only very cautiously in her direction. Whenever she turned to check on him, Patches quickly avoided eye contact and stared at the ground, because a stare can be an aggressive action and he was attempting to appease her.

I witnessed four copulations between Patches and Lady Bird. All these matings occurred away from the falls proper, because the latter is a scene of aggression and apparently inconducive to the long, complex activities of mating. Patches would follow Lady Bird from the falls as she left following a fishing bout and then would mount her on the secluded high embankment that parallels the river. These mountings were rarely prolonged as the constant arrivals and departures of fishing bears quickly spooked Lady Bird and caused her to run. During one of these brief mountings, Charlie Brown happened onto the pair and charged them head-on and rolled them both over, creating such turmoil that Patches managed to escape Charlie's wrath unscathed. A battle might have ensued between two boars of more equal rank, but Patches was no match for Charlie Brown.

The conflicts between boars vying for estrous sows were seldom observed, because the boars' wariness restricted direct observation. However, the profusion and extent of injuries on many boars indicated that battles were commonplace and extremely violent. For instance, a massive wound on a very large boar named Boxer involved the entire shoulder area where the skin and muscle on a space about eighteen inches across was ripped off to the bone. This violence may occur at any time and is not necessarily associated only with mating, as a boar will fight to maintain his position in the dominance hierarchy regardless of the situation. Although these dominance positions are fairly well defined and usually respected, the competition for estrous females may precipitate violent disputes between boars.

The unwary Patches had very little competition in his consort with Jeanne when she was in estrous in late July, because she meandered around the falls to areas where no wary male would dare venture. Jeanne seemed to be uneasy with Patches in consort, for she moved around constantly, changing her fishing spot incessantly, moving up and down the river, and then back and forth across the rapids with Patches close behind. Because Jeanne normally moved around very little while fishing, these erratic movements could only be construed as attempts to avoid her follower.

The unusual reproductive physiology of the female brown bear involves delayed implantation and premature birth. Matings in May, June, or July fertilize one or more eggs in the female. The fertilized egg, called a *zygote*, undergoes cell division and forms a tiny sphere of cells called a *blastocyst*. Further development is delayed at this point for an uncertain period of time, for instead of implanting on the uterine wall and commencing development, the blastocyst becomes dormant and is covered with a thick protective coating while it remains unattached and floats freely in the uterine horns for about four to six months.

Although reproduction in many animals involves a similar pattern of delayed implantation, very little is known of exactly how the process is regulated. One line of evidence suggests that estrogens may stimulate the uterine lining to produce a protein substance that controls the growth and differentiation of the blastocyst. When production of this growth factor is stopped, the blastocyst becomes dormant and is inactive until the factor is once again produced. Another theory postulates that the uterine lining must become sticky before a blastocyst can implant and begin development. In bears, this preparation of the uterus is delayed for several months. In the interim the blastocyst, unable to implant, simply remains dormant. Regardless of the method by which the delayed implantation is accomplished, there must be a means of preventing the expulsion of the blastocysts from the uterus. How this is done is not known, but a uterine "plug" may be produced during the period of dormancy.

There are indications that the reactivation of the blastocysts does not occur until late fall, perhaps in November or later, because the cubs that are born prematurely during January or February are pink, hairless, and weigh only about one pound. This suggests that active embryonic development probably does not exceed two or three months. If this is true, then reactivation of the dormant blastocysts may coincide with the sow's denning in late fall, which would concur nicely with the theory that estrogens control the reactivation. That is, because environmental stimuli, such as light, commonly control hormone levels in animals, it is possible that the darkness of the den may cause the level of estrogens to vary and prepare the uterine lining for implantation of the blastocysts. This would be a nice trick that evolution could easily have perfected.

This bizarre scheme of reproduction may seem round-about, as a more direct method would have mating in the fall, immediate embryonic development through the winter, and the birth of good-size cubs in the spring. Why have delayed implantation and premature birth? This strange pattern must be adaptive in some way for the bears, or it would not have evolved.

A cursory examination of their annual activities reveals that this pattern is adjusted so that the mating season does not interrupt the period of food abundance in summer and fall. The importance of a timing strategy to make eating and mating activities compatible becomes apparent when it is considered that these are the only two essential activities in a bear's life, for in order to be a success a bear must only survive and reproduce. It must eat when food is available, but mating is an activity that can take place at any time. Because a fall mating season would waste precious eating time in a season of food abundance, and because it could be cut short and end in failure because of early winter snows and early denning, the mating season occurs in late spring and early summer when food is scarce and the bears can spare the time. Later, when the sedge matures, the salmon spawn, and the berries ripen, they must eat and eat and eat.

The timing of the mating season in June makes delayed implantation necessary, for if implantation occurred soon after mating, then fetal development through the summer and fall would deny the sow her own winter fat reserves. Large precocial cubs would be born in late fall or early winter without fat reserves of their own, and the sow, lacking in fat because of gestation, would be hard-pressed to nurse the large cubs through the long winter.

Delayed implantation very neatly circumvents all of these problems by allowing a sow to accumulate fat through the summer and fall, enter her den, slip into a lethargic sleep, and begin gestation. Premature birth then becomes necessary because the deep torpid slumber of the hibernating sow results in a decreased metabolic rate, lower body temperature, and slower heartbeat, which do not provide an optimum environment for fetal development, which must proceed rapidly if the cubs are to be mature enough to survive the harsh spring conditions. Premature birth frees the young from the sow's torpid metabolism and allows them to complete their development more rapidly on their own.

The immature fetuses are capable of movement as soon as they are born and climb on the sow's hair until they find a teat to cling to and suckle. The sleeping sow continually provides super-rich milk for as many as four (perhaps five) fast-growing cubs from their birth in January or February until their emergence from the den in April. She must convert her fat into metabolic water for milk, as she does not eat or drink during the long nursing period. This makes the massive fat accumulation previous to denning an obvious necessity. Some mature sows, after the fishing season at the falls, resemble a basketball elevated on sticks as their bellies slide through the grass almost dragging along the ground.

8

Mothers
and Their Cubs

The brown bear family consists of only a sow and her cubs, as the boars have no further association with females after the brief mating season in early summer. During the two or three years before the weaning of her cubs, a sow provides them with consummate maternal protection. The interactions between sows and other bears that result from this extraordinary maternal protection, together with the ongoing interactions between the sows and cubs, combine to make maternal behavior the most interesting aspect of brown bear life.

Attacks on humans by sows with cubs have been sensationalized to the point that their irascible behavior is almost universal knowledge. This reputation may be accurate in some instances, but such generalizations on maternal behavior tend to gloss over this very fascinating phase of ursine natural history, which even today lacks accurate documentation. Much of the reported information has come from inexperienced observers whose reports are sketchy and questionable. The difficulty of conducting long-term studies on specific sows with cubs in the wild is largely responsible for the paucity of information. Sows in most wilderness situations will not tolerate human observers at close range and because they are solitary and range over many miles of open country, it is impossible to keep track of more than one sow for any length of time.

All of these obstacles are surmounted at McNeil where even sows with spring cubs wander past humans, seemingly oblivious to their presence. The same sows return year after year to the falls, and so it is possible to document their maternal behavior and its development over a period of years. Further, the social situation at the falls precipitates many interactions between sows and other bears that would not occur among solitary bears in open country. These features make McNeil an extraordinary outdoor laboratory for the study of bear behavior.

There were only two sows with cubs at McNeil during the first year of my study in 1973. Spooky had three spring cubs and Big Mamma had two yearling clubs. These two sows were very interesting but they gave me few clues to the incredible maternal behavior that I would witness during the following summers.

It was the summer of 1974 in which all my expectations were realized, for that summer five sows produced no less than fifteen cubs. It was impossible to assign any causal factors to this synchronized reproduction other than chance alone, so it was with a bit of luck that I had the unique opportunity to observe the development of maternal behavior of many sows separately, as well as in complex interactions with one another.

A sow and her new spring cubs emerge from their den in April or perhaps early May if spring is late. The size of cubs upon leaving the den may depend on the number of cubs in the litter, the quantity of milk they received, and the dates of their birth and emergence in the spring, but size differences are relative at this point, as they are all very small. Even though they grow rapidly, the cubs are still extremely small when we first see them on the flats or at the falls in July. In fact, they are so tiny one wonders how they survive the rigors of a McNeil spring.

Snow still covers most of the terrain in April when cubs get their first glimpse of the outside world. Violent north Pacific storms lash the Peninsula each winter and pile up deep snow that remains in the high country until July and August. The rugged, treeless land is stark white and totally bleak. The smooth, rolling coastal hills look like great drifts of sterile snow that slink slowly down to meet the muddy ocean waters where river outflows freeze and clog every cove and bay with miniature glaciers. The pounding surf gnaws away at these growing masses of ice and chisels a sheer blue wall in the frozen river mouths. Nothing moves. Ears ring in the silence, then elusive sound arrives as the roaring of surf drifts in and out with the wind. Incessant storms blow rain, then snow, rain, then snow, forming a world of snow and ice.

An awakened sow digs a hole in the bank of snow covering her den and plows through the opening to the outside. Standing at the entrance, she scans the frozen landscape for a moment, snorts once or twice, shakes her dense winter coat vigorously, licks her lips, glances back at her new cubs, and waddles off into the blinding whiteness. The family may stay in the vicinity of their den for a varying period of time. The sow will return to her winter-long bed to sleep with her tiny cubs or to take refuge from foul weather, but soon springtime foods beckon and they leave for the last time. The crusted snow smooths the rugged terrain and makes travel easier for the cubs as the family wanders.

Their foods are extremely scarce in April and May, because the ground is still locked in winter's grip and produces nothing green, while roots and ground squirrels are secure beneath the frozen surface. Carrion of animals that died over winter provide the only substantial food, but even this is rare and often secured by more dominant bears. Little food is available and little is eaten.

Some sows with cubs remain in remote areas until the salmon runs begin and are rarely seen near the coast before arriving at McNeil Falls in July. These wary mothers remain secluded in backcountry presumably because it is more remote and provides them with effective isolation. Of course boars also remain in remote areas in the spring, but the density of individuals is so low that sows can easily avoid other bears.

A few young sows shun the remote areas and occupy the coastal areas in early summer. This behavior may seem contradictory, but it occurs for essentially the same reason that other bears remain in backcountry. That is, they feel safer in one place than another. These sows have grown up around people and fear them less than they fear other bears, and consequently they avoid bears by staying with us near camp on the coast.

Red was one of the young mothers who arrived on the coast in June and remained in the vicinity of our camp throughout the summer, which allowed me to document her behavioral development thoroughly.

Utah State students first observed Red with her sisters, White and Blue, in the summer of 1970. The three sisters had been weaned earlier that summer by an unknown sow, but their brazen behavior in and around camp and at the falls was a strong indication that the trio had grown up as McNeil residents.

They stayed together in sibling bonds that summer and cooperated to present a common front when encountering other bears, thereby enabling them to obtain a much higher dominance ranking than any of the cubs would have had alone. White, who tended to be more irascible, more independent, less cooperative, and generally less amiable than Red or Blue, established herself as the more independent figure in the group. For instance, when the trio fished for salmon at the falls, White did most of the fishing.

White already had the distinctly asocial disposition that all females develop when they are older, so it was not surprising that she failed to rejoin Red and Blue the next summer. Just why she was more precocious than Red or Blue in acquiring this typical adult behavior is not known. As I explained earlier, she was not more dominant than her sisters, nor was she sexually mature at an earlier age. This illustrates that each bear's temperament and its development are potentially unique.

Red and Blue rejoined in their sibling bond in the summers of 1971, 1972, and 1973. It is doubtful that they had denned together in the later winters, because in 1973 Red arrived on the sedge flats in mid-June and grazed alone for two weeks before Blue appeared and joined her. They grazed near one another but made no contact. Their intolerance of one another occasionally erupted in brief bluff charges, which were nothing more than quick slaps at the ground with the front paws, combined with a huff. A short period of habituation was necessary before the sisters could rejoin in the bond for a fourth summer.

The next day the pair had become almost inseparable, and during the remainder of the summer they grazed, rested, played, slept, and fished together, combining their clout and giving them more freedom at the falls and elsewhere. As the summer progressed it became obvious that Blue was more dependent on their relationship than Red, who was more dominant and freewheeling. They were still together when we last saw them that summer.

The next summer (1974) I could hardly wait to discover the new developments in Red and Blue's remarkable relationship. Sibling bonds rarely last for more than one or two summers, so I was amazed when I first spotted the six-year-old sisters playing in Mikfik Creek in late June. They stood in 3 or 4 feet of water and splashed around in the clear, cold creek as though re-forming their old bond for an unprecedented fifth summer. It was possible that both bears could have been sexually mature with cubs of their own, yet here they were playing like newly weaned cubs!

This extraordinary relationship took on new dimensions the next day when I spotted Red in consort on the flats with

Arlo. This confirmed that Red was in estrous and so I felt sure that her attitude toward Blue would change immediately, but it did not. That same afternoon she joined Blue and Light, a six-year-old male, on the flats for grazing and playing. Several hours later all three approached camp and played at length in our front yard. Red and Light were the primary play partners with Blue an inactive onlooker for the most part. Light chased Blue away on two occasions, which indicated that his playful bond with Red may have been encouraged by Red's estrous condition.

Red left Blue grazing on the flats and disappeared for several days until the salmon run began at the falls. When the two sisters finally met again, their reactions were extraordinary. Their first encounter took place on the center rock of the falls. Red was already fishing when Blue arrived for the first time and approached her sister as casually as ever. Red instantly charged Blue and chased her 100 yards down the river before Blue finally turned and faced her new adversary in a classic encounter. Red was virtually on Blue's heels when the latter whirled around in a crouch with her head high, ears back, and mouth open. Red stopped just short of plowing into her sister and displayed the same threatening posture. Both heads were immediately thrown high with bite threats and then lowered almost to the ground as the challenge threats continued. Their standoff with these challenge threats continued for about twenty seconds before Red ended her threats and began to back away. Red was dominant to Blue so she could terminate the encounter by leaving. In contrast, Blue had to remain still and as inoffensive as possible and yet ready to defend herself against renewed aggression from Red. If Blue had tried to leave first, Red would have attacked her from behind in order to reassert her dominance. With the encounter over and Red withdrawn, Blue glanced around, licked her lips, yawned, and shook her shaggy summer coat, actions that appeared to relieve the tension of the situation.

Red and Blue had several more classic encounters that summer and all were initiated by Red charging Blue from a distance. It was obvious that Red was determined to break the old sibling bond that had lasted for so long, because Blue was the only target of this aggression and Red played frequently with many other bears. Because Red had successfully conceived in June and had two spring cubs the next summer, her timely moves to dissolve the ties with Blue were probably precipitated by hormonal factors caused by her reproductive state.

Red was a real pro at utilizing the falls, for she had spent every day of the fishing season every summer of her life fishing the cold glacial waters for chum salmon. She knew when the salmon were running the falls and how to catch them and she knew the best fishing spots and how best to occupy and hold them. She was familiar with every bear and was keenly aware of who could and could not be pushed around and she knew just how far to press her luck with bears ranking above her. She was a good fisherman and seldom stole fish from others, but she knew from whom she could steal and exactly how to do it. She ignored her human observers and dealt artfully and confidently with the fishing business at hand. She was an ultimate "falls hound" and epitomized the modern-day human-habituated McNeil bear.

Red's fishing that summer seemed to be desperate in its intensity and her eating was voracious and insatiable as she became fatter and fatter. This behavior was preparatory to nursing the cubs that she would have that winter, but this does not mean that she was cognizant of the great need for fat, as this type of behavior is probably under hormonal control. I suspect that hormonal changes also caused her thick coat to become shaggy during the summer and eventually to fall out altogether, leaving the beginning velvet of her new winter coat. Male bears shed their old coats in this fashion, but young sows and sows with cubs usually retain a dense coat through the summer.

August 10 was the last day that Jim and I took data at the falls in 1974. It was a dull day, as the vast majority of the bears had been gone for several days. Red and Zubin had fished earlier, but now only Zubin remained, and he slept soundly, submerged to the neck in a deep pool with his head resting on a large rock. Ripples of water bobbed his head gently but he slept undisturbed. We read and were lulled to drowsiness by the warm weather and the drone of the falls. When this last sample period of our summer at McNeil came to an end, we gladly packed up our equipment and prepared to leave, but before we could depart Red came scurrying down the trail licking her lips wildly with her eyes fixed steadily on the falls as if she were as ravenous for salmon as she had been when arriving for the first time in July. We left her fishing enthusiastically and saw no more of her that summer.

When Red did not make her usual early appearance on the flats the next summer (1975), I suspected that she had spring cubs because sows with cubs are often late in arriving. She finally appeared the first week in July with two tiny spring cubs. I first spotted her resting on a bluff across the river from camp where she remained almost motionless until the following afternoon. This unusual vigil was baffling at the time, but the supercautious behavior that she displayed later made me suspect she had simply been checking out the flats before taking her vulnerable cubs into the area. Precautions of this sort are not unusual, even among many mature boars, who may carefully inspect the falls before risking the open exposure involved in fishing.

The next afternoon Red finally began to search for a route down from her outpost on the bluff and disappeared with her two cubs into a steep ravine that spilled into the river. Moments later, after crossing the river's deepest, swiftest portion, Red came sauntering across the tidal mud with two wee wet cubs hurrying along to keep pace with her smooth easy stroll. The cubs stopped and began to protest when Red crossed yet another cold stream that was a mere trickle compared to the mouth of the McNeil that they had just crossed, but this was apparently one too many cold swims. They squalled and barked at her as she splashed through the icy water, so Red turned to watch the pair for a moment and then returned to fetch them. She led them upstream to a shallow stretch and crossed once more, but after venturing about a foot from shore they began to squall even louder and retreated to dry ground. Red stood in midstream and turned to watch her irritated cubs as though beckoning them to follow, then after several seconds of coaxing, one cub rushed into the current, squalling as he swam. The other cub followed immediately, and seconds later Red was smelling about their trembling heads while they barked and shook themselves dry. Then as the family waddled off toward the green sedge flats the cubs continued to bark their complaints at Red, but she paid them no heed.

The next morning I walked out on the flats and sat near Red and her cubs to observe them. The cubs became very distraught, which was an expected reaction as I was probably the first human they had ever seen. They stood on hind legs and held to Red's sides with their front paws and cautiously watched this strange new being from eyes that twinkled and twitched as their heads jerked back and forth from Red to me and back to Red (plate 25). They apparently expected some reaction from Red and were confused by her total apathy, but moments later this fascination lessened and the cubs returned to grazing with their mother. They pulled up long succulent shoots of sedge and pointed their mouths to the sky as if to let gravity pull the shoots into their mouths as they nibbled. During the next three hours they often turned to scrutinize me closely and occasionally they stood on hind legs for a better view.

Red and her two spring cubs resting after nursing on the Mikfik sedge flats in early July.

I was glad that Red was undisturbed by people being near her cubs, as this made close observation of the development of her maternal behavior a simple task. Unexpected aspects of her behavior appeared that afternoon. She suddenly stood erect and peered at an unknown bear who had walked onto the flats about 200 yards to the south. Then she returned to her feet, ran to a nearby sandbar, stood once again to survey the bear, huffed and puffed in alarm at her cubs, and made a frenzied dash up the beach and into the secluded alders behind camp. I watched this incident in disbelief, because she was at ease with me scarcely 60 feet away, but came unglued when another bear approached at 200 yards!

Red had retreated to the remote alder-covered hills that overlook the ocean east of our camp because no other bears used the area and she felt safe there. She apparently felt safer near the coast and never ventured inland past the sedge flats, as other bears grazing on the flats had their daybeds there.

During her first few days on the flats, Red grazed and nursed her cubs with few interruptions from other bears because the area remained almost vacant, but soon isolation became more difficult as the summer population of McNeil brownies began to concentrate in the area. Even though the mere appearance of another bear on the flats continued to frighten Red into fleeing the area, she slowly began to become habituated to the presence of other bears, and after five or six of these traumatic escapes, she was satisfied simply to increase the distance between her cubs and an intruder. Still later she would return to the same spot after running away a short distance and it was not long before she shared the flats with several bears and grazed near younger bears. This incredible habituation had taken only five days to complete.

The turnabout in Red's behavior in a relatively short time indicated that she had had very little contact with other bears before arriving at McNeil. The summer concentration of bears around the falls gives the mistaken impression that the whole area is literally crawling with bears, but this is not the case, as during the spring and fall the fifty or so bears that visit McNeil may disperse over an area of 20 to 50 miles. Using the keen sense of smell that Big Ears, Clara, and Rama displayed earlier, it was probably quite easy for Red to avoid the few bears that came close to her. The first encounters on the flats were in all probability her first prolonged contact with other bears that spring. As I described earlier, most bears go through a similar, though less spectacular, habituation process each summer, which is further evidence of the paucity of springtime association between bears.

When the fishing season finally got started on July 23, I wondered if Red had gained enough confidence to fish among so many bears. She had undergone a remarkable habituation, but she was still very scared of larger bears on the flats. I was a little surprised and very happy when I first spotted her creeping cautiously up the bank from the mouth of the river late one evening. She stopped and made token fishing attempts at the lower falls where no bears were fishing, but even in this isolated spot her constant surveillance of other bears interrupted her fishing and made it unsuccessful. The fishing spot that she used on the lower falls was a poor one that I had never seen her use before, but she was not yet ready to venture among the other bears at the better fishing spots on the upper falls. After an hour of erratic fishing, she slowly began to settle down and finally caught a fish before we left for the evening.

The next day Red once again waited until late in the evening to come to the falls. This time she wasted no time fishing on the unproductive lower falls and carefully crept into the midst of eight fishing bears on the upper falls, while eyeing her old familiar fishing spots. This was a totally new experience for her two cubs, who crouched and huddled at her side and occasionally stood to examine nearby bears with their wide-open eyes twinkling and their little heads jerking erratically as they glanced from one new sight to the next. It was a traumatic experience for the cubs to be more than 2 or 3 feet from Red's side, so they moved in unison with her as she moved about inspecting the salmon-filled waters.

Red quickly stationed herself at an excellent fishing spot on the first big rock out in the falls just below our cave. She had easily stepped over a fast-flowing rivulet of overflow water in order to reach her spot, but her cubs were too small to negotiate the swift current. They stopped at the water's edge and stood erect to watch Red and scream their objections at her, but she had already become so engrossed in her salmon prospects that she failed to notice their absence. It was apparent that one visit to the falls had greatly acclimated Red to the proximity of fishing bears, but she immediately ran to her cubs to check on them after detecting their frightened barking and squalling. A few brief sniffs at their trembling heads and a glance or two around seemed to ease her concern. The cubs then followed her down to a more accessible fishing spot along the middle of the falls where she could remain with them, but the lack of success at these poor spots soon brought her back to the upper falls. She again crossed the overflow stream and then wandered back and forth between her fishing spot and the stranded cubs, who were now desperate enough to try to cross the rushing water. The darker cub hesitantly waded out about halfway before he lost footing in the racing torrent and fell onto his stomach. He scratched frantically for a hold on the slimy rocks as he bounced down the rapids to the pool at the bottom. Once in calm water, he easily swam to the rock where Red was fishing and climbed up to join her. The light cub became more distraught than ever and ran up and down the stream several times before discovering that the top of the rapids was narrow enough to jump across. He learned from his success and the crossing became routine for the cubs in the future.

The cold, wet cubs crowded themselves together at Red's feet as she began her first fishing attempts on the crowded falls. The rocks were alive with the constant activity of bears arriving, searching and fishing for salmon, carrying their catches to the riverbank for eating, and then returning for more. Red Collar and her three large yearlings (the Marx Brothers), arrived and found Red eating a salmon in one of their favorite spots and began to edge her out. The two sows faced each other with open-mouth threats and held their positions (plate 26). Red's cubs backed up in fear to the edge of the main falls and clung with precarious footing to the last bit of slippery rock between Red and the rapids. The sight and sound of a flopping salmon on nearby rocks distracted Red Collar and drew her away in a sudden leap, which startled one cub sufficiently to cause him to lose his footing and fall into the main current. Frantic swimming helped him to catch a backflow into a deep pool just below Red, who was unaware of the mishap until the cub appeared on the rocks below her and shook himself dry.

This scene was repeated the next afternoon, except this time the cub failed to swim out of the current and shot straight into the treacherous main rapids. With ears flat and eyes wide open in terror, he pawed frantically to stay afloat, bobbing like a cork and disappearing in and out of view as the thunderous white water surged in long, graceful waves. Red seemed unconcerned on catching a glimpse of her cub being swept into the current, for he was halfway down the 300-foot rapids before she slowly started downriver after him. At the base of the falls the cub swam to shore, shook himself dry, and ran to meet Red before she arrived at the scene. Red turned without even inspecting her cub and sauntered back to the falls apparently unconcerned about the cub's accident. These swimming trips down the river became routine for the cubs during the remainder of the season.

Each day Red became more habituated to the presence of fishing bears. She began to roam all around the rocks of the main falls, while leaving her cubs stranded on the first rock to fend for themselves. Initially, an approaching bear would bring her running to guard them, but soon she became so immersed in fishing that she often ignored them. Their cries of distress were completely drowned by the roar of falling water. They soon learned to huddle together patiently on the rocks below the cave and wait for Red to return. Approaching bears always aroused them and any movements by people in the cave caused both cubs to stand with heads jerking around as they scrutinized each person with enormous sparkling eyes.

Approaching bears would occasionally cause the cubs to retreat from the falls in terror. They usually stopped on the grassy knolls above the falls where they would cry out in vain for their mother, who fished unaware among several bears in the deafening roar of water. When they were unable to locate Red or attract her attention, the confused and frightened cubs continued to retreat higher into the alder-covered bluffs along the river. Red often fished for five minutes and occasionally longer before realizing that her cubs were missing. She would then begin a deliberate investigative search by smelling at length on the rocks where they last rested and then tracking them into the alders. Her hunt was calm and unhurried in the beginning, but it became more and more intense as she worked through the grass and alders and stood erect at times for an instant to survey the area. While Red rummaged around in the brush, the cubs often circled back down to the river or up to the clearing on top of the bluffs, but Red always managed to locate the pair by using her fantastic sense of smell to ferret them out. When she finally found them, the cubs often ran from her in fear, which was an expected reaction because spring cubs cannot discriminate their own mother from any other bear at a distance. Therefore Red's approach was threatening and fearsome to the confused cubs and it caused them to continue their escape. They stopped at times to stand and watch her approach before running on further, but soon Red's persistent following allowed her to contact them and establish recognition.

Red had completed her habituation at the falls in a matter of days. Less than three weeks earlier the sight of another bear 200 yards away had driven her to distraction, but now she fished all day in the midst of ten or more bears and often ignored her cubs. The latter also began to habituate themselves to the falls situation, although more slowly than Red. They were no longer afraid of people, but they continued to watch our activities with great curiosity. Other bears still scared them, but soon they learned to stay near the falls and seldom fled the area in fear.

Their habituation to humans was perhaps too complete. Our constant contact with the cubs for several weeks on the flats and at the falls had mellowed their fear of us and had left only curiosity. This presented no problems until their curiosity about me became uncontrollable one day late in the summer as I was walking alone across the flats on my way to the falls. I rarely carried my shotgun anymore, but because I would be alone at the falls that afternoon I brought it along for a secure feeling. Red and her cubs were grazing steadily on sedge across Mikfik Creek directly in my line of travel, but I knew that Red would slowly move off and allow me to pass, so I continued on across the water. She was already moving away by the time I had traversed the shallow creek, but the cubs were not quick to follow and Red huffed at them instructively. This was nothing unusual and I hurried on around them. Then unexpectedly the light cub began to follow me in a playful manner with total attention directed at me. I was dumbfounded as he ran toward me with a brightness on his face that could only make me believe that he wanted to play with me, or at least investigate me at very close range. I knew I should turn and stand my ground with a display of aggression in order to deter the audacious cub, but I was almost to the narrow trail that leads between the river and the cliffs that border the cove, and for some reason I felt that the cub would stop following if I could get off the open flats and onto the trail. I hurried along at a jog even though I knew that was the worst possible thing to do under most circumstances, as running usually entices a bear to chase even faster. The light cub was no exception and he broke into a run on detecting my haste. Red had begun to follow along slowly at the beginning and now she speeded to a jog as the cub began to run. She was concerned but not aggressive and she glanced around aimlessly in the air as though trying to avoid looking directly at me or the cub. Her cub had been close to begin with and was now only 20 feet away, so I turned and pumped my shotgun in one motion and fired into the air. The cub froze in his tracks with a look of surprise on his face and Red meandered around behind him huffing alarms as I slowly backed away. Ten seconds later Red and cubs were grazing calmly as though nothing had happened. I always wondered what Red would have done if the cub had caught up with me. I trusted her more than any other bear, but I suppose there *are* limits.

The fishing season was brief that summer of 1975, but Red continued to fish long after most other bears had left for parts unknown. When I arrived for the final time at the falls to pick up the last of our equipment and any litter left behind, I found the rocks deserted except for Red and Zubin, who was again sleeping in a deep pool. As I threw the broken remains of an old wooden chair into the river to be carried to sea, Red became interested in the fragments and moved downwind to catch a whiff of them, and then swam out to inspect them at close range. Later, I left her fishing with both cubs huddled at her feet.

I was eager to catch up on Red's detailed history when I returned for a brief visit the summer of 1976, but unfortunately she had not visited the area that summer. Bears occasionally disappear from McNeil for a summer or two and then return, although others are never seen again. Red will never return to fish the falls, for she was shot and killed by a native near Lake Iliamna that autumn. Reportedly she was attracted to salmon in a subsistence fishing net and was shot as a troublesome bear. It was not reported if she still had her two cubs when she was killed, but chances are she did. I suspect that she ignored her killer as he took aim.

9

The Aggression Factor

Red was the only McNeil female whose behavioral development I was able to document so completely. Other females failed to have cubs or were already mature during my summers at McNeil. Nonetheless, other sows provided me with a great deal of information on maternal behavior and revealed that it is extremely variable. The major observable differences in maternal behavior result from variations in sows' reactions to other bears and to humans. These variations in behavior are controlled by each sow's social status and her own individual disposition, both of which are strongly influenced by changes in reproductive status. The presence of cubs makes a sow more irascible and raises her dominance ranking considerably, whereas the weaning of the same cubs will reduce her ranking and mellow her temperament.

The increase in dominance of a sow with cubs originates from her overtly aggressive protection of her young. The ultimate origin of this maternal protection results from the bizarre phenomenon of infanticide. The killing of cubs by other bears, usually boars, has been widely reported, and young weaned bears and even adults are sometimes killed. Although not strictly infanticide, generally young bears are killed, so I refer to it as infanticide.

This most perplexing bear behavior can best be explained by arguments from the field of sociobiology. This discipline explains behavior and ecology in evolutionary terms. That is, if a *basic behavior* (or the initial tendency to perform a behavior) is *genetically controlled* (innate), then the behavior will be subject to natural selection and will evolve accordingly. A key principle of sociobiology (or evolution) is that any behavior or trait that increases the reproductive success of an animal will be *selected for* (will be perpetuated) and any behavior or trait that decreases reproductive success will be *selected against* (will be eliminated). It is easy to understand how an innate behavior that increases reproductive success will increase in a population from generation to generation until it becomes typical of the species.

With this concept in mind, why do bears commit infanticide? Perhaps a more relevant question is Why should they *not* commit infanticide? What prevents any carnivore, particularly an asocial carnivore, from killing members of its own species? After all, they do represent a potential meal. Well, just as a behavior can evolve by increasing reproductive success, other behaviors are eliminated if they reduce reproductive success. It is obvious that infanticide would be a reproductive disadvantage under most circumstances and it has been selected against for this reason in most animals. Why not in bears?

Is it possible that infanticide could provide a reproductive advantage for an animal? Yes, in the golden langur, for instance, it is probable that certain males increase their reproductive success and decrease the success of other males by killing infants that are not their own offspring. This has resulted in the evolution of infanticide in the golden langur (Blaffer-Hrdy, 1974).

However, brown bear sows are very promiscuous and one sow may breed with several boars during a mating season, which makes it impossible for a boar to identify and selectively kill any cubs or young bears. Considering this, there is no certain way for a boar to increase his reproductive success through infanticide.

The only possible conclusion from this evidence is that ursine infanticide has not been selected for because of any reproductive benefits, and yet the behavior exists. Inherent in this observation is that there is no significant reproductive disadvantage in the behavior either. This may seem to be a contradiction, but, as boars cannot identify the young bears they kill, the phenomenon must be random. In this event, the guilty boars most likely reduce all boars' reproductive success equally through their actions, not just their own. This negates the possibility of selection for or against the action, so the behavior continues to exist.

If the laws of probability are invoked, then the chances of a boar killing his own young at random are very slim and he reduces the population so his own young have a better chance of survival. However, if boars in general are killing at random, then each boar's reproduction would be reduced equally (as percentage of population), so there would be no reproductive advantage (and no disadvantage) in the behavior.

A young boar that has not mated and is just reaching the age when he can successfully compete for estrous sows could possibly increase his reproductive success through infanticide. In so doing, he reduces other boars' reproduction, makes room in the population for his own future young, and speeds the return to estrous of those sows whose cubs he kills. However, the behavior of sows toward fully mature boars versus maturing boars indicates that this is not the case. Sows with cubs routinely tolerate young boars in the 500- to 600-pound class near their cubs, but they *never* allow fully mature (800 pounds and up) boars to approach their cubs. The alpha boar at McNeil, Charlie Brown, was the ultimate target of sow aggression, yet surely he had fathered more cubs than any McNeil boar.

Perhaps mature boars, such as Charlie Brown, could increase their reproduction by killing the young of unfamiliar sows or sows they have not mated with recently. If this is true, sows should be more aggressive to strange boars, but this is not the case. Again, Charlie Brown, who undoubtedly is one of the most familiar mates to McNeil sows, is the target of the most extreme sow aggression. In addition, young weaned bears and, rarely, even adults are killed and the identification of these bears by a boar would be impossible.

During a visit to McNeil in 1980, I witnessed the near death of a newly weaned two-year-old bear at the falls. The latter arrived with its sibling and together they quickly gained confidence in scavenging and even stealing fish on the falls. They became too bold, however, and soon Romeo, a fifteen-year-old boar, was eyeing the audacious youngsters from his fishing spot on the center rock. A few moments later one of the siblings carelessly took a chance and crept out onto the center rock among several bears to scavenge a salmon scrap. Romeo lunged from his spot and overran the escaping bear from behind and crushed him to the rock under 800 pounds of fury. Romeo was unable to pin the two-year-old down and they scrambled across the falls in a spray of white water (plate 27). It was clear that this was a death struggle for the young bear and only his bravest fighting and most intense threats prevented Romeo from killing him. I felt sure that Romeo would have succeeded if he had been able to pin the young bear down.

In another incident, a mature sow, Goldie, charged a yearling whose mother was fishing and failed to notice the aggression. Goldie obviously had violent intentions as she chased the yearling down the riverbank, but the yearling turned and gave Goldie its most intense threat and stood its ground until she backed away from the encounter. If the yearling had continued to run, I felt sure Goldie would have caught and attacked it from behind.

These incidents, plus other observations over the years, made me believe that most any bear, not just boars, have the potential to kill any young bear under certain low-risk circumstances. This conclusion was confirmed during the summer of 1985 through an incident reported by Larry Aumiller.

The venerable and productive seventeen-year-old-sow White was present in early summer on the Mikfik flats with three yearling cubs. One day, while fishing for red salmon on Mikfik Creek, she became separated from one of her yearlings. White never relocated this yearling and the lost cub spent the next month wandering alone on the flats near camp.

Later in July in front of camp, with people watching, the yearling cub wandered near a sow with two spring cubs. The sow reacted to the inquisitive yearling just as she would to any other bear—she charged it aggressively. The yearling, perhaps because of social inexperience, turned and fled rather than standing its ground with a challenge threat. This was a fatal mistake for the sow easily ran the cub down and killed it quickly. She ate a small amount of flesh but soon left the carcass and did not return.

This incident supported my belief that any bear may kill any other bear if given the chance in a low-risk situation. Fatal violence between bears of more equal age or size would obviously reduce reproductive fitness and should be selected against. However, there is very little danger for large boars or sows when they attack young bears. Similarly, there is little danger for a black bear to kill and cannibalize another black bear caught in a trap, which occurs in studies whenever traps are used (Jonkel, 1971). There is no significant evolutionary advantage or disadvantage in the behavior. I believe it is a quirk, if you will, that results from their overtly aggressive, asocial behavior, and it continues to exist because it cannot be selected against.

Because of infanticide, the female often develops behavioral strategies to ensure the survival of her young. One result of infanticide in bears has been the evolution of the infamous maternal protection that sows provide their cubs. Sows are most aggressive toward the dangerous boars, but unfortunately this irascibility extends to other bears, animals, and humans.

The basis of the irascible nature of sows becomes crystal clear in light of this phenomenon of infanticide. A 400-pound sow will not hesitate to charge and attack a 1,000-pound boar who has approached too close to her cubs. Boars are accustomed to the irascible ways of sows with cubs and usually steer clear of them and tolerate their threats. Boars have no reason to challenge aggressive sows as the latter pose no threat to their ranking in the dominance hierarchy. (Grizzly sows of the interior are apparently more aggressive than brown bear sows. Perhaps this increased aggression is due to a high incidence of infanticide brought about by greater environmental stresses that interior grizzlies experience in their lean habitat.)

There was one incident of cub killing at McNeil during my study. Rama, the newly weaned two-year-old cub of Goldie, was killed in late July 1973. The pilot of an oil company helicopter spotted her body and brought it to our camp. An autopsy gave us some details of her death. Extensive hemorrhaging in tissue surrounding large wounds on the neck indicated that these were the fatal wounds. The only other major wound was on Rama's left thigh, where about one-half of the flesh had been consumed and the femur and hip joint were badly broken. We knew that the crushing of these large bones could only have been accomplished by another bear. Rama had lost the protection of her mother, Goldie, only four weeks earlier.

Because sows will tolerate the close presence of most adolescent males but not mature males, I believe that only large mature boars (eight or nine years old or about 600 pounds) are a threat to a sow's protection of her cubs. Again, any bear is potentially a threat, but all bears that are equal or less in size and power to a sow with cubs are effectively eliminated as threats. Sows know they can control their peers and subordinates and this keeps the sows' aggression, as well as that of their peers, in check. There is a mutual respect—a mutual standoff. However, if push came to shove, mature sows could not defend their cubs against a mature boar. Therefore, sows fear primarily the large boars and this makes the latter the main target of sow aggression.

PLATE 1. (top) *A young Alaskan brown bear female pauses in her grazing on the Mikfik sedge flats early June. The snow-capped Aleutian Range rises to the south.*

PLATE 2. (bottom) *The entire length of McNeil Falls as viewed from downriver near the mouth of the river.*

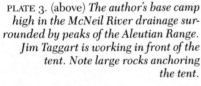

PLATE 3. (above) *The author's base camp high in the McNeil River drainage surrounded by peaks of the Aleutian Range. Jim Taggart is working in front of the tent. Note large rocks anchoring the tent.*

PLATE 4. (right) *Aerial view of the McNeil River area in late June with Kamishak Bay and Augustine Volcano in the background.*

PLATE 5. (opposite top) *Jim Taggart standing beside an area of alpine tundra dug up by a bear searching for arctic ground squirrels or roots.*

PLATE 6. (opposite center) *The mouth of McNeil River and McNeil Cove viewed from McNeil Head. The McNeil camp is visible along the lower shore of the cove and McNeil Falls is faintly visible beyond the second bend in the river in the center of the photo.*

PLATE 7. (opposite bottom) *A late spring McNeil landscape overlooking the Akumwarvik Bay and Cape Douglas area to the east of McNeil River.*

PLATE 8. (right) *Aerial view of McNeil Falls showing the upper and lower falls, and the first and second rocks (major fishing locations) in the upper falls.*

PLATE 9. (opposite top) *Observers and photographers on the observer's knoll overlooking McNeil Falls. Several bears are fishing and eating salmon on the falls.*

PLATE 10. (below) *McNeil Falls crowded with fishing brown bears during the peak of the fishing season in July.*

PLATE 11. (opposite bottom) *A young male brown bear executes a complete dive from the center rock in McNeil Falls into salmon-filled waters.*

PLATE 12. (opposite top) *A young brown bear performing the swim-and-lunge fishing technique in McNeil River. This technique was most often used unsuccessfully by young bears who seemed to enjoy the activity.*

PLATE 13. (below) *Siedelman surfaces from his underwater fishing technique with a chum salmon. This inventive young male sat underwater in the lee of the center rock and ambushed salmon as they were swept downstream.*

PLATE 14. (bottom) *Groucho observing and learning the underwater fishing technique used by Siedelman (plate 13), who is fishing underwater to the left.*

PLATE 15. (below) *Patches resting spread-eagl*
on the first rock in McNeil Fal

PLATE 16. (left) *Charlie Brown, the largest, m*
dominant boar at McNeil, in his prime in 19
Note the enormous paws, claws, musculatu
and cautious ey

PLATE 17. (opposite top) *An intense challer*
threat between a sow with cubs (right) an
young adolescent male. Note the body postur
head down, ears back, and the sow's open mo
and menacing sta

PLATE 18. (opposite center) *A bite threat eru*
between two brown bears on McNeil Falls. T
threat is the more aggressive progression c
challenge threat (plate 17). The bite thr
appears to be on the verge of combat bu
rarely ends in fighti

PLATE 19. (opposite bottom) *The end c*
challenge threat between two boars. Ron
(right) is backing away and ending the encoun
while Dark remains still in threat postu

PLATE 20. (right) *Encounter between two large adult boars. Charlie Brown (right), the dominant boar, turns his neck to Boxer, who snaps at Charlie's neck and pushes him with a forepaw. Note the large stream of saliva flowing from Charlie's mouth and the massive wounds on Boxer's right shoulder.*

PLATE 21. (below) *A typical aggressive encounter at the number-one fishing spot. A sow with cubs (left) whirls around to threaten an approaching bear, while on the right, a boar ignores the action. The sow will continue to threaten the approaching bear but will eventually allow it to move in and fish.*

PLATE 22. (above) *A bite threat erupts during an aggressive encounter between a large, mature sow (right), and a younger bear. Note the body postures, head high, ears back, and open-mouth threats.*

PLATE 23. (center) *An intense challenge threat between two bears on McNeil Falls. Note the sow on the left (dominant) lacks the intense threat components (crouching body, ears back, mouth open) that the younger, subordinate bear uses.*

PLATE 24. (bottom) *Tense fishing at the number-one fishing spot. A sow with cubs threatens a nearby boar with an open-mouth threat. Aggression such as this is often continual when several bears fish close together.*

PLATE 25. (opposite) *Red and her spring cubs grazing on the Mikfik sedge flats in July 1975.*

PLATE 26. (top) *Red Collar and her three yearling cubs (right) steal a salmon from Red. Note the yearling cubs boldly move in to steal fish while Red's spring cubs flee in fear.*

PLATE 27. (center) *Romeo, a large boar, attacks a two-year-old bear on McNeil Falls. The young bear barely escaped with its life.*

PLATE 28. (bottom) *Jezebel, a sow with cubs, attacks Dismay, a young male, while Goldie, also a sow with cubs, charges into the fight from the left. Outbreaks of aggression often caused nearby sows with cubs to join together in fights.*

PLATE 29. (top) *Goldie (left, a sow with cubs) attacks Patches, an old boar. Red Collar (right, another sow with cubs) prepares to join in the fight and both sows then fiercely attacked Patches from both sides.*

PLATE 30. (bottom left) *Reggie's two spring cubs eating a salmon on the banks of McNeil River while watching their mother fishing on the falls.*

PLATE 31. (bottom right) *Jeanne and Wingnut fishing on McNeil Falls.*

PLATE 32. (bottom left) *Lanky* (center) *stealing a salmon catch from Patch Butt, while her two spring cubs look on anxiously.*

PLATE 33. (top) *Red Collar roams around McNeil Falls searching for salmon while her five spring cubs wait on the center rock.*

PLATE 34. (bottom right) *Red Collar, at age twenty-three, fishing on the falls with a single spring cub. Note her dense coat and large, vigorous body at this old age.*

PLATE 35. (top) *Lady Bird stands while fishing to observe human observers with wide-eyed concern. Her three yearling cubs await the capture of salmon.*

PLATE 36. (bottom left) *Lady Bird hovers over her spring cubs and holds her ground against the approach of Charlie Brown at the number-one fishing spot. Charlie avoided the aggressive sow and moved downriver to fish. This was the only time Charlie was observed to defer to another bear.*

PLATE 37. (bottom right) *Red nurses her two spring cubs on a knoll overlooking the falls and anxiously observes the fishing action down on the river.*

PLATE 38. (bottom center) *White and yearling cubs eating salmon beside our observer's knoll. One yearling licks White's bloody mouth.*

PLATE 39. (top) *Reggie bites the back of her cub's neck to punish it for stealing her salmon. The* was undaunted and continued its attempts to steal from its mother.

PLATE 40. (bottom) *Jeanne gives a piggyback swimming ride to her spring cub, Wingnut. Sprin cubs often swam after their fishing mothers and then clung to them in deep water.*

41. (bottom) *The spring cubs of Lanky and Red Collar meet and cautiously approach to* *ct one another. Spring cubs in 1974 became accustomed to meeting and often waited in* *bled groups for their fishing mothers.*

42. (top) *Goldie and Red Collar fish side by side at the number-one fishing spot while their* *rowd together in a group behind them. These cubs often followed either sow away from the* *nd created cub-swapping situations.*

PLATE 43. (top) *Red Collar* (right) *and Lanky* (left) *in an aggressive encounter over their spring cubs. The latter often became confused and intermixed, which led to encounters between sows as they attempted to protect and separate their cubs.*

PLATE 44. (center) *Lanky holds her cubs beneath her as three of Red Collar's cubs approach to inspect them.*

PLATE 45. (above) *Complex encounter between Jeanne* (left) *and White* (right), *two sou with cubs. Jeanne's spring cub, Wingnut, failed to recognize her and ran to White and her two yearlings for protection. Here, Jeanne approaches to retrieve Wingnut, who crouches in front of White and her yearlings.*

E 46. *Two young McNeil bears play in waist-deep water above the falls. Note the
n of the mouths and paws.*

PLATE 47. (above) *A playful sow, Doogie (right), in a complex play-aggressive encounter with a juvenile bear (left). Doogie desired play, but the juvenile bear, as well as her yearling cub (far right), were apprehensive and active play never developed.*

PLATE 48. (right) *Patch Butt (left) and Zubin (right) stand on hind legs and play in open country near McNeil Falls.*

Dismay, an adolescent male about six or seven years old and weighing 450 pounds in 1973, was typical of young males that were sometimes allowed near cubs. His privileges were somewhat tenuous however, because he could not boldly approach a sow with cubs without incurring her wrath. A sow will not abide such impudence from any bear. Cautious maneuvering by Dismay was necessary before he could fish alongside one of these sows. He preferred a desirable location that was usually held by one or more dominant sows with cubs whenever a mature boar was not present. Dismay would work his way into the midst of these sows by gradually fishing closer and closer until he was directly alongside the fishing mothers.

It is most likely size alone that distinguishes an adolescent like Dismay from a mature boar. Males slightly older and larger than Dismay were viewed as mature boars, and were never allowed near cubs. In two or three years Dismay would probably not be tolerated by sows, but for the present he was allowed near these mothers as long as he maintained a submissive profile.

Dismay once made the mistake of turning and walking away from an encounter with Big Mamma, which is a move that only the dominant animal in an encounter can make. It was particularly unfortunate for Dismay, because Big Mamma was the largest, most dominant sow at McNeil and she had two yearling cubs at the time and was very aggressive. The instant Dismay turned his back on the encounter Big Mamma took a flying leap and landed on the middle of his back and knocked him to the ground and into the main rapids of the falls, where he was swept safely out of her reach.

Dismay's most traumatic experience with protective mothers came two years after his mishap with Big Mamma. He was still allowed to fish alongside the regular fishing sows with cubs—Goldie, Lady Bird, Red Collar—but a new sow, Jezebel, was not accustomed to such casual behavior by any bear. One day poor Dismay, unaware of Jezebel's presence or temperament, came walking calmly toward the number-one fishing spot where Goldie was fishing alone with her yearling cub. His approach directed him between Goldie and Jezebel, who was fishing downstream about 50 feet with her two large two-year-old cubs. Goldie showed little reaction to his approach, but Jezebel charged him without delay. He whirled around in a defensive crouch with ears back, head high, and mouth gaping in an open-mouth threat as Jezebel plowed into him at full speed and knocked him backward off his feet as she sank her teeth into his flanks. The sudden commotion surprised Goldie and caused her to charge into the disorder with Jezebel. Both sows flung themselves onto Dismay from opposite sides while he scrambled for a defensive position (plate 28). Submission or appeasement was impossible in this situation, so he fought to escape their reach, and then ran and did not look back.

Dismay had incurred the aggression of these sows simply by making some indiscreet moves, but there is no way for a mature boar to be discreet around a sow with cubs. Even a distant approach by a boar will evoke an attack from a sow. Patches, our sleepy old friend, often got into trouble with mothers around the number-one fishing spot, which was the spot he preferred over all others and one he always investigated, regardless of what bear was occupying it at the time. When a sow with cubs was fishing in this spot, she invariably met his approach with a charge. These encounters almost always ended without erupting into violence, as Patches was usually successful in appeasing the sows by stopping his advance and turning his head to one side to expose his neck. The latter was a gesture of appeasement that boars often use when confronted by sows.

Patches was not always so lucky in appeasing sows. Lady Bird, whose irascibility was second only to Jezebel's, often gave him a particularly rough time. She seldom let him leave before snapping and clawing at his face and neck. During one of these aggressive encounters, Lady Bird was joined by Red Collar, and the two sows cooperated in attacking him from opposite sides. They flipped him onto his back with powerful blows and bit viciously at his sides and flanks (plate 29). Patches tried to escape, but the two enraged mothers pressed their attack even harder as he retreated and continued to work him over for at least fifteen seconds before Lady Bird finally ran to find her cubs. It was amazing that Patches escaped without serious injuries.

Two mature sows attacking an old boar in unison from both sides.

10

Seven Mothers: Portraits

The behavioral metamorphosis that occurs when a sow has cubs can be more extreme in a submissive, low-ranking female than in a dominant, aggressive one. Reggie was one of these low-ranking sows whose maternal behavior development most dramatically illustrated the transformation that occurs when a sow becomes a mother. When I first saw the twelve-year-old Reggie in 1973, she was incredibly ugly and barely resembled a bear at all, for her wet coat revealed long legs and a narrow head that gave her the look of an anteater. Her appearance proved to be deceptive for I failed to recognize her the next day when she arrived at the falls with her long, dense platinum coat all dry and fluffy and shimmering as the sea breeze cut soft undulating patterns across her back. The great puffs of snowy fur covered up her unusual features and made her head and body round and plump and bearlike.

Reggie was always one of the first bears to arrive and begin fishing at the falls, but her fishing efforts were thwarted for the first few days by her fear of other bears. She scanned the waters for salmon for several seconds and then turned or stood to look all around for approaching bears. This sporadic fishing persisted even when she fished alone for hours. Her apprehension was not baseless, however, because early in the summer some dominant bears refuse to share the falls with others and will consistently chase away any bears attempting to fish nearby. I once watched Patches interrupt his fishing and walk downstream 300 feet to chase Reggie from her fishing spot at the lower falls. These incidents served to keep Reggie wary at all times.

Many bears adapt very quickly to the gregarious conditions at the falls, but most low-ranking bears, like Reggie, require several days to adjust to the new circumstances. All but the very youngest bears eventually gain enough confidence to utilize the falls successfully, and Reggie was no exception. Later in the summer she specialized in long, complex encounters with bears of equal rank for possession of choice fishing locations. Intense conflict of this sort might seem contrary to her submissive disposition, but a complex encounter is really nothing but a lot of testing and bluffing between participants, and such noncommittal actions are consistent with Reggie's character.

Reggie had never had cubs and so when she arrived without cubs at the falls in 1974 at age thirteen, I gave up on her reproductive potential. Then in 1975, when she was conspicuously absent from the falls early in the season, I once again had a twinge of hope that Reggie might have had cubs. I first saw her as she appeared on the bluff overlooking her favorite fishing spot at the lower falls. She stood and carefully surveyed the entire area before venturing down to the river. When she finally began to descend and two big spring cubs appeared from the deep grass behind her, I was totally flabbergasted at the sight. I dropped my binoculars and yelled at Jim to have a look at who had just arrived at the lower falls. After a quick glance we looked at each other and rolled over on the ground laughing, for McNeil's apparent celibate had finally given birth.

It was a major event when a fourteen-year-old sow had cubs for the first time in her life. She had waited a long time, but she had apparently made the most of her belated reproductive effort, for her cubs were fully twice as large as Red's two tiny cubs. They were blond like their mother, who retained a luxuriant white winter coat. One cub had an undercoat of soft blond hair with longer light-brown hair growing through it. The other cub was creamy white, even lighter than Reggie herself, and only the darker fur that surrounded her brilliant white claws and her coal-black eyes and nose highlighted the snowy fur (plate 30).

As the trio first approached the falls, it became obvious that Reggie was a newly transformed bear. She was still wary of other bears, but her status had suddenly skyrocketed. She had lost all fear for her own safety by transferring it to fear for her cubs and this caused her behavior to undergo a dramatic metamorphosis. The cowering submissive Reggie became a reckless tyrant, whose wrath had no limits or boundaries and granted immunity to no bear, no matter how dominant. Her intolerance of other bears was most extreme during the first few days after the trio arrived in the area, but she remained an aggressive mother throughout the season.

Reggie's extraordinary irascibility was most intense when she dealt with mature boars. The day after her arrival at the falls, Charlie Brown, the largest, most dominant boar at McNeil, came ambling up the riverbank while Reggie was fishing. Charlie was the epitome of brown bear boars as he confidently approached the falls carrying his 1,200-plus pounds in strong, smooth movements that bulged and shimmered his massive musculature with every step. Unusually small ears were set deep atop his impressive round head, which appeared small above the thick muscle of his neck. His shoulders and back were rounded and made smooth by great slabs of muscle that enveloped his entire body and expanded even his legs to the size of small tree trunks. The mere presence of this awesome form was sufficient to impose Charlie's dominance over the falls.

Charlie's absolute dominance made him an exceptional target for Reggie's maternal aggression, as she apparently viewed him as the greatest possible threat to her cubs. After noticing Charlie approaching, she immediately began to move away and pressed her ears back against her neck and glanced constantly in his direction as she climbed the grassy knoll beside the river. Charlie was completely unaware of Reggie watching him from atop the bluff 40 feet above the river as he slowly lumbered toward his number-one fishing spot. Finally, when he was directly below her, his presence became an unbearable threat to Reggie and she flew down the steep slope in three or four great bounds and plowed her 450 pounds into Charlie in a frenzied rage. He made no attempt to rebuff her attack, but he kept his head turned away with his neck exposed to her assaults and peered at her out of the corner of his eyes. Reggie pushed on his exposed neck with a forepaw while snapping repeatedly at his face. Charlie backed up slowly toward the river as Reggie continued to attack with her open mouth flashing bared white teeth directly in his face. When Reggie continued her attack long past the usual limits, Charlie became irritated and three times he pushed her away with his right forepaw, throwing her back several feet with each shove, but she continued to attack and eventually she forced him into the shallow rushing waters at the edge of the river. When she finally retreated to find her cubs, Charlie resumed his walk calmly as though nothing had happened, which was a move that Reggie apparently construed as being aggressive, because she made another frantic charge at him and snapped and clawed as fiercely as ever, but this time she quickly ended her attack and raced away to find her cubs.

I was absolutely amazed at Reggie's behavior, because I had never witnessed such aggression against Charlie Brown. Lady Bird once held her ground against his approach, but no other bear had ever unleashed such blatant fury directly in his face. This was a prime example of how tolerant of sows a boar can be and also an incredible display of the potential increase in a sow's aggressiveness when she has cubs. Reggie's intolerance of adult boars continued unabated during the summer and exploded in enraged attacks on virtually every boar that visited the falls, including two more unbelievable attacks on Charlie Brown.

Reggie never left her cubs alone while fishing, as Red had done. She fished mostly on the restricted side of the river where all the fishing spots were easily accessible to her cubs, which allowed them to follow her at all times. Nonetheless, Reggie's concern for their safety kept her constantly at their sides. Both cubs often clung to Reggie or to one another for security. It was obvious that touching and holding each other made them feel safer.

Reggie's excessive maternal protection did not carry over to a fear of people, which was surprising since she had always been wary of people before. In fact, during her rare appearances on our side of the falls, she seemed less concerned with us than before. She even nursed her cubs on the riverbank beside the cave while we watched. Considering her intolerant, explosive beginning, Reggie had adapted remarkably to the falls situation.

The changes in behavior that Reggie displayed when she had cubs occurred in all sows but generally not to the same extent. The more experienced, dominant sows were very much in control of the social situation at the falls. A prime example of these sows was Jeanne, a fifteen-year-old female.

Jeanne was something of a symbol at McNeil during the 1970s. She was one of the first bears to begin fishing in early summer and her departure in August always meant the end of the fishing season was near. In this way Jeanne literally signaled the beginning and end of the fishing season at the falls.

Jeanne had spent every summer of her life on the falls. She was first immobilized and tagged by the Alaska Department of Fish and Game in 1963 at age three. She bred at age four and had two cubs the next summer. Since that time she has had a sporadic and rather unsuccessful reproductive history. Just why a sow that appears to be highly successful in every visible respect and yet does not excel in reproductive efforts is not clear.

Jeanne was perhaps the most successful bear at utilizing the falls. She had a very businesslike, no-nonsense approach to dealing with the competition at the falls. She did not waste her fishing time competing with other bears for the number-one fishing spot. Instead, she maximized her efforts by fishing at slightly less desirable locations where she could fish without interruption. Jeanne was so successful at her fishing that she did not need the number-one spot. When competition did appear, she dealt with it quickly and effectively with the most expedient response possible.

Jeanne's straightforward behavior did not change much when she brought cubs to the falls. She was more aggressive, but not in the wild and seemingly inappropriate style of Reggie. The true test of Jeanne's maternal composure came during the summer of 1980 when she had the single spring cub aptly named Wingnut (plate 31). The latter was hands-down the most insecure cub I have ever seen. Wingnut was literally afraid of his own shadow. Whenever Jeanne left him to fish in the river, Wingnut would bark and squall hysterically until she returned. If another bear approached while he was alone,

Brown bear sow attacking a young boar that approached too close to her cubs.

Wingnut would run to hide and get lost in the brush along the river. Several times he even ran onto our knoll among ten tourists, and once he took refuge under Mo's folding chair! During two of these incidents, Jeanne waited 15 feet away while Larry shooed Wingnut away from people.

Jeanne never appeared to be too alarmed at Wingnut's wild behavior. When he ran to hide in the alder brush, Jeanne would calmly set out to locate him. I can vividly picture her fat form trotting along the river as she began her search. Jeanne was not only very fat, but her coat was extremely long and dense, to the point of making her appear like a great round ball of fur with four feet barely poking out underneath, and whenever she trotted in haste her great coat would shake and shimmer, further emphasizing her resemblance to a ball. As she passed by our observation knoll, Jeanne would quickly glance up at us and continue with her search. She knew the people present were no threat to her cub and she ignored us. But please pity any bear that crossed her path during such a search. Jeanne could launch a vicious charge, but she rarely wasted time pressing an attack while her cub was missing. When she located Wingnut, he would often fail to recognize his mother and would run from her. Persistent following was necessary before Jeanne could reclaim him.

For many years Jeanne's experience with her cubs at the falls was obviously a factor in the differences between her maternal behavior and that of Reggie. Jeanne was no less protective of her cubs, but she simply knew precisely what situations required action, whereas Reggie made no such distinctions. However, experience was not the sole factor involved in these differences. Many of the older, more experienced sows displayed varying degrees of the wildly aggressive maternal behavior exhibited by Reggie. Individual variations in temperament that are so prominent in brown bear behavior were largely responsible for these differences.

There were only five or six high-ranking, mature sows like Jeanne who dominated the falls each summer. The greatest of these sows in the early 1970s was Big Mamma, who was, as her name implies, a big bear. At a weight of 550 pounds or more, she was the largest, most dominant sow at McNeil and best exemplified my idea of the ultimate brown bear sow.

I first saw Big Mamma on the sedge flats in July 1973 when she was sixteen years old. Two small yearling cubs, who were the survivors of a litter of three from the year before, grazed on the sedge beside her. The loss of one cub from this large litter was not surprising but the retarded growth of the surviving cubs seemed inconsistent. I expected that Big Mamma would be unsurpassed in providing optimum growth conditions for her cubs, because her enormous size and superior fishing ability would logically result in a copious milk supply for her young. However, the rate of lactation has little to do with body size in most mammals and bears are apparently no exception.

Big Mamma arrived on the flats a few days after the start of the fishing season and grazed on sedge for a few days more before venturing to the falls for fishing. On the same day that Rama was found killed, Big Mamma was seen on the flats with only one cub. We initially assumed that the dead bear was her missing cub, but a closer examination of the teeth revealed the dead cub was a two-year-old instead of a yearling. The next day she once again had both yearlings with her on the flats. This was the only time I observed the separation of a yearling from its mother.

The dominance of Big Mamma at the falls was unquestionable. Her authority radiated in all directions and controlled almost every contest of rank. She was in control. Only the larger boars were more dominant than Big Mamma and even these behemoths steered clear of her sensitively fused wrath. She approached preferred fishing spots with a confidence that seemed calm and relaxed, but there was always the mysterious illusion that she was on the verge of erupting in fury. When she walked onto the crowded falls, there was the same tension as when someone holds a firecracker until the last second before throwing it, like feeling a brief earthquake tremor, then waiting in silence for greater shocks. There was always this feeling of impending violence when Big Mamma arrived at the falls, because a minor spark of insolence from a subordinate was the only stimulus needed to ignite her aggression.

Despite her explosive nature around other bears, Big Mamma was never aggressive toward people. One day on the way to the falls we met Big Mamma and her two yearlings on the trail and we immediately began to veer off to give them room to pass. She also angled off the path to avoid us, but her yearlings decided that we were worthy of closer inspection and playfully approached us as we circled wider and wider around them. Big Mamma followed after the pair huffing alarms at them as she became more concerned with their foolish behavior. The cubs finally heeded her warnings and followed her down the trail as we retreated in the opposite direction.

Big Mamma became even more relaxed around people after the cubs were weaned the next year (1974). She was grazing alone on a high section of the flats one day in late June when Jim and I spotted her while motoring about the submerged flats in our skiff at high tide. Jim steered the skiff in her direction so we could pass beside her for a good lateral view and make a positive identification. Unfortunately the thick emergent sedge eliminated all steering and aimed us directly at her. She lowered her head, swayed from side to side, and cast a horrifying glare at us, which were all signals that were aggressive in nature. Jim fumbled with the reverse switch as we drifted closer and closer to the irritated sow, but just before we rammed her, the motor reversed and slowly pulled us back and out of the entangling sedge. We had come dangerously close to forcing Big Mamma into aggressive action.

This encounter with Big Mamma had been dangerous for several reasons. First, it was early in the summer and she had not yet become rehabituated to our close presence. In addition, the situation in which the encounter took place was unusual, because the bears are only accustomed to close observers at the falls proper. We had definitely pressed our luck by crowding her with the skiff.

Later in the summer she vividly demonstrated to Jim just how different the falls was for contact between bears and people. Jim asked me to watch for bears while he went after a jug of water at the tiny stream behind the cave, where the bushes crowded the scene and made it possible for bears and people to meet unexpectedly. While Jim was hidden in the bushes, I became engrossed in an encounter between two bears and failed to notice that Big Mamma had left the falls with a fish and headed straight up the stream toward him. He was straddled and bent over the stream to fill the water bottle when he heard some splashing and looked up to see Big Mamma emerge from the bushes and meet him almost face to face with a bloody salmon clenched in her teeth. He automatically threw a hand in the air and yelled at her, but she had already turned and headed into the alders without any visible reaction at all. Jim didn't appreciate my explanation of how I had failed to notice Big Mamma's departure.

Big Mamma preferred to fish at the number-one spot, which often put her in competition with other sows and mature boars. When she had cubs, Big Mamma could hold the number-one spot against all but the largest boars. Most bears knew this and she was rarely challenged, but as the season progressed all bears became more accustomed to fishing near others and every day at least one younger bear would press its luck and crowd Big Mamma. Her response was often the most spectacular charge and attack I have witnessed by a bear. She would leap through the air and land squarely on the back of the subordinate bear, biting and clawing viciously. Only frantic scrambling would free the victim from her attack.

Big Mamma's dominance dropped significantly after the weaning of her cubs. This loss of dominance is always more noticeable in an irascible sow like Big Mamma, because most of her intense aggression was in the form of maternal protection. Much of her irascibility also disappeared with the weaning of her cubs and she became a less noticeable personality at the falls. She routinely allowed younger bears to pass near her and fish beside her and seldom did she resort to violence unless another bear attempted to steal her salmon catch. At times her fishing success was so phenomenal that she even allowed others to steal from her. I once recorded sixty-three salmon catches by her in a four-hour period. She let all the males go and ate only the eggs from the female salmon.

After Big Mamma weaned her cubs in 1974, she failed to reproduce through 1976, when she was nineteen years old. There was no record of a brown bear sow reproducing in the wild past this age, so I assumed that she was infertile. Even at this age her body was still impressive and well-muscled and her massive hips looked as though they belonged on a boar. She was ageless, as powerful as ever, and still very much a Big Mamma.

Because of her excellent condition, I always held out hope that Big Mamma might reproduce at an old age and extend the known reproductive age of wild brown bears. I visited McNeil for a week during the height of the fishing season in 1977, but Big Mamma had not arrived that summer. Then one afternoon I spotted a large sow with three spring cubs hurrying along the river out on the tidal flats. The sow was wet from swimming the river and she did not look familiar, especially from almost a mile away through a spotting scope. Later the same afternoon this sow wandered closer to camp with a fluffy dry coat and with one glance I was certain that it was Big Mamma.

What a magnificent animal she was! With her coat shimmering in the breeze, she appeared to be larger and more powerful than ever in her twentieth year. The three cubs that scurried along behind her were large and healthy. These three youngsters survived the winter and returned to the falls with Big Mamma as yearlings and again as two-year-olds. What an amazing sow she was.

Big Mamma had no equal in the small group of large, dominant sows. There were several younger or smaller sows who were not in the same class of bear represented by Big Mamma or Jeanne. One of the lowest ranking, mature sows was Lanky, a small sow whose size was a factor in her subordinate position at the falls. Early each summer Lanky was thin and gaunt at a weight of 300 pounds. Despite her size Lanky had a long, successful reproductive history.

She arrived early in the 1974 fishing season with three

spring cubs. Two of the cubs were medium-size, but the third cub was much smaller and definitely a runt, which was a rarity at McNeil. His creamy chocolate coat made him unusually fat and round, and his compact little head, topped with short ears, completed his cuteness. One of the larger cubs was very dark brown with a collar of light blond fur, called a *harness,* that circled his neck and ran several inches down his front legs. This harness is common on spring cubs, but it always disappears after the first year. The third cub was large, but a bit gaunt and had long stringy reddish-brown hair.

Lanky's three cubs habituated themselves very quickly to the separation from their fishing mother. They sat and watched her maneuver around the rocks in the falls and soon they were content to curl up and sleep while she fished. Other cubs were rarely satisfied until they reached their mother, and they often produced confusing situations by running around bawling, struggling to swim to their mother, or running away and becoming lost in the alders. The placid attitude of Lanky's cubs made it easy for her to keep track of them most of the time. She had one confusing experience after making a rare trip across the river to fish the restricted side of the falls one day early in the fishing season. Lady Bird and her three cubs fished nearby and later Red Collar arrived and added her five cubs to the crowded scene. It was not long before Lanky got her cubs all mixed up with the other cubs and lost them altogether for several minutes. Immediately after locating her three, she herded them back across the river to our side and she never again took them back.

Lanky had a low ranking for a sow with cubs, because she was not aggressive and lacked the size, power, and confidence that allowed sows like Big Mamma to utilize the falls skillfully. More often than not she seemed to be more of a spectator than a participant at the falls. She became progressively less active at fishing during each year of my study. Early in the summer of each year she was active in her fishing endeavors and moved constantly from spot to spot as though she had little patience with unproductive locations. The poor success rate that she experienced was largely due to this lack of persistence, but she

also suffered from poor fishing technique and an obvious defi-
ciency in real effort. Although most bears seemed to be very
intense in their fishing efforts, Lanky never expended much
energy in her halfhearted attempts. Stealing and scavenging
the catches of other bears provided her with as much salmon
to eat as her own catches. Each day she spent more time
stealing and scavenging and soon she developed these activities into a real art. During the last week or two of the season
she rarely fished at all, preferring instead to sit along the riverbank and wait for other bears to catch fish that she could steal
or scavenge (plate 32).

One clear cold day Lanky displayed her fearless attitude
toward people and thoroughly tested my nerves in the process.
I had moved from the cold shade of the cave to a warm sunny
spot nearer the riverbank. I was sitting in my chair recording
data when Lanky came walking along the river's edge with her
cubs following close behind. She was directly below me on the
river about 15 feet away when she suddenly started up a trail
that passed literally inches from my feet. It was instantly too
late for me to move, so I froze in my chair and tried to look
inoffensive by staring at the ground and holding my breath as
she literally brushed past my feet with the cubs following in
line behind her. It occurred to me that one of the cubs could
put me in an incriminating position by doing something
unusual, but she passed without acknowledging my presence
in any way.

Late that summer Lanky often fished the shallow waters
near the mouth of the river for spawning or deteriorated
salmon. Because only two or three bears remained in the area,
we had stopped taking data at the falls and were concentrating
on catching some silver salmon to smoke before we left
McNeil. While we fished, Lanky often splashed around us as
she searched the shallow pools for an easy catch of dying
salmon. She once left her cubs on a gravel bar near us and
crossed the river to fish new areas. She continued on toward
the falls and left her cubs half a mile behind. Her cubs were
disturbed when she first left, but soon they relaxed and fell
asleep on the gravel. Meanwhile, we caught several beautiful

silver salmon that were splashing around on a string at our feet when Lanky decided to return to her cubs on our side of the river. We knew a bad situation was rapidly developing. There we were, stuck on a narrow bank between a sow and her cubs with salmon flopping at our feet and a cliff at our backs. I thought that Lanky would voluntarily circle up and around us, but she walked straight ahead. She was a very coolheaded sow, but we *were* separating her from her cubs, so I shoved the salmon into deeper water and Jim waved his arms in the air and yelled at Lanky. She did not appear to be the least bit concerned by all our commotion and approached to within 20 feet before she finally turned and headed up the steep bluff without breaking stride and emerged from the alders downstream beside her sleeping cubs a minute later. It was just routine fishing for her.

Despite her retiring disposition, Lanky was fearless in protecting her cubs when real danger threatened them. Unlike the more aggressive sows who usually threatened any bear who came near their cubs, Lanky seemed capable of discriminating between dangerous and nondangerous situations. She normally restricted her threats to the situations where potential danger to her cubs was obvious. Zubin, an 800-pound male, once made the mistake of chasing her cubs off the first big rock in the falls. Lanky weighed barely 300 pounds but she made three great leaps and hit Zubin broadside with such force that he was flipped onto his back as she tore fiercely at his flanks.

Lanky lost one of her offspring to unknown causes late in the fishing season. The runt cub and the dark cub with the harness were still with her when we last saw them in mid-August. The next summer she returned with only one yearling, who wore a faint outline of a harness, revealing that it was the dark cub with the harness who had survived.

The salmon run started very slowly that summer and except for one brief spurt it remained slow all summer. Lanky's fishing success was hurt by the lack of salmon, so she quickly reverted to her stealing and scavenging techniques. She often sat with her yearling for hours without obtaining a morsel of salmon. The data on fishing success later revealed that she had eaten very few fish that summer. She weaned her yearling before the next summer and was alone at the falls. The absence of cubs apparently relieved a considerable drain on her, because she was at least 75 pounds heavier and wore a thick shiny coat that made her look much better than in years past.

The McNeil sows were always a study in contrasts. Perhaps the best example of this is a comparison of Lanky and the incredible sow Red Collar. The latter had all the necessary attributes that were required for maximum utilization of the falls. Like Red, she was adept at handling the social situation at the falls, but in addition she had the size, dominance, power, and confidence to do anything she pleased. A freewheeling, opportunistic style helped her to catch and steal more fish than most bears, and although she was an excellent mother, she seldom let maternal duties slow her down at the falls. She kept one eye on the fish and one eye on her cubs.

Red Collar was a big, beautiful twelve-year-old sow when I first saw her in 1973, but she did not stand out among the fishing bears, because she was inoffensive and did not waste precious fishing time quarreling over fish or fishing spots. She seemed impatient as she roamed boldly around the falls in a constant quest for salmon. If her fishing spot proved unfruitful, she left it immediately and boldly approached another, regardless of the dominance of the bear occupying it, and either ignored or dealt quickly with any aggression she incurred in the process. When she was unsuccessful in catching fish, Red Collar often tried stealing another's catch, but she was impatient with this also and if the bear fought to keep its catch, she quickly abandoned the effort and searched elsewhere.

Red Collar had an incredible reproductive history from 1974 to 1976. She had four spring cubs when I first saw her in July 1974. She then disappeared for two days before returning to the falls with only three good-size spring cubs. Earlier that morning we had observed two lost spring cubs running around the sedge flats frantically searching for their mother, but we made no connection at the time between Red Collar and these

Red Collar and five spring cubs along the McNeil River.

lost cubs. She left the falls about noon and wandered down-river toward the flats, where we next saw her with a veritable pack of five cubs following along behind her. She had apparently picked up the two lost cubs on the flats.

We never knew if Red Collar had given birth to all five cubs, but I believe that they may well have been all hers. We had seen her with three, four, and five cubs on three different occasions, but because a sow with several cubs can easily lose some for short periods of time, I suspected that she had simply lost and regained different cubs on each occasion. All five cubs were exactly the same size, which was further evidence that they were all Red Collar's, as cubs from different litters usually vary considerably in size. The chances were slim that she had adopted one or two cubs that were identical in size to her own. Further, there were no McNeil sows in the area that could have lost two cubs to Red Collar. Red Collar made this reproductive effort more believable in 1978 when she appeared at the falls with four spring cubs.

Red Collar's quintet was surprisingly fearless and enterprising at the falls from the outset (plate 33). They were often marooned on the riverbank while Red Collar fished from the center rocks, but they remained collected and soon learned to swim across deep, calm pools to join her as she fished. Once on the rocks, they huddled together and patiently waited until she caught a salmon, when they all fought fiercely for a portion. They had to do a lot of dangerous swimming, because Red Collar changed her fishing location constantly and she was not always sensitive to their swimming capabilities. For instance, when they once attempted to follow her across the river in the middle of the fastest rapids, Red Collar seemed unaware of their futile efforts and continued across until one cub was swept away in the rapids. Only then did she return to the stranded cubs and attempt to herd them back to dry ground from their shallow refuge in the violent white water. Two more cubs were washed away on the return trip, but all three swam safely ashore and ran to meet their mother and siblings before they arrived below the falls to find them.

The cubs were thoroughly introduced to people one rainy afternoon when Red Collar came strolling into the cave where Jim and I were sitting. When she first saw us she stopped, only 5 feet from my side, which was so close that I could almost have reached out and touched her on the nose, but without flinching she turned and waddled down another trail to the falls and left her cubs behind to inspect us for a moment. They stood on hind legs and nervously glanced around, watching us with their big, wet eyes for several seconds, and then turned and ran down the trail to join their mother, who had never bothered to look back at the cave to check on them. Red was the only other sow who was so completely unconcerned with our presence.

On rare occasions I experienced unexplained intuition about certain bears' behavior. This was true of Red Collar and Red and their nonchalance toward us. I had absolute, complete trust in Red and never doubted for a moment my safety around her, but sometimes I had my doubts about Red Collar. While circling close behind us on our knoll, she would edge closer and closer and cast a menacing stare from under her brow. I believe she was testing us, pushing us to determine something of what we were and what she could do with us. This happened only two or three times and I was never really afraid of her, but I could not trust her the way I trusted Red.

Red Collar and her five cubs had an incredible summer of unusual experiences with both people and bears, but their most interesting experiences occurred in complex interactions with other sows and cubs. The bizarre details of these interactions, which involved the swapping and adoption of cubs between sows, will be discussed later. Suffice it to say at this point that Red Collar retained only three of her five cubs at the end of the summer.

These three cubs survived the winter and appeared with Red Collar the next summer in mid-July. They were the most beautiful group of bears I had ever seen. Red Collar still wore an unusually dense, blond winter coat that strongly resembled deep velvet from a distance, and her three cubs also retained thick winter coats. Together the four golden bears were an impressive and formidable group.

The yearlings, later known as the Marx Brothers, had learned from their mother's freewheeling activities and they became aggressive and brazen during their second summer at the falls. Because Red Collar was always on hand to back them up in any situation that might challenge their authority, they made bold bluff charges at older bears, who usually yielded to their threats for fear of retaliation from their mother. This taught them to be dominant and soon they were helping Red Collar steal fish from other bears.

Red Collar usually left the falls to eat fish that she caught and her yearlings always followed after her to fight for a portion. She always tried to avoid them and keep the fish for herself, but the cubs invariably produced a gory scene while stealing some of the salmon. All four bears roared and growled as they tore the fish apart with powerful jaws and reduced the salmon to shreds in seconds. Each bear was lucky to salvage a morsel.

The yearlings usually lingered over the remains after Red Collar returned to fish, and then they invariably wandered around our knoll on their return to the falls. I was alone on top of the cave one afternoon when the audacious trio came nosing around behind me. One of the yearlings ventured ahead of the others to smell my backpack, which stood upright about 4 feet away with my down parka partially protruding from the top. Unfortunately I failed to notice the cub until he had grabbed my parka and begun dragging it off. I stood and yelled in an attempt to scare him into dropping his find, but he was undaunted by my aggression. The parka must have been really loaded with exotic smells, because his two siblings soon joined him in a thorough inspection of the garment and all three started clawing and biting at it and rolling around in its strong scents. I was contemplating more aggressive action when Red Collar became interested in the action and joined the trio. I could hear the nylon being ripped as globs of down began floating about in the air above them. I was livid, to say the least, and stood about 20 feet from the orgy yelling while showering them with empty film canisters. Red Collar stopped for a moment and lifted her down-covered head above the turmoil to glance in my direction, but the sight of me, jumping up and down and waving my arms wildly in the air as I screamed and flung various objects at them, failed to impress her and she fell onto the parka with renewed enthusiasm. I kept telling myself that I didn't have to take this kind of abuse from these clowns, so I considered hurling my 30-pound wooden chair into their midst, but I decided that was a bit extreme and instead secured a large granite rock, wound up, and propelled this weapon directly into Red Collar's fat haunches. She gave a sudden start and ran away three or four steps before lapsing into her waddle as she strolled back down to the falls. She never looked back for her cubs, who slowly followed her away. I walked over to the scene of the crime and surveyed the ruins of my parka. They had kneaded the torn remains deep into the soggy muskeg.

These three yearlings had only begun to abuse their human observers. Later in the season, two young tourists made the mistake of leaving their equipment on top of the knoll while visiting below in the cave with other photographers. The yearlings rummaged through their gear and made off with a nylon poncho that they promptly tore to shreds. Although the young lady who owned the poncho was in tears, I found it hard to keep a straight face.

A week later the yearlings got into more trouble at the cave when they tried to steal a fish from an older bear without the assistance of Red Collar and got chased through the middle of a group of photographers. A tripod and camera were knocked over in their wake and fell off the top of the cave, crashing to the ground in front of the people below. The cubs continued their escape, seemingly oblivious to the people they had just terrorized.

Red Collar failed to wean these cubs the following year

(1976) and kept them that summer for a third season at the falls. I observed them for only a few days during a brief visit in late summer, but I was told the trio, who by that time had been named the Marx Brothers, had been brazen though undestructive around the falls that summer. They remained together in close sibling bonds through the summer of 1979. This extended sibling relationship was best summed up by Mo Aumiller, who said in her delightful Australian accent that they were "thicker than thieves." I was able to observe Groucho, Chico, and Harpo during a visit in 1980 when they were six years old. Their sibling bonds had ended, but they played together a great deal at the falls. Their life histories at McNeil would have been fascinating to follow, but unfortunately two of the brothers had disappeared by 1984. It is assumed that they were taken in legal hunts that continue to this day at selected times within two miles of the falls.

Red Collar's reproductive history did not end with the Marx Brothers. She appeared in 1978 at age seventeen with four spring cubs, but only one of these survived to be a yearling. Following this effort, she was alone at the falls until age twenty-two. It was a safe assumption that Red Collar would have no more cubs. We had no record of a sow reproducing past this age.

Our information on brown bear reproduction was certainly sparse in the 1970s. At that time much of what was known came from a population study by the Alaska Department of Fish and Game at Black Lake on the Alaska Peninsula. The oldest sow that reproduced during that study had cubs at age seventeen. However, hunting is so intense in the Black Lake area that it is probably rare for a sow to survive to age seventeen, much less older. The data at McNeil were scant. For instance, one old sow named Blue Flapps was unproductive from age seventeen until she was shot in 1972 at age twenty-two. Lady Bird and Goldie, two large, dominant, aggressive sows were both without cubs from 1976 to 1985. There seemed to be a pattern suggesting the maximum age of reproduction was around seventeen years.

There is evidence that females of many species are capable of reproducing until death, but brown bears may be different. They have no "natural" predators and there are no obvious factors to prevent them from living to an older age than most prey species. For instance, I cannot imagine a deer or elk surviving to the stage of decrepit senility that Patches reached at age twenty-six in 1980. Sows can also survive until they appear feeble with age, so there is reason to suspect that they live beyond a reproductive age.

The benefits of long-term recordkeeping at McNeil were realized by the late 1970s. This was entirely due to the diligence and genuine care of Larry Aumiller, who has kept detailed data on the bears each summer from 1976 to the present. Larry's work had resulted in over twenty years of data by 1986.

Big Mamma was the first sow to advance the documented age of reproduction. As I described earlier, this incredible sow had three spring cubs at age twenty in 1977. This record held for three years until Jeanne also had a single cub, the infamous Wingnut, at age twenty. But the incomparable Red Collar was not to be outdone. In 1984, following four unproductive years, she arrived at the falls with a single cub at age twenty-three. Red Collar was as beautiful and powerful as ever at this age. She wore perhaps the most luxuriant coat I have ever seen on a bear. There was no sign of old age (plate 34).

So now the age to beat is twenty-three, but I suspect this record will hold for a while. There are not many sows like Red Collar. On the other hand the McNeil sows have been steadily advancing the known reproductive age of wild brown bears and they may well prove in years to come that some exceptional sows reproduce at an even more advanced age.

The age at which a sow first reproduces will strongly influence the number of potential litters she could produce. A sow conceiving at age three could obviously have more young than one first conceiving at seven or eight. Theoretically, a sow could breed first at age three and then every three years thereafter, but this no doubt would be rare. Many sows do not conceive until ages ranging from five to nine years, and as mentioned earlier, Reggie first conceived at the age of thirteen. In addition, sows commonly skip one or more years between reproductive cycles and many sows have young and lose them before they are weaned. All these factors drastically reduce a sow's actual reproduction from the theoretical maximum.

Reproduction must be limited in these ways, because a stable unhunted population could never begin to absorb all the young that its member females could potentially produce. The sows of such a population need only produce two surviving adults to replace themselves and their mates. Even allowing for some mortality after weaning, a sow would have to wean only a few cubs to ensure replacement. Because recent brown bear evolution most likely took place in the absence of predators, their reproductive potential may seem excessive, but reproductive redundancy is an expected phenomenon because the evolution of reproductive rates occurs at the individual level. In other words, it is in the best evolutionary interest of each individual to produce as many offspring as possible. Therefore, reproductive rates are not determined by what the population needs to remain stable, but by the maximum rate that is physiologically attainable by females.

During my study the McNeil sows were comparatively retarded in attaining sexual maturity. There were exceptions to this in the years before and after my study, but the delayed maturity of many sows in the 1970s remains interesting. In general, female brown bears first breed successfully at ages ranging from three to eight years or more. The reasons for such wide variation are obscure. It is doubtful that nutrition could be an absolute factor controlling the maturity of Alaska Peninsula brown bears, as they are opportunistic omnivores and their potential foods, particularly salmon and vegetation, are abundant and widespread. Although nutrition is a major factor, it alone should not delay maturation for five years or more.

A possible answer to the puzzle of retarded sexual maturation may well be found in the area of social stress, which is known to suppress reproductive development in many animal species by altering hormone levels that control reproductive physiology. Social stress, in the form of increased conflict and competition, provides increased stimuli to the central nervous system, which in turn affects the pituitary gland in the brain. The pituitary responds by decreasing its secretion of gonado-tropins, which are hormones that stimulate and control the reproductive organs. The result may be suppressed reproductive development and functions, as well as decreased intra-uterine and postnatal survival of young.

This social stress hypothesis is supported by ursine behavior. It is expected that an asocial, solitary animal that generally shuns close contact with its own kind would be greatly stressed by high population density and the accompanying increase in contact and strife. In fact, most any bear will violently chase a subordinate bear that encroaches into its *individual space.*

Many animals have an individual space, or critical distance, within which they feel safe. If another animal violates this space or distance, then the animal is threatened and will either fight or flee. The individual space of a brown bear is highly variable, but is generally quite large, so violations of this space increase as population density increases, and this results in greater stress.

If stress suppresses the development and function of bear reproduction, then there should be observable differences between populations of high densities and those of lower densities. Data from two such populations of the Alaska Peninsula tend to support this conclusion. The McNeil population receives light hunting pressure, and as the bears have no other predator, the population is probably stable and near its upper limit. The population of bears inhabiting the Black Lake area of the Peninsula is subjected to intense hunting pressure each year (Glenn, 1975). As a result the McNeil and Black Lake populations have very different controls, with McNeil bears being partly limited by natural factors and the Black Lake population largely controlled by hunters.

Almost invariably an animal population that is heavily hunted will respond to the decrease in density by increasing its productivity. Females will mature earlier, breed earlier and sometimes more often, and have more young per litter with less infant and juvenile mortality. The Black Lake females, as expected, increase their reproduction, as many three-year-old females come into estrous and a few conceive successfully at this young age. Litter size, which was not unusually high at 2.3, was probably reduced by the high percentage of young females reproducing, but their cub mortality was very low at 9 percent.

The McNeil females mature late, breed late, produce good-size litters, and have high cub mortality between the first and second year of age. The youngest female to breed during my five-year study was Spooky, who conceived at five years. Others first conceived successfully at six, seven, eight, ten, thirteen, and still others were without young at eight years of age. My sample size was small, but it seems improbable that the sexual maturity of these females, all of them successful at fishing, could be delayed so long by lack of food alone. Litter size from 1972 to 1976 averaged 2.64, which is large, but somewhat expected from older, more mature sows who gorged annually on McNeil salmon. Cub mortality for the same period was 58 percent. I seriously doubt that a mature McNeil sow suffers such high cub mortality because of low food availability. The stress resulting from high population density (in relation to habitat) could be a factor in this high mortality.

It could be argued that stress as a factor in maturation is unfounded. First, the sows in the heavily hunted Black Lake population may well mature earlier because the annual population reduction from hunting provides increased or more available food sources, particularly salmon. Further, in arctic and interior Alaska and in the Yukon, where the winters are long and severe and food sources scarce, the resident grizzly sows are very late in maturing despite low population densities (Pearson, 1976; Reynolds et al., 1976). In addition, on Kodiak Island, where salmon are very abundant and mild winters provide a long growing season and lush vegetation, the brown bear population is very productive, with females maturing early and having low cub mortality despite one of the highest densities of bears in the world (Hensel et al., 1969; Troyer and Hensel, 1964a). All this evidence can be used to argue that nutrition largely controls the maturation of female brown bears, and yet the McNeil females remain a puzzling mystery. One only has to glance at the large, fat McNeil sows to see that they have adequate food.

Perhaps there is a generalized stress factor operating in bear populations that may include environmental factors (for example, food shortages, climatic extremes, disease organisms) as well as social stress factors (for example, crowding at the falls, intense competition, abnormal sex ratios, lack of stability of social organization). Environmental stresses may have the same physiological effects as social stress and they are not necessarily mutually exclusive. Therefore, the potential for social stress must be evaluated in terms of the carrying capacity of the habitat. For instance, the high density of bears on Kodiak Island may not be crowded in an ecological sense, while the lower density of grizzlies in interior Alaska or McNeil may well be. The potential for stress factors operating at McNeil is obvious.

Some investigators have suggested that bears may be *induced ovulators* (Craighead et al., 1969). That is, ovulation is induced by coital stimulation. Induced ovulation is simply a timing mechanism that tends to ensure fertilization, especially among animals in which chances for copulation are rare. This method of ovulation is common among asocial, solitary animals, and so it is logical to expect that brown bears are also induced ovulators. However, as induced ovulation is only a timing mechanism, it is probably not directly involved as a factor in sexual maturity.

Obviously the development of the ovaries is the ultimate factor in sexual maturity. Environmental variables such as nutrition and social stress would certainly influence ovarian development and successful ovulation. Thus, young sows will not conceive until body requirements for ovulation are met, and older sows may skip a year or even several years between reproductive efforts whenever environmental variables restrict necessary body requirements for ovulation.

It may appear that the earliest possible reproduction would be in the best interests of the individual sow, because this would extend the length of her reproductive life. How-

ever, in terms of energy investment versus reproductive returns there may be a selective disadvantage in an early reproductive effort. If a young sow conceives, she is committed to
a huge energy investment, which might be jeopardized if her
chances of successfully rearing her cubs are poor. It might be
a better strategy to wait a few years to conserve energy and
accumulate experience until the chances of successful reproduction are improved. There may have been selection for a
rigid set of body requirements that must be met before ovulation can occur. Thus, in rigorous climates or in areas of high
population density (for example, McNeil), sows mature later
than in milder climates (Kodiak) or where hunting is heavy
(Black Lake).

When McNeil sows finally mature, they usually come into
estrous in late May and June, though an occasional sow will not
be in estrous until late July. Duration of estrous is apparently
quite variable—just like everything else about bears. Craighead et al. (1969) gave evidence that Yellowstone grizzlies
experience two distinct estrous cycles separated by a brief
period of anestrous. The two cycles, each lasting up to ten days,
are separated by a period of anestrous of four to eighteen days.
My observations of estrous sows were too limited to form any
conclusions on this question.

There was no apparent correlation in the McNeil sows
between reproductive success and their age of sexual maturation, dominance, size, or temperament. Lanky, the smallest
and least aggressive sow, weaned as many cubs (seven) as any
other sow from 1970 to 1984. During this period Lady Bird, a
large, dominant, aggressive sow, weaned only three cubs. Lady
Bird was a mature sow that I considered in the small class of
large, dominant sows. Her age was unknown but I estimated
it at about fifteen in 1975, since she had been fully mature
during the six years of our study. She had three spring cubs in
the summer of 1972, but she lost all of these before the next
summer when she was again in estrous, which resulted in three
more spring cubs in 1974.

Lady Bird was the classic frantic sow at McNeil River. Early in
the summer she moved around the falls like a tautly coiled

spring that grew tighter and tighter until released in an attack on any bear that wandered too close to her cubs. Sometimes the sudden movement of a fishing attempt by a nearby bear was all that was necessary to elicit an attack from Lady Bird. She slowly habituated herself to the crowded conditions at the falls and even fished alongside other sows and younger bears after a few days of fishing, but she remained a fused bomb at all times.

She stayed exclusively on the restricted side of the river, because she was too afraid of people to venture onto our side. She was so wary of us that her fishing was often interrupted by sudden movements of observers at the cave. People arriving at the falls usually spooked her into fleeing the area for extended periods of time. Most bears approached their fishing spots in a slow, cautious manner in order to check for other bears that they feared, but Lady Bird always ran down the riverbanks at full speed and flung herself into the river without delay. This first wild belly flop fishing attempt was surprisingly successful, and although her subsequent fishing attempts were more conventional, she often made these sporadic diving leaps into deep water.

No bear willingly tangled with Lady Bird, as she was a big, aggressive sow and her social status was extremely high. Her lower lip hung loose from the jaw and exposed the base of her teeth as it flopped about wildly whenever she was excited. This, added to the wide, wild stare in her eyes, gave Lady Bird an excited, frantic look that perfectly matched her behavior (plate 35).

Charlie Brown was one of the few bears that Lady Bird could not dominate. She avoided him whenever possible, but late one evening in July he made an unseen approach from behind her while she was fishing at his favorite spot. He was scarcely 15 feet away when Lady Bird suddenly detected his presence and whirled around and crashed over her cubs as she charged him. She cut the charge short and stopped directly in front of him, depressed her ears, and crouched close to the ground as she raised her head high to meet his advance with bared teeth flashing in his face and sharp claws slapping at his neck. He stood still and offered no resistance to her aggression. Lady Bird retreated to her cubs, hovered over them, and continued to direct open-mouth threats at Charlie, who stood still and surveyed the river as though contemplating a course of action (plate 36). Lady Bird's response was a combination of aggression and fear, or a conflict between fighting and running away. She was terrified of Charlie, but she was also prepared to stand her ground in order to protect her cubs. Both bears held their positions for twenty to thirty seconds, then Charlie finally turned and slowly ambled downriver to a less desirable fishing spot. He obviously wanted his favorite fishing spot, but he apparently did not care to press the issue with such an irate sow. This was the only time during five summers that I observed Charlie actively defer to another bear. Although Lady Bird had technically won the encounter, it was rather by default, because Charlie Brown had simply avoided a nasty situation.

There was a quantum leap in aggressiveness between Lady Bird and Jezebel, who could only be described as hysterical. Every nerve in her body was an overloaded power line ready to be grounded on anything in sight. Jezebel was a thrill a minute and she kept us on our toes.

Our first experiences with Jezebel came late in the summer of 1973. The sun was just setting as she came scurrying up the river toward the falls at an anxious pace, with two dark spring cubs struggling to keep up with her. We had no idea who she was, so I stood to make myself as conspicuous as possible, because I wanted to find out at a safe distance if she was a new sow and how she was going to react to humans. She failed to notice me, so I walked on top of the cave and waved a hand in the air. She saw me at about 200 feet and exploded on the spot. Fear sprang instantly to her face and her eyes widened as she lunged toward us in a raging charge, veritably flying along the riverbank with her feet a blond blur as they spun beneath her hurtling form. I had already pumped my shotgun when she broke off the charge at 100 feet and raced back to the startled cubs with her lips fluttering wildly from alarm huffs, but she turned before reaching her cubs and charged us again. She had worked her 400 pounds of flying fury into an uncontrollable frenzy of unbelievable speed. Again she broke the charge and raced back to her confused cubs, plowed through their midst, and charged down the river away from us and completely out of sight.

This debut at the falls had apparently been sufficiently traumatic to cause Jezebel to avoid the area for the remainder of the summer and she made no known appearances the next summer. I had practically forgotten about her by June 1975, when one day in the middle of the month, while I was scanning the sedge flats with my scope, I spotted a sow with two large two-year-old cubs—a trio that gave me a slight twinge of déjà vu the instant I saw them. I rationalized that the chances were very remote that the sow was Jezebel, but she gave me a very uneasy feeling. I mentioned her to Jim but quickly dismissed any real concern about the sow.

Two hours later we left camp for a fishing trip on Mikfik Creek. I had scanned the flats just before we left and had located only two young bears grazing near the creek, so I was satisfied that the strange sow and her cubs had vacated the premises. We crossed the grass-covered beaches near camp and edged along the snowbanks that still covered the leeward sides of the rocky bluffs and occasionally extended 200 feet out onto the sedge flats. We were talking and laughing as we circled around one of these large drifts that crossed our trail, unaware that Jezebel was grazing calmly on the other side. As we walked on unaware of the ticking time bomb, Jim carefully watched the icy, muddy footing and held our only shotgun absently at his side, while I plodded along in the thick mud behind him. Then suddenly aware of some guttural crescendo, I looked up to see Jezebel burst over the ridge in an explosion of flying wet snow, and almost involuntarily I threw my hands in the air and let out a warning yell at her. The instant she saw what we were she turned on the crest of the drift and ran up its length to the adjoining bluff. She was already retreating by the time Jim looked up and pumped his gun.

The two cubs appeared on top of the snow and casually

began to inspect us as Jezebel crashed into the alders on the
bluff. She immediately came ripping back through the brush
and raced onto the snow to retrieve her cubs. Her blasting
guttural roar sporadically lapsed into staccato huffs of alarm as
she emitted violent hoarse gusts of air from her lungs. These
alarm calls failed to attract the attention of her inquisitive
cubs, who began stalking us by creeping down the snow with
their eyes fixed steadily on us and their heads close to the
ground. The sight of her cubs approaching us drove Jezebel
into an even greater frenzy. I thought every hair on her body
was going to shoot into the air like skyrockets as she ran huffing
and puffing back into the alder brush. Jim and I had slowly
backed away from the snowdrift as we yelled and waved our
arms at the brazen cubs, but they continued to stalk us. We
decided that our situation called for a warning shot in the air
to discourage the cubs, so while hoping that the sudden shot
would not detonate Jezebel, Jim raised the shotgun and fired
a .12-gauge slug into the air. Jezebel instantly lunged from the
alders and flung herself down the snowdrift while huffing
madly as she roared toward us. Jim pumped and fired again
and she reversed her charge at the base of the drift and returned to the bluff and zigzagged in and out of the brush while
huffing at her cubs, who reluctantly began to heed their
mother's warnings. They turned occasionally to peer menacingly back at us, while slowly climbing the snow to Jezebel.

This encounter with Jezebel emphasized to us that quite
often cubs are more dangerous than sows. Jezebel had been
eager to run from us, but the persistent curiosity of her cubs
had almost forced her into violence for their own protection.
We were in all probability the first humans the two-year-old
cubs had contacted at close range and so it was logical that they
should be curious. They might have been fearful of us a year
or two earlier, but now they were larger than we were and two
years with Jezebel's backing had made them very bold. The
only unusual aspect of their behavior was their total disregard
of Jezebel's instruction. Throughout our encounter, while Jezebel ran around in a frenzy, huffing and puffing alarms on the

snow, the cubs had remained mesmerized by our presence, seemingly unaware of Jezebel's actions.

I hoped that Jezebel's intolerance of people would drive her from the area, but she continued to graze on the flats. Whenever we approached her in open country, she spotted us at great distances and ran into hiding. Our only other direct encounter with the unpredictable trio occurred while we were busy fishing on Mikfik Creek and failed to notice their approach until they appeared on the opposite bank about 100 feet upstream from us. Jezebel fell to pieces, as usual, but the cubs seemed to be less interested in us and followed her away after making a few clumsy fishing attempts in the creek.

Jezebel disappeared with her cubs in late June and was absent for a full month, which led me to hope that she had left the area for the summer. It seemed inconceivable that she would ever visit the falls and mingle with the bears and people, but Jezebel always appeared at unexpected times, so we tried to stay alert for a possible encounter with her.

After this thirty-day respite from the threat of Jezebel, the fishing season began and proceeded rather routinely for several days, until late one evening, when she suddenly appeared from the alders near the cave and surveyed the misty, fog-shrouded falls. She was unaware of our presence, as the cold east wind had forced us to huddle out of sight in the deepest section of our cave. Jim noticed her first and nudged me in the ribs as he cautiously reached for his shotgun. We gave each other a knowing look of dread and stood with guns in hand to make our presence known.

Her cubs were already nosing about in shallow water in search of fish, but Jezebel remained still and hesitantly continued to inspect the surroundings. Oddly enough, she did not explode on detecting our movements. Instead she froze on the spot and stared at us for a couple of seconds, and then circled around on the rocks in a stealthy manner before stopping to stare at us again. I stepped up a few feet onto higher ground to give her a more complete view of me. She began to huff quietly, moved in tighter circles, and then broke off into jumpy abstract movements as though confined in a small cage. She was still very afraid of us, but it appeared as though our earlier encounters had helped to habituate Jezebel to our presence.

The longer the cubs remained on the riverbank, the more engrossed they became in the fishing scene. They smelled salmon and saw other bears catching salmon, and even Jezebel appeared to be on the verge of fishing. It occurred to me that the reinforcement of catching one fish might be sufficient to keep Jezebel fishing all summer.

She was in no hurry to leave, so Jim and I decided to keep an eye on her from on top of the cave. I hoped we could scare her away for the evening and perhaps for the entire summer, because there was no way for us to get any work done with this lunatic sow meandering around. As we began to climb on top of the cave, our initial moves triggered her into an immediate charge of lightning quickness that wildly vibrated her thick coat as she lunged at us, but again she broke off the charge as suddenly as it had begun and returned to her cubs. Then she huffed quietly at her offspring and led them slowly off into the brush while staring at us menacingly.

We continued our surveillance long after Jezebel disappeared over the ridge behind the cave. The chances were excellent that she would return later in the evening, so we decided to move on top of the cave where we had a better view of her arrival routes. I went below and handed our gear up to Jim and then as I climbed up to join him I noticed Jezebel's silhouette against the twilight on a knoll overlooking the cave. The instant that I appeared from below she launched herself downhill at a speed far exceeding that of a free fall. She touched ground only two or three times in descending the 30-foot knoll, but she ended her sprinting charge in the muskeg 50 feet in front of us. It was over before I had time to react in any way and Jim had never even seen her. It was obvious that we had no real defense against Jezebel if she ever completed a charge, but of course this is true for any bear.

The tremendous lure of the salmon soon brought Jezebel and her cubs back onto the rocks of the falls. She apparently was prepared to tolerate our presence as long as we sat still and made no sudden movements. I still thought it was feasible and desirable to try to scare her away from the falls, so I tossed a rock in her direction. When it hit and shattered about five feet in front of her, she practically jumped out of her skin and crouched as she danced around scratching for footing as if the ground were revolving beneath her. As she was unable to locate the source of the disturbance, she began to investigate the fishing prospects.

Much to our dismay, she caught three fish before we left the falls that night, which was probably enough success to entice her to return for more fishing in the days to come. She made two more bluff charges at us that night. The first came as we moved around to pack up our gear and the second was triggered as we started out on the trail to camp. Each charge had become progressively shorter and less hysterical.

During the next week, Jezebel returned every evening to fish and succeeded in charging many visitors at the falls. Fortunately all of these charges were bluffs. We became very religious in carrying our weapons to the falls, but we knew our guns were useless against Jezebel because she always appeared so suddenly and at the most unexpected times. One evening I stayed at the falls to collect more data after everyone else had gone back to camp. When it came time to pack up and leave, I carefully surveyed for signs of Jezebel before going below to stash my gear in the cave. No bears were approaching, so I carried my things down the trail and shoved them into the cave. When I stood up to leave I saw our hysterical friend standing with her two cubs about 30 feet away. Surprise! With my heart suddenly in my throat, I crouched slowly and hoped they would move on down to fish. I had discovered from experience that the best way to elicit a charge from Jezebel was to climb the trail that led up from the cave, so I remained still and waited until she started down the riverbank and passed behind a small clump of brush. Then I scrambled up the trail and raced for my shotgun. While I was hurrying up the path, I envisioned her charging at the speed of light, but once on top I discovered that she was calmly fishing on the rocks below. Late evening fun and games at the falls.

The danger of Jezebel around unsuspecting tourists was

obvious. If she were to approach the cave when Jim and I were not there, some unwary tourist might attempt to photograph her at such close range that she would have no room for a bluff charge. With this in mind the Department of Fish and Game considered closing all access to the falls after 7:00 P.M., which was about the time that Jezebel arrived to fish each evening. There was even the suggestion of drugging and transporting her to a more remote area. Then, just before any action was taken to alleviate the problem, Jezebel did what I had hoped she would do all along. She moved to the restricted side of the river and stayed there. She joined the other wary bears, such as Lady Bird, Goldie, and most large boars, who avoided people by fishing at a safe distance on the far side of the falls.

Fortunately I had no more encounters with Jezebel during my visits after 1975. She never became a regular McNeil resident, but every two or three years she continued to make surprise appearances. Larry Aumiller told me that one summer at the falls she charged a man to within 4 feet before halting. Larry was able to measure this distance, since her paw prints were clearly visible in the mud where she skidded to a halt.

Our experiences and problems with Jezebel vividly demonstrated just how broad the spectrum of bear behavior can be. At one end of the scale were sows like Red, Lanky, and Red Collar, who were coolheaded and very tolerant of people and other bears. Then came Big Mamma and Reggie with their intolerance of other bears and fairly calm attitude toward people. Frantic sows, like Lady Bird and Goldie, continued the progression with their pugnacious reactions to bears and extreme wariness of people. The final extreme was Jezebel, the hysterical sow. These sows displayed, perhaps more dramatically than other bears, the individualism that characterizes bear personalities and behavior.

11

The Young Cubs

Despite their remarkable variations in behavior, the sows' relationships with their cubs were very similar, because the latter are independent of the sows' temperament. For instance, Red and Jezebel, who were as different as two sows could be in most of their behavior, were very similar when dealing directly with their cubs. This behavior would vacillate from callous sternness, to neglect, to real tenderness, depending on the situation.

The sight of a sow nursing her cubs is an extraordinarily intimate and tender scene in an otherwise rugged ursine life. It is seldom witnessed, as few sows are sufficiently at ease to nurse in the presence of people. The atmosphere of tension at the falls is a deterrent to nursing, so most sows seek out more secluded areas before nursing their cubs.

Red was an obvious exception to the habit of nursing in seclusion. While she was grazing on the flats in early July, she often allowed me to watch as she rolled over and gently nursed her cubs. Even though the cubs grazed continually on the protein-rich sedge, they frequently became hungry for milk and begged Red to stop her grazing for a brief nursing break. When they were grazing on sedge, the cubs usually became hungry for milk more often than at the falls where they had access to the rich salmon.

The cubs began to beg by attempting to suckle while Red remained standing, but no sow will allow her cubs to nurse from a standing position. If a sow is busy with other activities and does not choose to nurse on demand, she may punish persistent cubs with a bite on the back of the neck. If Red did not immediately prepare to nurse them, the cubs next began to beg by squalling while following her around and struggling to nurse. I know of no other sound comparable to this begging squall of spring cubs. It is a low guttural growl that is sometimes continuous for several seconds with many crescendos of volume, and at other times, particularly when the sow is uncooperative and the cubs are really hungry and irritable, the squalling is broken into staccato barks. The barks are very similar to the cries of alarm the cubs emit when separated or lost from their mothers, although the latter are more intense than the begging barks.

Red usually responded quickly to her cubs' cries of hunger on the flats, as grazing was an activity that she could easily suspend for nursing. Later, at the falls, she would be more preoccupied with fishing and would often ignore their hungry demands. Soon after the cubs began to squall, Red would begin to search for a suitable location. She preferred a spot with a slight slope where she could lean back and remain partially erect and still see all around while nursing.

The sand- and gravel bars that undulate around the flats and form the battle lines between the river and sea were Red's favorite nursing spots, so whenever one of these bars was reasonably close, she invariably made the trip over to lean against its slope and nurse her cubs. Red usually sauntered up the side of these gravel bars and settled on a spot with a commanding view of the surrounding flats where she could watch for approaching bears. Once a good spot was found, she sat down with a strong, graceful motion and allowed the cubs to climb onto her thighs as they grappled for a teat to suckle. As soon as the cubs had obtained a nursing position, she extended her massive front paws around them and held them gently as she leaned back into a reclining position. The cubs cradled on Red's stomach and immediately began to nurse with enthusiasm.

Each cub lay flat on Red's stomach and enveloped an entire teat with its mouth in strong suction. The six teats were black and hairless and the entire breasts were dark and thinly haired. They were not pendulous, but protruded only slightly. Four breasts are located on her chest just behind the front legs and the remaining two are between the hind legs.

Red generally nursed her two cubs for several minutes. The cubs purred constantly with a low, muffled growl that was a contented sound, much like a cat purring softly while being stroked. They would suckle on one teat for varying lengths of time and then quickly move to another in search of more milk. They often moved back and forth many times between teats and nursed intensely as though each second was very precious. Red gently supported them from the side with her front legs and from the rear with curled-up hind legs, thus forming a protective bowl in which the purring cubs could nurse hungrily. Sometimes she sprawled in complete relaxation with all four legs limp on the ground and allowed the cubs to maneuver freely about her chest. If other bears or people were around, she usually nursed them from a sitting position with the cubs standing on her thighs or stomach.

Red would immediately stand and end the nursing at the approach of another bear, for she apparently felt vulnerable in her reclining nursing position. Early in the summer she also broke off the nursing prematurely whenever I approached within 150 to 200 feet, even though she routinely allowed me three times as close when she was not nursing. She watched my distant approach from her reclined position by twisting her head around and peering over the gravel surface and then raising her head a bit, she scrutinized me carefully as I came closer. If I continued on, she rose to a sitting position and let her cubs slide down her belly from their secure positions. As she stood and ended a period of nursing, her cubs often stubbornly hung on to her teats and then ran along under her as they tried to continue nursing as she ambled along. Red never punished them for this persistence as other sows sometimes did. Instead, she ignored them and continued walking until they broke away.

A short nap usually followed an uninterrupted nursing period on the flats where the atmosphere was relaxed and conducive to leisurely resting and napping. When she was fishing at the falls, Red and other sows were too busy to nap after nursing, but during the easygoing days on the flats, Red would roll over from her nursing position and cuddle with her cubs for a nap that lasted as long as an hour. Their naps were often cut short by intruding bears, but people seldom restricted their nap time and they often slept with me sitting on a nearby log. The cubs snuggled beside her and slept soundly in the soft warmth of her deep, thick coat. The fold that formed between her hind leg and side as she slept on her

Red nursing her two spring cubs beside the cave.

stomach was a prime napping spot for the cubs. A head propped up in this deep soft crevice looked very comfortable on a cold, wet day.

The cubs engaged in rough play bouts after their naps. Their play was characterized by a certain ungainliness that is typical of spring cubs, because they do not yet have the coordination that marks the strong, graceful movements of older bears. They stood on hind legs and batted at each other with tiny paws, bit at one another's faces and necks, fell over and wrestled around in the sand, jumped up and chased each other around in circles, then wrestled some more. Red often continued to rest after the cubs had begun to play. She ignored them as they ran in circles around her playing hide and seek and climbed all over her fluffy back, frolicking about on the varied contours of her form. Regardless of how rough they played, Red seemed oblivious to their activities and never became irritated.

Even though sows generally did not nurse in the immediate vicinity of the falls, a few of them engaged in rare nursing bouts around the falls during my summers at McNeil. Lanky, Lady Bird, and Goldie nursed frequently in 1974, Reggie and Red were observed in 1975, and Jeanne put on many nursing shows in 1976. I never witnessed a nursing episode by Red Collar, Big Mamma, or Spooky.

Goldie would carry her salmon catch away from the falls to eat on the grassy bluffs along the river, and then she occasionally nursed her cubs on the same spot before returning to fish. This was the most common nursing routine at the falls, because sows seldom made a special trip away from the river to nurse. If a sow was busy fishing when her cubs became hungry and began to beg, she ignored them and continued with the more important business at hand—fishing.

Lanky, Red, Reggie, and Jeanne were sufficiently at ease around people to nurse near the cave and Jeanne would sometimes nurse her cubs on the first rock in the falls. Red was too wary of other bears to nurse at the falls proper, but she frequently nursed right beside the cave within 20 feet of me. She had become more relaxed in nursing near people as the summer progressed, but the sudden movement of a photographer attempting to shoot at close range always spooked her into moving away. She usually retreated to the grassy knoll that overlooked the river from upstream, where she would sit upright and survey the fishing activities while quietly nursing her cubs (plate 37).

Spring cubs are voracious salmon eaters and they can eat enormous quantities of fish in relation to their small size. They must fight for every scrap of salmon they obtain, because a sow never catches and delivers a fish expressly for her cubs. Hungry sows always try to avoid their aggressive cubs in order to eat the entire catch themselves. This is particularly true of sows with yearlings, as the latter can rip a 7-pound salmon to shreds and devour it quickly. Sows that fished exclusively on the far side of the falls could never avoid their hungry cubs, as all of their fishing spots were easily accessible to their young (plate 38). Sows that fished from the center rock, however, could sometimes isolate themselves from their cubs and hog their entire catch.

Red and Lanky often ate their catches out on these rocks, while ignoring the protests of their cubs on the riverbank. Red Collar, however, had a particularly difficult time in salvaging much of her fish for herself. Like many bears, she often left the falls before eating, which was a behavior that was probably a tradition or habit that she retained from her youth. That is, because older bears commonly steal fish from younger bears, the latter often retreat from the crowded falls before eating their fish and this becomes a tradition that many bears continue throughout their lives. Whenever Red Collar left with a catch, her cubs met her at the river's edge and immediately began their struggle for part of her fish. She ran at full speed into the brush and grass behind the cave, but her cubs quickly fell behind and all four mouths converged simultaneously on the salmon the instant she stopped to eat. A chorus of growling, grunting, roaring, and squalling arose from the gory scene as every cub fought for a taste of salmon. A tug of war over the torn fragments of the fish usually occupied the cubs long after

Red Collar had lost interest in the remaining morsels. If one cub escaped with a bit of skin, a tail, or jaw, one or two cubs would chase him down and begin the stealing scene again. This stealing continued back and forth until the last of the salmon had been consumed. Occasionally when a cub managed to abscond with a fair-size hunk of salmon, Red Collar would pursue the thief and reclaim her fish.

Aggressive cubs were sometimes punished for their persistent stealing attempts. Yearlings, who were stronger and more aggressive, were punished more often than spring cubs. Red Collar never punished her spring cubs, but she severely chastised them many times a year later. Reggie demonstrated that spring cubs are not immune to punishment by giving stern discipline to her two young on several occasions. These latter incidents always occurred when a cub tried repeatedly to steal from Reggie while she was very hungry for salmon. The family would be violently tearing away at a recent catch when Reggie would suddenly pounce on a cub and slap it across the back with a paw and bite it viciously at the back of the neck. The cub crouched to the ground with ears back, mouth open, and eyes wide with terror as he peered around at his attacker (plate 39). These disciplinary attacks were not as violent as they appeared and they were always over in two or three seconds. The cubs were completely undaunted by such maternal violence and continued their stealing attempts immediately.

There was an interesting development after Lanky punished one of her cubs. She was nursing the trio in the grass about 40 feet to the right of the cave when a young bear walked by with a salmon. Lanky recognized a stealing opportunity and quickly got up to pursue the juvenile, but one persistent cub continued to nurse as she walked away, so she whirled around and bit the cub's neck and shook him fiercely in her mouth. The cub let out a piercing shriek of alarm and then continued to squall for several seconds. I left the falls soon after this incident and thought nothing more about it until the next day, when Lanky returned without the cub she had punished. I never had convincing evidence that Lanky's action had contributed to the loss of her cub, but the coincidence of the two events was certainly suspicious. The cub was never seen again.

Punishment is a very rare maternal behavior. Sows spend infinitely more time protecting and assisting their cubs. Big Mamma once swam out to one of her spring cubs that was being washed into the rapids and assisted it onto her back and then swam ashore with the cub clinging to her neck. Goldie and Jeanne also gave these piggyback rides to their spring cubs (plate 40). Red's two tiny cubs often swam out to join her in deep, quiet pools where she frequently scavenged for dead salmon, and then they treaded water around her and clung to her back as she swam back to shore.

Sows as a rule are not playful with their cubs or any other bears. Between 1973 and 1977 there was not one observation of a sow playing with her cubs. Occasionally some sows might playfully cuff their cub or cubs for a moment, but extended play was unheard of. However there is always an exception to the rule in brown bear behavior, and this time it was Blue who provided the exception. She appeared in 1978 at age ten with her first spring cub and later she was observed playing for long periods with the cub on the alpine bluffs around the flats. At times she rolled over on her back and played with her cub as it frolicked around on her stomach.

12

The Cub Swappers

My most interesting observations of maternal behavior involved the swapping and adoption of cubs between sows. This extraordinary phenomenon has been reported in the past but the majority of these reports has been brief and sketchy. The phenomenon had never been accurately documented in detail until 1974 at McNeil Falls, when all the causal factors combined to make cub swapping an everyday occurrence.

I had never witnessed even a clue that McNeil sows would swap their cubs until one beautiful evening in late July. Jim and I were alone at the falls as the last streaks of a rich gold sunset were sparkling on the rapids, while the shadows of late evening crept along the banks of the river and slowly covered twelve fishing bears. Red Collar and Goldie fished side by side in the gathering darkness at the number-one spot, while their seven spring cubs (five and two, respectively) rested behind them (plate 41). I was busy recording data on other bears when suddenly Jim yelled at me and pointed across the river. On the opposite bank Goldie was waddling up the steep bank with a salmon in her mouth and an entourage of seven cubs behind her!

Although Goldie was completely unaware of what was behind her, some of the cubs knew that something was wrong. The last two cubs in the line, who belonged to Red Collar, stopped and looked back at their mother a couple of times before finally following the other cubs. When Goldie stopped on top of the bluff to eat her fish, she did not seem to notice anything unusual about suddenly having so many cubs. She tore at her salmon voraciously and ignored the congregation of cubs around her. Some of the cubs appeared to be uneasy or confused at first, but soon they all moved in to try for a piece of Goldie's salmon. Down on the falls Red Collar was so engrossed in her fishing that she failed to notice the absence of her cubs before Goldie returned to fish and brought all seven cubs back to the river.

I was dumbfounded. Goldie and the seven cubs had acted as though such swapping of cubs by sows was nothing unusual, and yet I had never witnessed a clue that this could happen. In retrospect, however, there were many unusual circumstances that contributed to this phenomenon. For instance, the summer of 1974 was an anomaly because of the large number of cubs present at the falls. The following sows arrived with spring cubs: Red Collar—five cubs, Lady Bird—three cubs, Goldie—two cubs, Lanky—three cubs, and Reagan—two cubs. Two other sows were present with yearlings but they had no part in the drama of cub swapping, and Reagan was only an occasional visitor to the area who was never involved in swapping. The other four sows and their thirteen cubs created most of the swapping situations during complex interactions with one another.

The behavior of both sows and cubs contributed to the confusion that led to the swapping of cubs. The location at which a sow fished was the most critical factor. Goldie, Red Collar, and Lady Bird habitually fished together on the number-one spot and these three sows were most often involved in swapping. Their cubs mingled together in the crowd, and because they had little ability to distinguish their mother from the other two sows, some of the cubs often left the falls with the wrong sow. Most of the swapping occurred in this way. Perhaps a more accurate term would be *sow swapping* instead of cub swapping.

The river was low in 1974 since the early arrival and continuation of warm, sunny weather had eliminated much of the snowpack in the mountains that normally feeds the river and keeps it high all summer. Many of the good fishing spots on the falls disappeared as the river level dropped, because the water was directed almost entirely through one main channel rather than cascading over the massive rocks in the river. This concentrated the available fishing spots and moved the bears closer together. Red Collar, Goldie, and Lady Bird were forced to fish close together. As a result, their cubs were routinely mixed up behind their fishing mothers. The number-one fishing spot was by far the best location and because each of these sows was sufficiently dominant to hold the spot for extended periods, it was common to see them fishing shoulder to shoulder on this prime spot.

A typical swapping situation developed in the following manner. Sometime around noon Red Collar arrived at the falls with her pack of five cubs, ambled up the riverbank on our side of the river, and passed under the cave en route to the fishing spots on the center rocks out in the falls. If these spots yielded fish, she continued to work the area until it became unproductive and then she moved to the far side of the river to the number-one spot. When the river level dropped later in the season, she opted for the number-one spot most of the time.

Red Collar was seldom alone at this prime position for long, for Goldie and Lady Bird also preferred it. Goldie usually arrived first and joined Red Collar sometime during the afternoon. She had to approach Red Collar with caution, just as she

Spring cubs from two different litters inspecting each other after first meeting along McNeil Falls.

would any other high-ranking bear. She moved in a wide circling path to give Red Collar advance warning of her approach, and then she crept slowly along with ears back and eyes cautiously glancing at Red Collar. The latter might occasionally bluff charge Goldie, but usually a few open-mouth threats were the only signals used as Goldie moved in to fish.

Goldie's cubs followed closely behind her as she approached Red Collar and then they huddled in fear behind their mother as she settled down to fish. They sometimes became frightened at the closeness of Red Collar and her cubs and ran back up the trail to watch from a distance, but soon they rejoined Goldie as she moved in to fish. The five cubs of Red Collar, who were huddled and half asleep behind their mother when Goldie first approached, held their positions during the encounter between the two sows. When aroused, they stood excitedly on hind legs and held on to one another as they stared at Goldie approaching, but eventually their interest became centered on the two tiny cubs that followed Goldie.

The two groups of cubs carefully inspected each other from a distance as though it were their first close contact with other spring cubs. Red Collar's five took the first initiative in approaching the other two, who were smaller and certainly outnumbered. The quintet crept along slowly, all bunched together, in a stealthy stalk with ears back as they sneaked along with outstretched noses searching for clues of the smaller cubs (plate 42). Goldie's tiny pair crouched behind their mother in fear as their inspectors approached. Once together there was a furious, though delicate, touching of noses in a sensitive tangle of sniffs and greetings. The seven infants mingled for a minute or so and then separated, having apparently completed a cursory inspection of each other. At this point they could obviously distinguish their own siblings from others, because they separated into litters and huddled behind their respective mothers.

As the cubs were very curious about each other, they rarely stayed separated for long and soon a reinvestigation was under way. After several of these meetings at the falls, the litters would huddle together behind the fishing sows without delay. Whenever their mothers fished for long periods, the cubs curled up and slept in one great pile behind their mothers. If other bears were meandering about, or if their mothers were frequently leaving the falls with fish, the cubs stayed alert and crowded close to their mothers. They often sat in a long line with each cub extending its forelegs around the middle of the cub in front in a piggyback fashion. When Lady Bird's three young joined them, all ten cubs sat piggyback parallel to the river behind three fishing sows. What a sight!

Lady Bird was not seen at the falls as often as Goldie and Red Collar, as she was wary of people and preferred to fish in the late evening when few people were present. Goldie and Red Collar were often fishing together when she arrived in the late afternoon. She seldom had to contend with any aggression from the other two sows, as they had already contested ownership of the spot and had become accustomed to sharing it with each other. A few open-mouth threats and some cautious glances with ears pinned back against the head were the only signals used by Lady Bird as she slipped into place on the river.

Lady Bird's three creamy blond cubs followed directly behind her and were immediately faced with the battalion of seven other cubs. They froze and stared as the group of seven began to approach inquisitively with one or two bold cubs edging ahead to lead the others toward the three frightened cubs. Sniffing inspections were soon under way as all ten cubs mingled like fish in an aquarium. Moments later they were all huddled close behind the three sows.

Because the area around them was buzzing with bear

activity, the ten cubs huddled together in fear rather than separating into distinct litters. The cubs never played with each other in this situation, because the intense action around them suppressed such carefree activities. They frequently ran away after being spooked by an outbreak of aggression between their mothers, or by the approach of another bear. It was this constant fear and readiness to leave the area that set the stage for the drama of cub swapping.

The events that immediately followed the catching of a salmon were the most crucial elements of cub swapping. For instance, if Goldie caught a salmon and turned to leave the river, the cubs were presented with a confusing problem. In the existing situation they were afraid, hungry, and obviously eager to leave the area, so the sight of Goldie retreating was a delightful invitation that would eliminate all of their problems. She had real nursing potential, a big tasty salmon in her teeth, and most important, she was departing for safer areas. The cubs would look back and forth between Goldie and the other two sows as though trying to figure out what was going on, then one or two cubs would hesitantly begin to follow Goldie up the trail. These leaders may or may not have been her own young, because any one of the ten cubs could begin the ensuing exodus. The departure of a few cubs had a contagious effect on those remaining and soon all the cubs followed the lone sow away from the falls. Depending on which sows were fishing, Goldie variously left with two, five, eight, or ten cubs. A few confused cubs occasionally remained with the other fishing sows.

Red Collar and Lady Bird, as well as other sows, failed to miss their cubs for varying lengths of time. If they were busy fishing, they usually did not notice the absence of cubs until a fish was caught and they withdrew from the river to eat the catch. This could vary from a few seconds to five or ten minutes or more. If three or four cubs had remained behind when Goldie left, the remaining sows usually failed to notice if any of their own young were absent. It apparently did not matter if the remaining cubs were theirs or not, because they allowed those present to move in and fight for a piece of salmon, and then they moved back to the river and continued to fish as if nothing were amiss. The number of cubs present normally did not matter. The sows seemed satisfied if three to ten cubs were on hand, even if some of their own were missing. Red Collar, who had five cubs, was more prone to overlook missing cubs than were Goldie or Lady Bird.

All of these sows eventually noticed that some or all of their young were missing. Their search for the missing cubs was immediate and frantic. If Red Collar became aware of missing cubs, she scanned the riverbank, then raced up one of the many steep trails that led to the top of the bluffs along the river and rummaged around the grassy slopes for the lost cubs at an ever-increasing pace. Her head bobbed in and out of view as she loped along and stood on hind legs for a better view, with her head jerking around wildly as she huffed with foaming saliva dripping from her mouth. This wild search continued to intensify for one or two minutes and then it began to fizzle out, even if the cubs were not found. She would soon return to the river and begin to fish once again.

All three sows quickly gave up their searches for lost cubs as Red Collar had done and their cub quests became shorter as cub swapping became more common. There was a rapid transition back to normality following a brief search, for the sows seemed to forget all about their cubs as they resumed fishing, undisturbed until their young returned with the temporary mother.

These searches were rarely futile, however, because the sow with all the newly acquired cubs was almost always in the immediate area. A few seconds of frantic searching brought the two mothers into very complex encounters with each other. Red Collar often found Goldie nursing the cubs, including Red Collar's, or eating salmon on the bluffs beside the river. The two sows immediately approached each other with heads down, ears back, and mouths opening and closing in threats, as they reached a standoff at a distance of 5 feet or so (see a similar encounter in plate 43). Goldie would not allow Red Collar any closer to the cubs, who crowded under and behind her in fear. Red Collar obviously knew that some of the

Red Collar approaching Goldie, who is nursing several cubs (both her own and Red Collar's) on a bluff overlooking McNeil Falls.

cubs were hers but she was unable to approach and segregate them from Goldie's. I always believed that Goldie could distinguish her own cubs from the others in the group, but her defense could not be selective. She had to protect them all because they were in one big group.

These encounters were even more complex if Red Collar had two or three of her own cubs, for in such an encounter neither sow would allow the other to approach her accompanying young. The cubs were absolutely bewildered. Occasionally, when the two sows were very close together, a few of Red Collar's swapped cubs would venture ahead of Goldie to investigate their mother and siblings. They were very curious about them, but hesitant about leaving the very real security of Goldie. There were a few rare instances in which a cub or two of Red Collar's would not only approach her, but would then follow her as she left the scene of the encounter. These were the only instances that ever indicated the cubs were capable of distinguishing their real mother, but as these incidents were so rare, they could easily be attributed to chance alone. A sow was very lucky to regain her own cubs during an encounter. I noticed two encounters in which Goldie tried to hold back some of the cubs that were underneath her with her nose and forepaws, while leaving other cubs around her free to come or go. Although it was possible that the cubs she restrained just happened by chance to be her own, I believe that Goldie, and perhaps all sows, could detect their own young in groups of cubs (see a similar encounter in plate 44). Indeed, considering their keen sense of smell it would be surprising if they could not.

Cub swapping became more common as the fishing season progressed. The sows fished more often and caught more salmon and this increased the potential for swapping cubs. There was a continual cycle of sows leaving the falls with fish and returning for more, and each time a sow left, some or all of the cubs left with her. The sows and cubs became accustomed to this constant exchange and soon the sows rarely interrupted their fishing to search for missing cubs.

The first swapping occurred on July 21, when Goldie first left with two of Red Collar's cubs, and the last occurred on August 6. During this time the incidence of swapping increased and then ended abruptly on August 6, when the fishing season began to fizzle out and the three sows never visited the falls together again.

The list below illustrates the swapping of cubs that occurred between Red Collar and Goldie during a three-hour period on August 3, at the number-one fishing spot. (Note: Red Collar has only four cubs in this list. She lost one cub to Lady Bird earlier in the season and Lady Bird subsequently lost one of her four cubs to unknown causes. Whether or not the lost cub was Red Collar's is not known).

2:30 P.M.   Goldie arrives to fish with four cubs; two of her own and two of Red Collar's that she had left with the night before.

3:10 P.M.   Red Collar arrives to fish with two cubs.

3:10 P.M.   Red Collar and Goldie fish with all six cubs.

3:34 P.M.   Red Collar leaves with three cubs, returns to fish.

3:55 P.M.   Goldie leaves with all six cubs, nurses, and returns to fish.

4:15 P.M.   Red Collar leaves with four cubs, returns to
            fish.
4:28 P.M.   Goldie leaves with five cubs, returns to fish.
4:50 P.M.   Goldie leaves with three cubs, returns to fish.
5:20 P.M.   Goldie leaves with four cubs, nurses, returns
            to fish.
5:31 P.M.   Goldie leaves with all six cubs, returns to fish.
6:05 P.M.   Red Collar leaves with four cubs, returns to fish.
6:25 P.M.   Goldie leaves the falls for the night with three
            cubs.

This list shows that Goldie was the most frequently involved in cub exchanges. This was because she usually left the
river to eat her fish and the cubs followed her. The cubs were
never discouraged from following Goldie as she left the falls.
On the contrary, these mistaken departures were reinforced
by the salmon and nursing that the cubs received in the process. Goldie frequently lay down in the grass and allowed the
cubs to swarm over her stomach and chest as they jockeyed for
a nursing position. The eager nursing of as many as nine cubs
left each black teat outlined with rich, white milk.

Soon after the cubs had finished nursing, Goldie would
return to her fishing and set the stage for another round of
swapping. This temporary afternoon swapping came a step
closer to actual adoption when a sow ended a day's fishing and
departed with cub(s) that were not her own.

When Goldie, for instance, left for the night with varying
numbers of Red Collar's cubs, she treated these adopted waifs
as if they were her own, protecting and nursing them all without a hint of prejudice. The cubs adjusted instantly to their
surrogate mother. They never displayed signs of being disturbed or uneasy with their new family. Goldie would keep
these adopted cubs until she again fished with Red Collar,
which gave Red Collar a chance to regain her cubs in the same
way that she had lost them. There was a three-day period in
late July in which the two sows never crossed paths at the falls.
During this time Goldie had uninterrupted possession of two
of Red Collar's cubs. However, because the two sows usually

fished together every afternoon or evening, most of the adoptions were rarely long-lived. They routinely exchanged cubs every twenty-four hours.

This sort of free exchange of young between females must be considered unusual and it brings up the question of why it occurs. Sociobiology again provides the best insight into this curious phenomenon and the key again is the matter of social versus asocial behavior. First, consider the social or gregarious animals (herding ungulates, colony nesting birds, social primates). If females of these gregarious species did not have the ability to distinguish and care for only their own young, there would be utter chaos and the chances that a female could ensure the survival of her own young would be reduced. There has obviously been strong selection pressure for this ability of discrimination in gregarious animals.

Now consider asocial animals or animals that typically raise their young in isolation. An example is most passerine birds whose nests are isolated and the young are raised in the absence of other young. These birds have no ability to distinguish their own young from others. Switch the chicks in two robins' nests and the parents raise the wrong young unawares. They will even raise an entirely different species without knowing the difference. This is logical, for there have never been any selection pressures to make it necessary for robins to distinguish their own young. They normally do not have to deal with such problems, and the ability has not evolved. In contrast, some birds that experience heavy nest parasitism from cowbirds (for example, cowbirds lay their eggs in other birds' nests and let foster parents raise their young for them) have evolved the ability to distinguish cowbird eggs and young from their own and will push them out of the nest. This is a good example of behavioral evolution.

Bears and passerine birds may not be quite comparable, but the behavioral analogy is good. In both examples the young are raised in isolation from other young and the adults cannot or will not discriminate against other young. Passerines distinguish their fledglings once they leave the nest, and sows and yearling cubs also develop abilities to distinguish their own family members after their first year.

Brown bear sows normally do not have to deal with the problems of identifying their cubs. Sows are wary of other bears and it is almost a certainty that they keep their cubs in isolation during most of the year. Only when several sows with spring cubs assemble in one area does the swapping problem develop. McNeil Falls is something of an enigma in this respect. It is obvious that brown bear sows have rarely had cub swapping problems during recent evolutionary history, and there has not been significant selection pressure for an ability to distinguish and segregate their cubs.

For example, if a sow adopted the unrelated offspring of another female, then she would have more mouths to feed and this would reduce the chances that her own young would survive to reproduce. Therefore, the reproductive success of the adopting sows would be minimized by their lack of discrimination and this could decrease adoption in the next generation.

The above process would require that cub swapping be a common phenomenon in bear populations before abilities to negate the problem would evolve. Even though McNeil is an ideal setting for the swapping of cubs between sows, it is still rare. Between 1970 and 1985 cub swapping occurred only in 1974, and there is only one sketchy report of swapping from the fifteen years of various studies and casual observations prior to 1970 (Erickson and Miller, 1963). Larry Aumiller reported no evidence of cub swapping in 1985, despite the presence of a record twenty-eight cubs at the falls. This is strong evidence that cub swapping is very rare, so selection against the behavior would be insignificant. In addition, there is little reason to believe that sows who swap cubs experience any significant reproductive failure because of their actions. This is because sows who swap cubs probably rear the wrong cubs with similar success; only by gaining or losing in the ultimate struggle for genetic representation in succeeding generations can a behavior be selected for or against. This evidence suggests that cub swapping will always be a behavioral quirk that can occur rarely among brown bear sows when conditions are right.

Lanky was the only sow who managed to avoid the confusion of cub swapping in 1974. She temporarily lost her cubs to Lady Bird early in the season and then avoided potential swapping situations for the rest of the summer. This one experience with swapping occurred after she crossed the river to fish the far side of the falls, where Lady Bird, Goldie, and Red Collar were fishing as she approached to inspect the area. Lanky failed to notice that her three cubs were approached and surrounded by the nine curious cubs of the other sows. A few moments later, just as the twelve cubs began to relax following their meeting, Lady Bird caught a fish and left the falls. Three cubs began to follow her immediately and then the others fell into line as all twelve left in one great caravan.

Lanky quickly noticed the absence of her cubs and ran up the nearest trail in search of them. She thrashed about in the high grass and stood erect on hind legs so often that she seemed to be hopping rather than running. Her frantic search was in vain as Lady Bird had retreated over 100 yards upstream with the cubs, and so Lanky returned to the river and ran up and down the banks smelling for the trail of her cubs. I thought Lady Bird had left for the day, but she soon came ambling back down to the river with her entourage of cubs. Lanky saw their approach and practically attacked Lady Bird, which spooked the cubs and caused them all to run back up the trail in wild confusion. Lanky pursued the cubs with an enraged Lady Bird right behind her. Lady Bird jumped Lanky from behind as they reached the top of the bluff and rolled her over as she sank her teeth into Lanky's haunches. This sudden battle scattered the horrified cubs in all directions. Lanky was worked into a frenzy by the time she scrambled from under Lady Bird's attack and pursued her cubs downriver, while Lady Bird ran huffing in the opposite direction. Lanky found her cubs, who had fled the scene together, and gathered them up for a quick escape. She never slowed down until they had crossed the river and were isolated from the madness of the number-one fishing spot. She never took them back across the river that summer.

While Lanky seemed actually to avoid cub-swapping situations, the other sows made no moves to simplify their time at the falls. But despite their incessant problems, the other three sows somehow ended the summer with most of their own young, which was a good indication that they were capable of distinguishing their own young from other cubs. The last time we saw Lady Bird that summer she had three cubs. When Goldie and Red Collar met for the last time at the falls, they almost separated their six cubs into distinct litters. During this final encounter, Red Collar reclaimed one of her two cubs who was with Goldie, and although the fourth cub approached Red Collar and came very close to following her away, he turned at the last moment and rejoined Goldie. The two sows then separated and never met at the falls again. Goldie still had one of Red Collar's cubs when we last saw her that summer.

I hoped that Goldie would return in 1975 with three yearlings, thereby providing absolute proof of a permanent adoption, but unfortunately she had only one yearling with her the next summer. I was fairly certain that Goldie had actually adopted Red Collar's fourth cub, but McNeil's high cub mortality rate denied me the proof. Lanky lost another cub and returned with one yearling. Lady Bird and Red Collar had the only significant success in rearing cubs, as each had three surviving yearlings in 1975. They both kept these litters of three for a third summer at the falls instead of weaning them at the usual time during their third spring.

The behavior of these mothers and their cubs changed considerably from one year to the next, which provided observations that helped solve some of the mysteries of cub swapping.

Goldie, Lady Bird, and Red Collar had none of the swapping problems with their yearlings that had plagued them the year before with their spring cubs. The cubs had initiated most of the swapping because of their tendency to follow any sow away from the falls. The sows were not blameless because they were perfectly willing to accept and care for any and all cubs, and then the sows' own intolerance of one another would not allow an orderly division of the cubs. A year later these same sows and cubs had developed abilities to recognize their own family members and they would not join other groups.

The four sows had eight yearlings in 1975 as opposed to thirteen spring cubs in 1974, which made these families more manageable from the outset. In addition, the river was high throughout the 1975 season, which made more fishing spots available and allowed the sows to fish separately. The yearlings rarely congregated as they had done the year before, and the confusing swapping situations seldom developed.

Whenever an encounter occurred between two of these sows or when they otherwise came into close contact, the behavior of both the sows and yearlings indicated that they could now distinguish their own family members from all other bears. The sows aggressively chased away any strange yearlings or spring cubs that approached them, just as they would any older bear. A year earlier they accepted and cared for any wandering spring cub. It was obvious that the sows could easily differentiate their yearlings from all others.

The yearlings had also developed their perception of bear identities. They were still very curious about other cubs, but they never joined groups or played with other young. During the past year and a half, they had learned to be aggressive and dominant as a result of their mothers' protection of them in encounters with other bears. Because they had learned that other bears, including cubs, represented a threat to their food supply, they were more inclined to chase away other cubs and even young juvenile bears. They had become more asocial.

The yearlings were capable of following their mothers to any fishing spot on the falls, so they were separated for only brief periods during the summer. After a separation, both the sows and yearlings rejoined with confident familiarity. Lanky's single yearling would occasionally run from her in fear after a long separation. This wariness is probably advantageous to the survival of single cubs, because if a cub made one mistake in approaching a mature bear other than its mother, that mistake could well be fatal. Groups of yearlings had more confidence in identifying their mother.

There were other interesting incidents in later years that did not involve actual cub swapping, but provided some insight into the phenomenon. In 1980, Jeanne had the insecure cub named Wingnut, and White had two yearlings. The two sows never experienced any swapping problems with these cubs, but Wingnut once demonstrated the confusion that spring cubs can have about their mothers and other sows.

Jeanne had left Wingnut stranded on the first rock in the falls while she fished from the center rock. White and her yearlings were fishing on the first rock not far from Wingnut. When another bear approached the first rock, Jeanne ran to protect her cub, and White also turned to meet any aggression. Thus Wingnut was suddenly trapped by three approaching bears. He did not recognize Jeanne and so he ran to White instead. When he reached the trio he hesitated and touched noses with her yearlings before huddling with them beneath White's guard. Jeanne approached so quickly that White and her yearlings turned their attention to her rather than her cub. During a brief standoff between the sows, Wingnut seemed more afraid of his mother and remained huddled beside the yearlings (plate 45). White would not allow Jeanne to approach, so the latter pressed ahead with an aggressive encounter, which scattered the cubs and allowed Jeanne to depart with her cub.

This bizarre incident again made clear that it is usually spring cubs that create situations leading to cub swapping. There are some reports in bear literature of sows attempting to steal cubs from other sows, but this had never been observed at McNeil. Then, in 1984, a young sow named Melody arrived with one spring cub. She was five or six years old and this was definitely her first cub. I noticed nothing unusual about Melody's behavior until she arrived at the falls and encountered White, who had three spring cubs. Melody displayed an immediate and intense interest in White's three cubs. She almost ran to the trio as if they were her own cubs that she had temporarily lost. White was fishing close by and ran to intervene, much to Melody's surprise. White challenged the young sow with a typical aggressive display, but Melody could not be bothered by aggression—she was too interested in the swarm of alarmed cubs. White continued her challenge with open-mouth threats, roaring, her ears depressed, and her haunches crouched to the ground. Melody appeared bewildered by the scene and grudgingly gave up her pursuit of the cubs. During the following days, Melody continued to display interest in White's cubs.

I could only surmise that perhaps Melody had recently lost one or more cubs to unknown causes, and when she happened onto White's trio, she assumed that they were her own misplaced young. This is only speculation, but it is the only logical explanation. Melody's youth and inexperience no doubt contributed to her confusion. Nonetheless, this demonstrated that sows can be a factor in cub adoption.

This was further emphasized during the summer of 1986, after another incident of infanticide at the falls. McBride, a mature sow with three spring cubs, had a long, violent encounter with Fossey, a young sow with two spring cubs. During this long encounter, McBride suddenly reached down and with two quick chomps instantly killed Fossey's two cubs. The young Fossey then displayed intense interest in McBride's cubs for several days, as if she were trying to claim the cubs as her own.

The summer of 1975 was a more normal one for sows and spring cubs. Red and Reggie each had two spring cubs, which was a more typical number of spring cubs for one summer. Red and Reggie fished on opposite sides of the river almost all summer and therefore had few opportunities to swap cubs. Even when the two sows fished on the same side they had very little contact, because Reggie was very intolerant of all bears. Their cubs never came into close contact and were never swapped.

There was one interesting incident between Red and Reggie that involved a number of implications. Red made a rare trip to the far side of the falls one afternoon and was fishing on the upper falls when Reggie arrived to fish on the lower falls. Red soon became jaded with unsuccessful fishing and started back across the river to her favorite spots. She chose to cross in the swiftest portion of the river and never looked back for her cubs as she trudged through the raging white water at depths in excess of three feet. She had either forgotten all about her cubs or was unaware that they had absolutely no chance of negotiating the treacherous waters. Both cubs edged cautiously into the river and struggled to keep their footing on the slick rocky bottom. The dark cub made a foolish lunge into the white water and tried in vain to reach Red, but the current grabbed and thrust him helplessly downstream. He drifted in and out of view on the surging waves of the rapids and pawed furiously at the overwhelming waters and squalled in terror for his mother. The current shot the cub very close to the riverbank and carried him under Reggie's nose at her fishing spot. Reggie was unaware of other cubs nearby, so she instantly assumed that the cub in the river was her own. Then without turning to inspect or account for her cubs, she raced in a huffing panic downstream and threw herself into the river and swam toward Red's cub, who had just reached the quiet waters below the falls and was churning toward Reggie's side of the river. Meanwhile, Red had traversed the rapids and turned to look for her cubs about the time that Reggie sighted the dark cub and started after it. Red saw what was happening and immediately started downstream to retrieve her cub. Both sows swam toward the cub from opposite sides, but Reggie reached the terrified cub first. The cub apparently realized that Reggie was not his mother because he met her concerned approach with a squalling protest, which caused Reggie to jump back with her mouth wide open and her ears back as though totally surprised by the cub's reaction. Red reached the cub and calmly turned to swim back across the river, but the cub continued to tread water in confusion for a moment before turning to follow Red. Reggie was still bewildered and swam after the cub and huffed alarms at him. She overtook the cub twice more, only to have him scream in her face. Each time she reponded by jumping back with her mouth open and her ears depressed, which were displays that indicated she was under a great deal of stress. After her third attempt to retrieve the cub, Reggie turned and swam back to shore and ran huffing into the brush in search of her own cubs. Red and her cub reached the opposite side and calmly waited on shore for her second cub, who was also crossing the river behind them. The trio then proceeded toward the falls as though nothing had happened. Reggie found her cubs after a brief search and fled the area huffing wildly. They were two very different sows.

This encounter suggested that Red's cub could distinguish between a strange sow and its mother It also demonstrated that Reggie could have a difficult time in determining the identity of a strange cub. Of course, the encounter had occurred in the middle of the river and Reggie had begun with the assumption that the cub was her own. In addition, Red's cub was trying to reach its mother on one side of the river and upstream, so it might be expected to fear a bear approaching from the wrong direction.

Red's dark cub made another correct decision about bear identities the next week. He tried to swim out to Red on the center rock and was again swept down the length of the rapids and bobbed like a cork through the roughest water before reaching the base of the rapids unharmed. The current had directed him closer to the opposite shore so he swam to the wrong side, shook himself dry, and started to walk upstream. When he saw Jeanne fishing on the lower falls, he apparently realized his mistake, because he retreated and began to swim back across the river. He was halfway across when Red reached the lower falls and calmly waited for him on the opposite bank. She gave him a brief inspection and then returned to her fishing. The light cub had been very upset during the absence of its sibling and it stood squalling on hind legs and scanned constantly about until the dark cub returned.

The life history of Red provided me with an extraordinary amount of information on brown bear natural history in general, and maternal behavior in particular. Had she survived another fifteen years her life history at McNeil would have indeed been remarkable. Thus, her death from a native's bullet was especially tragic. So much information went down with that bullet; so much was lost. This reiterated once again the need for an enlargement of the McNeil Sanctuary or its inclusion in Katmai National Park, so that the entire range of the bears would be under protection from hunting. The McNeil bears are research subjects, not trophies.

13

The Play Factor

A description of play among the McNeil bears may seem to be a contradiction following all the previous discussions of asocial behavior, aggression, and infanticide, but it is not. The young of many mammals engage in play and bears are no exception. Actually, the absence of play would be more surprising, because it is generally agreed that play has biological significance for animals. That is, the essential motor skills needed for survival (coordination for catching prey, evading predators, sexual mounts, and so on) are developed during play bouts among young animals. The young train themselves in the skills they need to survive. Thus, play has survival value and this selects for the evolution of play behavior.

During my study, play was very common at McNeil. The bears played on the tidal flats, in and around camp, on the

185

surrounding bluffs, in the river, and at the falls they played on the rocks, in the rushing water, in the deep pools, and all around the falls (plate 46). High-ranking mature boars never played and sows usually did not play after they first had cubs. Play was most common among cubs, and, in general, all play behavior decreased with age.

Red and Blue played together and with others until age six, when Red first conceived, and then Red never played again. Blue was playful until she had one cub at age ten, after which she continued her playful ways by engaging in extended and vigorous play bouts with her spring cub. With the exception of Blue, no mature sow had ever been observed in extended play with her cubs or another bear. Occasionally I had seen sows playfully cuff or mouth a cub, but no involved play ever occurred.

However, in 1984 I learned once again that one cannot make generalized "rules" of bear behavior. "Sows do not play with other bears after they have cubs." Wrong again. A young sow name Doogie and her yearling broke all the rules in 1984.

Doogie was a beautiful young sow and her single yearling was large and vigorous. This pair played frequently and both of them seemed equally interested in initiating play bouts. But Doogie carried this one step further by initiating play with another young bear at the falls. This young bear, who was about four or five years old, was very apprehensive of Doogie's intentions as she approached. He was obviously not accustomed to playful sows with cubs. Indeed, such behavior was unprecedented in fourteen years of observations at the falls. However, Doogie was persistent and soon she engaged the young bear in cautious play. Her yearling crouched beside her in fear and responded aggressively to the third bear. The cub appeared to be puzzled by his mother's outgoing playfulness (plate 47).

Doogie was the only bear in this trio who knew what she wanted—play. There was considerable conflict in the actions of the other two. The young bear was never at ease with this playful sow and he constantly retreated to fish in the river.

Doogie's cub eventually managed some playful overtures, but he alternated these with aggressive swats at the young bear. There was too much tension in this arrangement and soon the lone bear left, in order to avoid Doogie.

Males tend to play more than females and they continue to play to an older age than females. For instance, I last observed Romeo playing at the age of ten and Zubin was still playful at an estimated minimum age of fifteen. Zubin was a special case because no other boars were playful at his mature age, and most other aspects of his behavior were also atypical of a mature boar. Putting it simply, he was a bit of a clown.

Zubin often had difficulty in finding a playmate because his massive 800-pound body usually frightened away smaller bears when he approached to play. Patch Butt was often his play partner, but sometimes Zubin even had trouble enticing the playful and dauntless Patch Butt into play. For example: One clear, beautiful morning in early August I arrived at the falls after dawn and found Patch Butt fishing alone on the center rock. He sat on his haunches and propped himself up with his left foreleg and rested the elbow of his right foreleg comfortably on the knee of his right hind leg. From this unusual and relaxed position, he casually scanned the rushing water for the sudden movement of running salmon.

Patch Butt fished alone for over an hour before Zubin arrived and headed for the center rock. Zubin ambled down the riverbank with his labored, ponderous walk as though each step was carefully planned and executed with considerable effort. He seemed to exist in a state of perpetual slow motion. Patch Butt watched him approach and then left his fishing spot when Zubin was 40 feet away and moved to the opposite end of the center rock to give Zubin a wide berth. Patch Butt returned to his fishing as soon as Zubin settled into a spot and then both bears fished for over an hour, ignoring each other.

When Zubin failed to catch a salmon, he left his spot and casually approached Patch Butt, who immediately began to retreat. I was certain that Zubin only wanted to play, but Patch Butt was not so sure and avoided Zubin rather than taking any chances with the big fellow. Unlike some social animals that have "play initiation behaviors," Zubin had no clear way of signaling or indicating his playful intentions to Patch Butt. He flicked his ears up and down and moved his head actively, while avoiding a direct stare at Patch Butt. Had he been in an aggressive mood, Zubin's head would have been lowered, his ears depressed, and his eyes locked on Patch Butt in a stare. However, Patch Butt was not certain of Zubin's intentions, so the latter could only follow slowly after Patch Butt and avoid any quick or sudden movements that might appear aggressive.

Patch Butt stayed about 30 feet in front of his pursuer as they left the falls and headed up the bluff behind our cave. I knew it was only a matter of time before they would begin to play, so I waited until they disappeared over the ridge and then followed them. These two playful bears routinely frolicked within 30 feet of us at the falls, but in open country I knew they would not play with me nearby, so I approached carefully and knelt down to watch them about 150 feet away.

They appeared to be ready to play on a large open area covered with colorful tundra lichens, surrounded by glistening green dwarf willow and swaying stands of blazing fireweed. Patch Butt stopped every few feet and glanced back at Zubin with his ears back and his head slightly down, and each time he did this Zubin came closer and closer. Finally Zubin was nipping softly at his haunches and Patch Butt turned and bit softly at Zubin's neck and face. They raised their heads and bit at each other's mouths at right angles and occasionally straight on with their jaws fully extended so that only the tips of their noses and lower jaws touched.

Play bouts always begin with soft biting and mouthing around the head before more vigorous play would occur. Bears who were not familiar play partners may continue with this precursory play biting and never pass this stage in their play. But Zubin and Patch Butt had played for many summers, so it was only a few seconds before Patch Butt threw his right forepaw over Zubin's neck and then rose on hind legs and gripped Zubin's neck and shoulders with both forelegs while biting at his ears and neck and then down his back, where Patch Butt

Patch Butt and Zubin on hind legs, playing in open country near McNeil Falls.

grabbed big wads of hide and twisted back and forth. Zubin whirled around with his mouth open and Patch Butt jumped down and away and then they resumed their play bites for a few seconds before Patch Butt reared up on his hind legs and lunged straight ahead to lock his forelegs around Zubin's neck. Just as he did this, Zubin also stood on hind legs and met Patch Butt's lunge by wrapping his forelegs around him to produce a dramatic, playful struggle as they stood upright. What a sight! Two large male brownies standing and wrestling with their arms locked around each other in deep morning light amidst a field of willows and fireweed, with the blue McNeil and snow-capped Aleutian Range in the background (plate 48).

Once Patch Butt and Zubin reached this vigorous stage of play they might continue for thirty minutes or longer if they were not disturbed. Play at the falls was usually brief and rarely lasted longer than a few minutes because the activities of other bears produced constant interruptions. Fortunately Patch Butt and Zubin had no interruptions in their secluded location and they continued to play for twenty minutes.

Perhaps the best way to describe their play in general would be to say it most resembles the play of dogs. Bears do not move quite as quickly and they do not chase each other like dogs, but otherwise the basic features of canid play and bear play are remarkably similar.

Patch Butt and Zubin used their mouths and forepaws in most of their play. While standing on hind legs, they used their forepaws mostly for pushing, shoving, and holding each other.

Their mouths were always open and biting at the other's neck, ears, face, and shoulders. They could not remain standing for more than a few seconds before losing balance and falling to all fours, but they would immediately rise to resume their play. Patch Butt seized a hunk of skin on Zubin's neck and twisted him around until they both fell to the ground with their forelegs still locked around each other. Patch Butt landed on top of Zubin, who was flat on his back, pushing, shoving, and biting at Patch Butt. This went on for thirty seconds before Zubin forced his way from under Patch Butt and rose to continue playing. They repeated all the play activities described previously many times, but their play while standing on hind legs was most common. This appeared to be their most intense and uninhibited play activity, and it is possible that their isolation on open, flat terrain provided the freedom for such uninhibited play.

Not all bears were as playful as Patch Butt and Zubin and some never played at all. The difference in playfulness is best illustrated by the familiar history of Red, White, and Blue. White was never observed to actively play after leaving her sisters at age three. Red and Blue, however, remained playful until they had cubs at age seven and ten years, respectively. Similar differences were apparent in the siblings Miss Kitty and M.J. These observations illustrate that there are simply great differences in the disposition of individual bears. Some bears are playful and others are not.

It is possible that the social situation at the falls promotes play through a familiarization and learning process. All spring cubs and yearling cubs play with siblings, and often two- and three-year-old bears continue to play with siblings as well as with other young bears. The close association of young bears with their peers year after year at McNeil may enable them to recognize each other and quickly become habituated to the social environment at the falls. It only seems logical that playful McNeil bears would continue to play with one another year after year.

Unfortunately, play among the McNeil bears is not so eas-

ily explained. During the summers of 1970 through 1972 play
was virtually nonexistent at the falls. The siblings Red and Blue
played occasionally, but no other bears were observed playing
during this period (Allan Egbert, personal communication,
July 1973). Then during the summer of 1973 many bears
played intensely during the fishing season at the falls. Since the
salmon run in 1973 was unusually large, we initially suspected
that the increased incidence of play was a product of the
salmon run. That is, the bears had tremendous fishing success,
which satiated their hunger, reduced the incidence of aggression, and thus created a setting conducive to play. However
there are some annual variations that are contrary to this explanation. For instance, the salmon run in 1971 was enormous,
yet the bears did not play that summer. Then, to confuse the
matter further, McNeil bears continued to play every summer
from 1973 to the present. During this period there were several small salmon runs at the falls and yet the bears played just
as they did during the summers with large runs. These observations make it impossible to explain annual variations of play
in terms of fishing success, and the absence of play at McNeil
during the early 1970s remains unexplained.

I was not present at McNeil in the early 1970s, but I suspect that the absence of play among the bears was probably
due to the constantly changing social environment at the falls.
Perhaps the recruitment of cubs was low and there were few
young bears present to engage in play. Also, because bear
"personalities" vary greatly and change from year to year, it
is possible that there were simply no playful bears present
during this time.

14

Indian Summer

Fall weather usually begins in mid-August at McNeil. Low-pressure systems generate over the Aleutian Islands and travel up the Alaska Peninsula to pound McNeil with wind and rain. But my last full summer at McNeil was blessed with beautiful, sunny weather that extended into August with a solid month of Indian summer. Long, hazy days continued after most of our bears had left for parts unknown.

This was an ideal end to three summers of research at McNeil. Jim and I picked blueberries, salmonberries, nagoonberries, and huckleberries and got fat making pies and berry pancakes. Low tides provided buckets of clams for thick chowders, and the silver salmon run on the McNeil had a strong beginning. Up went our improvised salmon smoker that was quickly filled with narrow strips of coho salmon.

Between all this food gathering, we squeezed in long hikes on the surrounding alpine tundra and beaches. One of these hikes turned into more than a hike when Jim talked me into climbing the 4,000-foot peak just north of the falls. Jim had this climb in mind all along, but he knew I would never agree to the attempt, so he started us off in the right direction under the guise of a day hike up the McNeil. Once we reached a point directly across from the mountain, Jim revealed his plan. I assumed the peak was unreachable because the first thousand feet of the slopes were completely blanketed in dense alder brush. Jim argued that we could follow one of the larger streams up the slope and avoid most, if not all, of the brush. The idea of reaching the highest peak in the area with its spectacular view was tempting, so I agreed and we crossed the McNeil at a shallow point and began the climb.

Jim's plan turned out to be feasible and we reached the alpine tundra with only a few bouts of thrashing through the unrelenting alders. The climb above the brush was nothing more than a very steep hike, but we did not reach the summit until 6:00 P.M. The view was worth every step. Lake Iliamna stretched across the north horizon, flanked by all the peaks of the Aleutian Range. The snow-covered peaks and glaciers of Cape Douglas appeared surprisingly close to the west, and further on Kodiak Island broke the horizon.

I wanted to linger with this overwhelming view, but we had to reach camp by dark (now 11:00 P.M.). Fortunately, the downhill side of any climb goes fast and we reached the river in only forty-five minutes. It was not so easy to find our way on bear trails in near darkness. Occasionally these trails became nothing more than round tunnels cutting through dense stands of alder brush. How disconcerting to be crawling on hands and knees along bear trail tunnels in the brush at dark. It was night when at last we reached the familiar trail near the falls that led to camp and a midnight dinner that was literally inhaled. I had never been so hungry or so tired in my life.

Such were our adventures at the end of a wonderful, productive summer. We had accomplished all our research goals and then some. The icing on the cake involved rare observations like Goldie parting with her cubs, and then watching her cubs, Clara and Rama, adapting to life without Goldie. There was the long, detailed history of the three sisters Red, White, and Blue from the time they were newly weaned siblings until they were mature sows with cubs. Perhaps most important were the unexpected observations of maternal behavior, the vast diversity of sow behavior, conclusions on infanticide and aggression, and the amazing incidents of cub swapping and the resulting implications. I was fascinated when Siedelman developed a unique fishing technique, which Groucho quickly picked up through learning. And best of all, I had gathered ample data for a quantitative analysis of brown bear communication. It would be hard to imagine more eventful summers.

It was a shame that organized research at McNeil ended in 1975. I had realized some of the benefits of long-term research, but the life-history information from a fifteen- or twenty-year study (an entire generation) would have been outstanding. Unfortunately, such a study did not fit into the Alaska Department of Fish and Game's management plan for McNeil River. By 1970 the department had decided that population studies at McNeil were not feasible and the management of the sanctuary was geared exclusively for tourism, and especially photography. They had little or no interest in our behavioral study, as the latter was not directly related to their management of brown bear populations.

Brown bear management in the state of Alaska means determining the maximum number of bears that can be killed in annual or biannual hunts and still maintain a healthy population. This is a rather crude way to put it, but the state's management of bears boils down to precisely this goal. Why is this the goal? Who decides this? Who benefits from this management? What effect does it have on the brown bear? What does it deprive other people of? By other people, I mean the 99.999 percent of the U.S. population that is never involved in brown bear hunting.

The state of Alaska makes money on the sale of brown bear hunting licenses. Today, this income is an insignificant pittance compared to Alaska's oil revenues and taxes. I doubt if the income from brown bear licenses would pay for the

janitorial services of even one small state office building in
Juneau, much less the salaries of the game biologists who man-
age the bears. Airlines and hotels make a little on hunters, but
it is the hunting guides who really benefit from bear hunting.
Thus the financial benefits of brown bear hunting are reaped
by a handful of hunting guides for the pleasure and sport of a
tiny group of big game hunters.

Just how brown bear hunting got started is no mystery. There
have always been some people who enjoy killing big, beautiful
animals. There was money to be made doing it, people wanted
to do it, few people seemed to care otherwise, and the technol-
ogy to deliver blobs of molten lead at great speed was present,
so it was done.

Many prey species of game animals require hunting as
part of modern game management. Natural predators have
been eliminated, so without annual hunting, animals may
overpopulate, overgraze their range, and starve. Do brown
bears fit this category? No. Omnivorous brown bears do not
need to be managed to regulate their populations. Granted,
heavily hunted bear populations may be more productive in
that sows may breed younger, more frequently, and have
lower cub mortality, but productivity is not necessarily desirable except for the business of hunting bears.

The losers in this bear management play—beyond the
bears—are those people who would enjoy seeing brown bears
roaming freely about their natural environment. Only in protected areas like McNeil and Katmai National Monument are
there fearless bears that behave as they did before man became their predator. Surely anyone with a yen to shoot a bear
would lose his desire if he could sit at McNeil Falls and watch
the brownies fish and interact without fear of man. But move
beyond the boundaries of protected areas and one will not
have the pleasure of observing brown bears. They will run
away and hide before anyone even sees them.

The effects of intense hunting may go beyond transform-
ing brown bears into wary, reclusive, often nocturnal creatures. The potential is present for changes in the genetic

structure of some brown bear populations. Boars are two to three times larger than sows because of intense reproductive competition. The largest, most powerful boars do most of the breeding. A simple fact that creates strong natural selection for large body size in boars. Intense hunting may cause reverse artificial selection for boar size. If hunters are selectively killing the larger boars, then the smaller boars may be granted a reproductive advantage in that they will live longer and have more reproductive opportunities in the absence of large boars. Thus, hunting theoretically could produce populations of small, wary, reclusive, and nocturnal boars. A sad state for the mighty brown bear.

It is hard to believe that the great white hunter mentality continues to exist today. But it is promoted in Alaska and remains unchallenged because most people are ignorant and apathetic toward such goings on. The state held steadfastly to a section of land on Akumwarvik Bay that is sandwiched between McNeil Sanctuary and Katmai National Monument where hunting was allowed until 1986 when the Board of Game finally closed the area to hunting. However, the area just north of the falls remains open to hunting and bears continue to be taken in legal hunts within two miles of the falls. Zubin was killed in this open area near Chenik Lake.

Actually, the layout of McNeil River Sanctuary is absurd. The bulk of the protected land (see map on p. xiv) is in the remote reaches of the McNeil River drainage, which is rugged, brush-covered country that is totally inaccessible by boat or plane. No hunter would ever venture there, and the bears rarely utilize this area. However, on the coast, where the bears concentrate and hunting is easy, the sanctuary is barely two miles wide. Any bear could cross the width in a matter of minutes.

Every year that hunting is open McNeil bears are lost to unlikely living rooms in Texas, California, and other parts of the world. Doomed to lie in front of fireplaces or stand with paws outstretched and mouth snarled in absurd manmade poses that the bears never realized. The awesome and playful Zubin was shot near Chenik Lake scarcely four miles from

Red and two spring cubs sitting together beside McNeil Falls.

McNeil Falls. In reference to Zubin, I remember an incident that summarizes the attitude of some people in the Alaska Department of Fish and Game. I was sitting at the falls with the man who was administering the sanctuary that summer (previous to Larry Aumiller), when Zubin ambled past us about 15 feet away. He appeared suddenly in my side vision and glided past in his slow, labored waddle as muscle rippled beneath summer fat and the velvet stubble of his fall coat. The man beside me watched him pass and said, "that bear is gonna make some hunter mighty happy." Indeed, it is a matter of record that Zubin now resides in Tulsa.

What a blatant and arrogant contradiction in policy for the state aggressively to protect the bears at McNeil in the summer and exploit them for tourism, and then open adjacent areas to hunting two months later. There must be an immediate push to expand the sanctuary in all directions to meet the boundaries of Katmai National Monument. This would provide protection for virtually all the range of the McNeil bears. Ideally, all Alaskan brown bears should be granted nongame protective status, but such an enlightened policy remains in the future.

Indian summer extended into late August with hazy, warm days ended by lingering gold sunsets. We longed to stay into the fall, but school and the real world would not wait. Our bears were all gone. They were off doing bear things. We would not return the next summer so we left most of our equipment and supplies for visitors the following summer. Nine years later, on one of my future visits, I discovered little evidence that our camp ever existed. The McNeil wilderness quickly reclaims its own.

Appendix

The major objective of our research project was to determine if the asocial brown bears adapted their behavior in the essentially social situation of McNeil Falls in order more efficiently to use the salmon food source. Also, what were the social and environmental variables that influenced their behavior?

The following presentation of data reveals that the bears' behavior at the falls was always subject to change and was influenced by multiple factors. These factors, in approximate order of importance, were individual recognition (involved the dominance of the bears or their size, age, sex, reproductive class, and temperament), habituation, the number of bears present, fishing success, and the spacing of bears (crowding).

The composition of brown bears at McNeil Falls, Alaska, in 1974 and 1975, by age and sex.

Age-sex class	1974	1975
Adult males (10 years and older)	10 + 4[1,2]	10 + 2[1]
Adult females (7 years and older)	4	4
Females with cubs	7	9
Adolescent males (5–9 years)	7	4
Adolescent females (5–6 Years)	4	2
Juveniles (2–4 years)	3	2
Yearlings (1½ years)	3	14
Cubs (6–9 months)	15	4
Unclassified	6[1]	4[1]
Total bears	63	55

[1]Occasional visitors sighted only one or two times
[2]Includes three males seen only on all-night observation

The hypothesis that asocial brown bears adapt their behavior in a social feeding situation is not entirely valid. It is logical to propose that an asocial animal would not predictably adapt to a social situation. The McNeil bears do whatever is most successful in terms of obtaining salmon. There is nothing

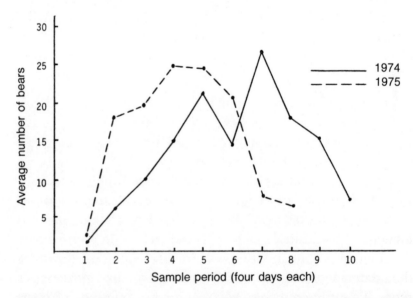

Figure A-1. Seasonal variation in the number of brown bears visiting McNeil Falls. Figures are the average number during four-day sample periods—July 7 to August 10, 1974, and July 20 to August 19, 1975.

to be gained by accepting subordinate roles, so their behavior is very dynamic as conditions and situations change.

The number of bears present at the falls varied seasonally and annually. Within a fishing season the number of bears increased until midseason and then rapidly declined (figure A-1). Any further variation in bear numbers within a season was due to the increased water level of the falls and resulting decrease in availability of salmon. Annual variations in bear numbers are not easily explained. Total numbers of bears visiting the falls varied from a low of fifty-five in 1975 and 1979 to a high of ninety-seven in 1985 (Larry Aumiller, personal communication, September 1975). Egbert (1978) suggested that increased numbers of salmon led to increased numbers of bears. This is logical and I agree with Egbert. However, Larry Aumiller suggests that poor salmon runs may also increase the number of bears at the falls. That is, when salmon are scarce, nonresident bears may be drawn to McNeil Falls where salmon are at least more accessible.

The resident population of bears at the falls tends to be stable. The same bears return year after year. I suggested in Chapter 5 that most resident bears were brought to the falls by their mothers as spring cubs and yearlings. This early experience prepares them for dealing with the falls later on, on their own. However, population data reveals that few young bears become McNeil residents. There were forty-five yearling cubs present from 1970 to 1974. These young would make up the two- to six-year-old age group in 1975, but there were only four bears in this age group present in 1975. Clearly few offspring of McNeil sows return to the falls on their own at an early age. Whether a significant number return at an older age is not known. Why some young bears, such as Red, White, Blue, Light, Dark, Patch Butt, and the Marx Brothers, become such regular McNeil residents while others do not is not known.

Figure A-2 illustrates that the McNeil population was dominated by cubs and fully mature adults age ten years or more. This is in contrast to the Black Lake population, which was primarily composed of young animals because of intense hunting.

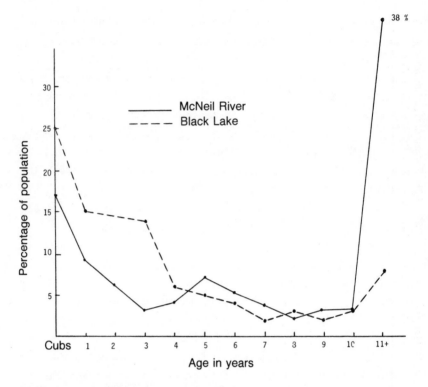

Figure A-2. The age structure of the McNeil River brown bear population (1973–1975) compared to the population inhabiting the Black Lake region of the Alaska Peninsula (Glenn, 1975).

The reproductive histories of nine McNeil sows over the past twenty-three years is documented in table A-2. Lanky, the smallest and lowest ranking sow, produced more yearling cubs (seven) than any other sow. Red Collar's late effort at age twenty-three may have been succeeded by Reggie's at age twenty-four. There is controversy over Reggie's age, which was determined from a single tooth taken in 1972. However, she was a fairly large sow with long claws in Derek Stonorov's 1971 film, which would place her minimum age at five during that year. Thus, her age could not be overestimated by more than two or three years.

The fishing success of the bears was correlated with dominance (table A-3). Adult males had the greatest success, and Charlie Brown, the alpha boar, was the clear winner with 4.29

The reproductive history of brown bear females of known age at McNeil River, Alaska, 1963–1985. Females of unknown age not included. Year of first capture in parentheses. Adapted from a table by Larry Aumiller. See foot of table for key to symbols.

Age, in years	Jeanne (1963)	Big Mamma (1963)	Red Collar (1967)	Lanky (1967)	Spooky (1968)	Red (1970)	Blue (1970)	White (1970)	Reggie[1] (1972)
2.5	C-IE			C-N	C-IE	C-N	C-N	C-N	O-WOY
3.5	O-MS			C-IE	O-MS	O-WOY	O-WOY	O-WOY	C-N
4.5	C-WC2*					O-WOY	O-WOY	O-WOY	O-WOY
5.5	—		C-MS	O-MS	O-WC1*	O-WOY	O-WOY	O-WOY	O-WOY
6.5	C-MS	C-IE	O-WC3	O-WY1*	O-WOY	O-MS	O-WOY	O-WOY	O-WC2*?
7.5	C-WC3	—	O-WY1	C-W2Y1	C-MS	O-WC2*	O-WOY	O-MS	O-WY1
8.5	O-WY2	—	C-N	O-MS	C-WC3	killed	O-WOY	O-WC2*	O-W2Y1
9.5	C-MS	C-IE	C-IE	O-WC3(1)	O-WY1		O-MS	O-WY1	O-WOY
10.5	C-WC1	—	C-WOY	O-WY1	O-WOY		O-WC1*	O-MS	O-WC1(1)
11.5	O-WOY	C-MS	O-MS	O-WOY	—		—	O-WC3(1)	O-WOY
12.5	O-IE	O-WC3	O-WC5(2)	O-WC2	O-WY3		—	O-WY2	O-WC1
13.5	O-WOY	C-WY3	O-WY3	O-WY2	O-WOY		—	O-W2Y2	O-WY1
14.5	O-WOY	O-MS	O-W2Y3	—	—		—	O-WOY	O-W2Y1
15.5	O-WC3	O-WC3	O-WOY	O-WOY	—		—	O-WOY	O-WOY
16.5	O-WY2	O-WY2	O-WC4(1)	O-WOY	O-WY2		—	O-WC3	O-WC1
17.5	O-W2Y2	O-WOY	O-WY1	O-WC3	O-WOY		—	O-WY3(1)	
18.5	O-WOY	O-WOY	O-WOY	O-WY3	O-WOY				
19.5	O-WC1	—	O-WOY	O-WOY	O-WOY				
20.5	O-WY1	O-WC3	O-WOY	O-WC3	O-WOY				
21.5	—	O-WY3(1)	O-WC1						
22.5	—	O-WOY							
23.5		—							
24.5		—							

C = captured; O = observed; — = not observed; IE = in estrous; N = not in estrous; WOY = without young; WC = with spring cubs, followed by number; WY = with yearling cubs, followed by number; * = first litter; W2Y = with two-year-old cubs, followed by number; MS = mated successfully; ( ) = number of young lost during observation.

[1]Reggie's age may be incorrect; see text.

TABLE A-3

The number of salmon caught and the rate caught per hour (salmon/bear hour) for each age and sex class of brown bears at McNeil Falls in 1974 and 1975.

Age-sex Class	1974			1975		
	Salmon caught	Bear hours	Salmon/ bear hour	Salmon caught	Bear hours	Salmon/ bear hour
Adult males	309	188	1.64	468	258	1.81
Females with young	154	136	1.13	633	374	1.69
Adult females	224	173	1.29	380	239	1.59
Adolescent males	434	339	1.28	297	180	1.65
Adolescent females	159	184	0.86	17	29	0.59
Juveniles	17	28	0.61	13	42	0.31
Totals	1,308	1,130	1.16	1,808	1,122	1.61

and 9.13 fish per hour in 1974 and 1975, respectively. The figure of 9.13 fish per hour in 1975 translates into about fifty to sixty pounds of salmon per hour of fishing. The success of females with young in 1974 (1.13 per hour) was probably reduced by the confusion and problems they experienced that summer with cub swapping. Adolescent males enjoyed high success for their dominance ranking, but as a group they were bold and reckless, which increased their success.

Seasonal fishing success increased until midseason and then declined with some variation. The 1975 season was late in getting started but immediately became intense. The level of fishing success in period two of 1975 was not equaled until period five in 1974 (figure A-3). The high success rate in period two of 1975 was owing to increased bear numbers rather than salmon numbers. Fishing success in periods nine and ten in 1974 increased, despite decreasing salmon numbers and bear numbers. This was because of extremely low water on the falls, which made the salmon more vulnerable for the few remaining bears (see figs. A-6, A-7, and A-8 in later discussion).

The hourly variation in salmon numbers (fig. A-4) reveals that during the hours of peak bear fishing activity (1400–2000 hours), the number of salmon present were generally at the lowest diurnal levels. I suggested in Chapter 5 that the bears

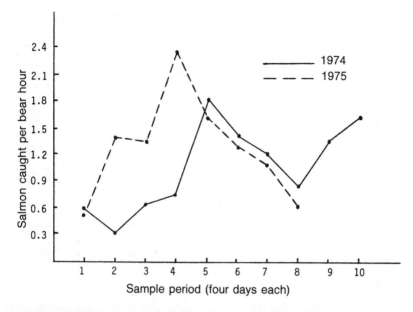

Figure A-3. Seasonal variation in the fishing success of brown bears at McNeil Falls. Figures are the number of salmon caught per bear hour during four-day sample periods.

apparently endured greater competition in the evening hours rather than adjust their diurnal patterns to exploit the salmon during morning hours.

The number of salmon at the falls generally increased steadily until midseason and then declined (fig. A-5). The midseason decreases in salmon in periods six and five in 1974 and 1975, respectively, were due to periods of high water. The salmon were undoubtedly present in greater numbers than shown, however, our census method involved counting the number of salmon surfacing in a quiet pool below the falls during two-minute sample periods every hour. This method was ineffective during high water but it was still a good indicator of the availability of salmon to the bears.

The summer of 1975 was perhaps a more "normal" season than 1974. The primary difference being the unusually low water level in 1974 which eliminated fishing locations, crowded the bears, reduced fishing success, and increased aggression (table A-4). The mean bear hours were greater in 1975

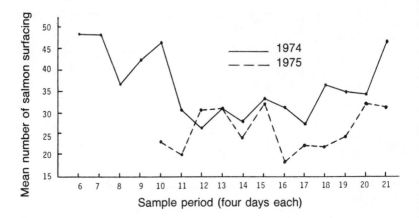

Figure A-4. Hourly variation in the number of salmon observed on McNeil Falls. Figures represent the number of salmon surfacing during a two-minute period in a quiet pool below the main falls during four-day sample periods.

because bear numbers peaked and declined abruptly, whereas in 1974 bear numbers increased and decreased gradually, reducing the mean numbers for the season.

Fishing success had a positive correlation with salmon and bear numbers. These three variables generally mirrored one

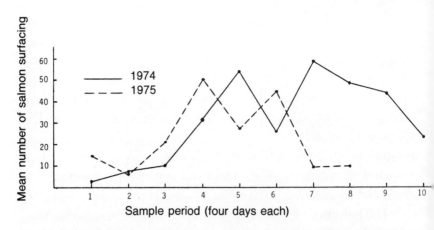

Figure A-5. Seasonal variation in the number of salmon present at McNeil Falls. Figures represent the number of salmon surfacing during a two-minute period in a quiet pool below the main falls in hourly scans during four-day sample periods.

Summary of the major behavioral and ecological variables at McNeil Falls in 1974 and 1975.

	1974	1975
Mean fishing bear hours/day	30.54	52.32
Mean activity bear hours/day	39.58	64.89*
Salmon caught/fishing bear hour	1.15	1.61
Mean salmon abundance	30.63	23.47
Mean water level (inches)	14.06	18.20
Mean encounter rate (encounters/activity bear hour)	1.20	1.24

*Hours adjusted proportionally

another with a few exceptions. The sharp increase in fishing success in period two of 1975 occurred because of a similar increase in bear numbers despite very low salmon numbers (fig. A-6). The sudden increase in fishing success in periods eight and nine in 1974 occurred as salmon and bear numbers decreased because the water level dropped and made salmon more vulnerable to the few remaining bears (figs. A-7 and A-8). In contrast, the high water level in period seven of 1975 sharply reduced salmon and bear numbers and fishing success and caused a premature end to the normal forty-day fishing season (fig. A-8). Bear numbers were strongly and logically correlated with salmon numbers (Figure A-9).

The aggressive encounter rate (expressed as the number of encounters per bear hour) at the falls increased to a peak in midseason and then gradually declined with minor exceptions (fig. A-10). The rate of encounters was strongly correlated with dominance (table A-5). The more dominant animals were involved in more encounters as they obtained and held choice fishing locations. Within a season the rate of aggression was more correlated with bear numbers than with fishing success or other variables (figs. A-11 and A-12). The one exception occurred in periods two and three in 1974 when poor fishing success led to a sharply increased rate of aggression even though bear numbers remained low. However, fishing success did influence the intensity of aggression through the season (see below).

Large changes in the water level of the falls had effects on

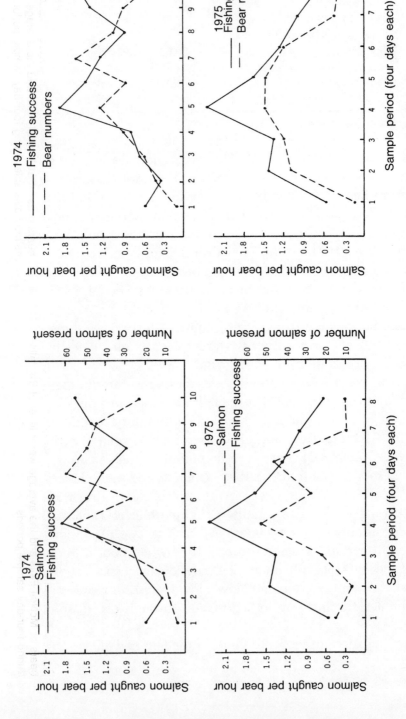

Figure A-7. Relation between the fishing success of brown bears at McNeil Falls and the number of bears present at the falls during four-day sample periods.

Figure A-6. Relation between the fishing success of brown bears at McNeil Falls and the number of salmon present during four-day sample periods.

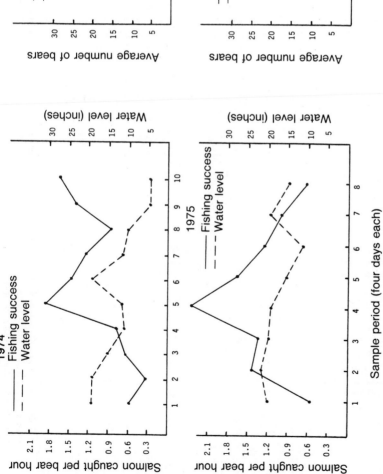

Figure A-9. Relation between the average number of brown bears present at McNeil Falls and the average number of salmon available during four-day sample periods.

Figure A-8. Relation between the fishing success of brown bears at McNeil Falls and the average water level of the falls during four-day sample periods.

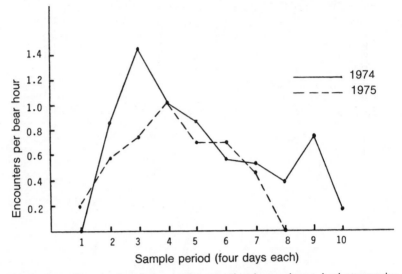

Figure A-10. Seasonal variation in the rate that brown bears had aggressive encounters at McNeil Falls. Figures are the number of encounters per bear hour during four-day sample periods—July 7 to August 10, 1974, and July 20 to August 17, 1975.

aggression (fig. A-13). The extremely low water level in period nine of 1974 sharply increased the rate of aggression as fishing locations dried up and forced the few remaining bears to fish closer together and compete for scarce locations. This occurred despite decreased bear numbers and increased fishing success. High water in period seven of 1975 did not increase the rate of aggression (fig. A-13).

TABLE A-5

Encounter rate (number of encounters per bear hour) for each sex-age class of brown bears at McNeil Falls 1974 and 1975.

Sex-age class	1974		1975	
	Encounters	Rate/hour	Encounters	Rate/hour
Adult males	419	1.74	590	1.67
Females with young	200	1.29	697	1.42
Adult females	241	1.14	251	0.84
Adolescent males	462	1.09	269	1.14
Adolescent females	209	0.95	27	0.71
Juveniles	9	0.28	64	0.69

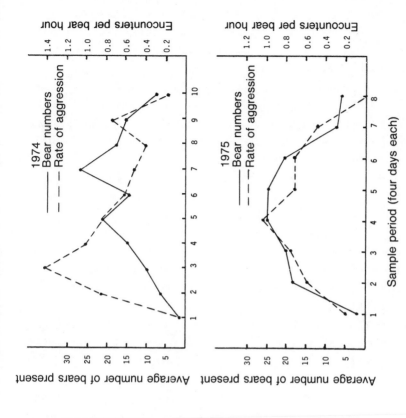

Figure A-12. Relation between the number of bears at McNeil Falls and the rate of aggressive encounters during four-day sample periods.

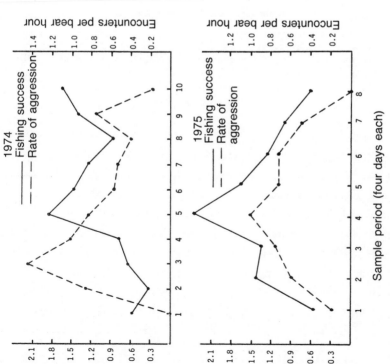

Figure A-11. Relation between the fishing success of brown bears at McNeil Falls and the rate of aggressive encounters during four-day sample periods.

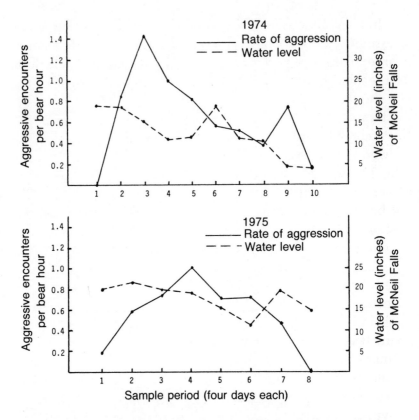

Figure A-13. Relation between the rate of aggression (as the number of encounters per bear hour) and the average water level of McNeil Falls during four-day sample periods.

Dominance relationships were often ambiguous except among the largest mature males, who presumably made a point of maintaining their dominance for reproductive benefits. The dominance relations of virtually all other groups was subject to change. In general, adult males ranked the highest, followed by females with young, adult females, adolescent males, adolescent females, and last, the juveniles. Early in the fishing season this rank order is more predictable; however, later in the season individual recognition, habituation, learning, and increased fishing success will increase reversals and ambiguity in this rank order.

Initial reactions may be based primarily on a distant visual assessment of an opponent. For instance, early in 1975, Jeanne, a large, mature sow, ran away at the approach of Patch Butt, a large adolescent male. Patch Butt was unusually large for his age and Jeanne simply did not recognize him initially, mistaking him most likely for a mature male. Jeanne was dominant to Patch Butt and individual recognition later in the season allowed her to respond correctly and maintain her rank above him. The importance of individual recognition and learning was obvious in the decline of the old boar Patches, who rapidly lost his dominance in the period 1975 to 1977. Despite initial caution owing to Patches' size, most bears learned of his decline and gradually ignored him.

Females with young ranked very high and often dominated all but the largest boars. These mothers won 55 and 37 percent of their encounters with adult males in 1974 and 1975 (table A-6). After some habituation, even these females with young became tolerant of most other bears, with the exception of mature males. They were especially tolerant of other females with young and adolescent males. There was considerable variation in the aggressiveness of sows with cubs and some individuals remained intolerant of all bears throughout the summer.

Adolescent males as a group became quite bold and reckless as the season progressed. Because of their boldness, they won 30 and 60 percent of their encounters with adult females in 1974 and 1975, respectively (table A-6). They often "pushed their luck" and elicited aggression from more dominant animals, but I doubt if this was due to misjudging a situation, or that they were not "socially keyed." More likely, they simply learned what they could get away with by being audacious.

The incidence of the four major forms of aggression (challenge threat, bite threat, charge, and attack) was influenced by habituation (season), dominance (age-sex class), fishing success, bear numbers, and water level (as effects on spacing and fishing success). These social and environmental variables controlled encounter intensity, whereas the overall encounter rate was primarily correlated with bear numbers (fig. A-12).

TABLE A-6

Dominance relationships between age and sex classes of brown bears in 1974 and 1975 at McNeil Falls. Figures represent the percentage of encounters won or lost.

Encounter won by		Encounter lost by						Total wins	Percentage wins
		Adult males	Females with young	Adult females	Adolescent males	Adolescent females	Juveniles		
Adult males	1974	—	45	96	100	100	0	239	87
	1975	—	63	92	99	100	100	227	81
Females with young	1974	55	—	80	94	100	0	86	74
	1975	37	—	78	97	100	100	211	68
Adult females	1974	4	20	—	70	100	0	77	43
	1975	8	22	—	40	100	100	41	29
Adolescent males	1974	0	6	30	—	87.5	100	56	22
	1975	1	3	60	—	0.0	100	20	11
Adolescent females	1974	0	0	0	12.5	—	100	5	5
	1975	0	0	0	0.0	—	100	1	3
Juveniles	1974	0	0	0	0	0	—	0	0
	1975	0	0	0	0	0	—	0	0
Total losses	1974	36	30	104	96	194	3	—	—
	1975	53	99	111	24	154	59	—	—
Percentage losses	1974	13	26	57	95	78	100	—	—
	1975	19	32	71	97	89	100	—	—

Challenge threats were the most common form of aggression, occurring in 35.5 and 36.0 percent of encounters in 1974 and 1975 (table A-7). Approximately one-third of the challenge threats erupted into bite threats, which occurred in 13.4 and 13.0 percent of all encounters. Charges were slightly more frequent than bite threats (13.9 in 1974 and 17.6 percent in 1975). Attacks (fighting) occurred rarely (3.6 in 1974 and 6.6 percent in 1975) when a charge was completed and ended with an attack, or when a bite threat erupted into fighting. Challenge threats and bite threats did not vary annually, however, both charges and attacks were more frequent in 1975 (table A-7).

There was considerable variation in the incidence of aggression by age-sex class (table A-8). Females with young were responsible for approximately one-half of all threats, attacks, and charges or twice the number expected. Other age-sex classes were involved in an expected percentage of aggression as compared to their percent involvement in all encounters. Adolescent males were the only other exception, with one-half to one-quarter of the expected threats, charges, and attacks.

Challenge threats and bite threats occurred more often between bears of the same age-sex class than between bears of different classes (tables A-9 and A-10). The exceptions being females with young, who threatened all bears equally, and adolescent males, who threatened other age-sex classes most often. These two forms of threat often occurred in contesting

TABLE A-7

The incidence (percentage) of four major forms of aggression during encounters between brown bears at McNeil Falls. Figures are the percentage of encounters that included each behavior. Figures in parentheses are the number of encounters that included each behavior.

Behavior	1974	1975	Probability less than
Challenge threats	35.5 (273)	36.0 (343)	0.95
Bite threats	13.4 (103)	13.0 (124)	0.90
Charges	13.9 (107)	17.6 (168)	0.05
Attacks	3.6 (28)	6.6 (63)	0.001

The incidence of aggressive encounters and four major forms of aggression by age and sex class. Figures are the percentage of total encounters and aggression that involved each age-sex class.

Sex-age class	% of encounters	Challenge threats	Bite threats	Charges	Attacks
Adult males	27.5	24.8	25.2	30.3	25.3
Females with young	24.4	43.8	54.7	45.2	53.8
Adult females	13.4	13.6	9.9	11.0	12.1
Adolescent males	26.3	12.0	6.6	7.9	6.6
Adolescent females	6.4	5.5	2.9	4.0	1.1
Juveniles	2.0	0.1	0.0	0.4	0.0

encounters between peers, hence the higher incidence within age-sex classes.

The pattern of charges was more varied (table A-11). Adult males and adolescent females charged their own class most often, while females with young and adolescent males charged other age-sex classes more often. Attacks were rare (table A-12) and only females with young initiated enough attacks (53.8 percent of all attacks) to reveal a definite pattern of attacking other age-sex classes more than within their own class.

The four major forms of aggression were described in detail in Chapter 6, so I shall not reiterate the descriptions here. Challenge threats and bite threats are analogous to the "jawing" and "sparring" described by Stonorov and Stokes (1972) and Egbert (1978). Because these behaviors are complex, ritualized threats with multiple components, I chose the more descriptive terms *challenge threat* and *bite threat.* My findings also differ from Egbert (1978) in that I analyzed only agonistic encounters, while Egbert quantified all encounters. Also, since I filmed encounters for analysis, I often missed simultaneous encounters, and this reduced the total numbers documented. Nonetheless, my selection of encounters was random.

The seasonal variation in the incidence of challenge threats and bite threats were similar (fig. A-14). This relationship results from the fact that bite threats are often an aggressive progression from a challenge threat. A similar relation

TABLE A-9

Incidence of challenge threats during aggressive encounters. Figures represent the percentage of encounters with challenge threats. Figures in parentheses are the number of threats observed.

| Aggressor | Recipient of aggression | | |
	Same sex-age class	Different sex-age class	Probability less than
Adult males	32.4 (57)	19.5 (96)	0.50
Females with young	55.9 (80)	50.3 (190)	0.50
Adult females	57.9 (11)	36.5 (73)	0.20
Adolescent males	21.7 (15)	33.9 (59)	0.001
Adolescent females	72.0 (18)	38.1 (16)	0.001
Juveniles	50.0 (1)	0 (0)	

existed between charges and attacks (fig. A-15). Early-season intolerance is obvious in the high incidence of charges in period two. The sudden drop in charges in period three illustrates that habituation and increased tolerance occurred quickly.

Annual variations in aggression were correlated with bear numbers, fishing success, and water level. Challenge threats in 1974 were correlated with bear numbers, except for a decline in period five (fig. A-16) that corresponded to the season peak of fishing success (fig. A-17). Challenge threats increased gradually in 1975. The drop in threats in period four was associated with the season peak of fishing success, and the peak of threats in period seven was because of the increasing water level and declining fishing success.

TABLE A-10

Incidence of bite threats during aggressive encounters. Figures represent the percentage of encounters with bite threats. Figures in parentheses are the number of threats observed.

| Aggressor | Recipient of aggression | | |
	Same sex-age class	Different sex-age class	Probability less than
Adult males	13.1 (23)	9.3 (46)	0.20
Females with young	27.3 (39)	29.4 (111)	0.50
Adult females	21.1 (4)	11.5 (23)	0.50
Adolescent males	2.9 (2)	10.3 (18)	0.20
Adolescent females	16.0 (4)	9.5 (4)	0.001
Juveniles	0 (0)	0 (0)	

Incidence of charges during aggressive encounters. Figures represent the percentage of encounters with charges. Figures in parentheses are the number of charges observed.

| | Recipient of aggression | | |
Aggressor	Same age-sex class	Different age-sex class	Probability less than
Adult males	11.9 (21)	9.8 (48)	0.10
Females with young	11.9 (17)	22.7 (86)	0.01
Adult females	15.8 (3)	11.0 (22)	0.80
Adolescent males	2.9 (2)	9.2 (16)	0.20
Adolescent females	36.0 (9)	4.8 (2)	0.001
Juveniles	50.0 (1)	0 (0)	

Charges were not correlated with fishing success or bear numbers. Bite threats and attacks were correlated with bear numbers in 1974 and 1975. The only exceptions were increases in both bite threats and attacks in period seven of 1975, which was again because of increased water level and decreased fishing success (figs. A-18 and A-19).

The importance of individual recognition in animal communication has been stressed in countless studies. I am convinced that individual recognition is the single most important factor influencing bear behavior at the falls. The majority of encounters consisted merely of the approach of a dominant bear and the immediate withdrawal of a subordinate. The importance of recognition had to be taken into account, so I

TABLE A-12

Incidence of attacks during aggressive encounters. Figures represent the percentage of encounters with attacks. Figures in parentheses are the number of attacks observed.

| | Recipient of aggression | | |
Aggressor	Same age-sex class	Different age-sex class	Probability less than
Adult males	3.4 (6)	3.5 (17)	0.20
Females with young	4.9 (7)	11.1 (42)	0.20
Adult females	5.3 (1)	5.0 (10)	0.80
Adolescent males	1.9 (2)	2.3 (4)	0.20
Adolescent females	4.0 (2)	2.4 (1)	0.001
Juveniles	0 (0)	0 (0)	

included the recognition of a dominant, a subordinate, and a peer as three "signals" in communication (table A-13).

I recounted earlier that Jeanne initially failed to recognize Patch Butt, but thereafter she recognized him and maintained

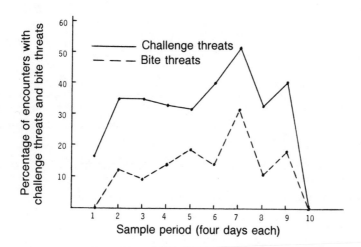

Figure A-14. Seasonal variation in the percentage incidence of challenge threats and bite threats during aggressive encounters between brown bears at McNeil Falls.

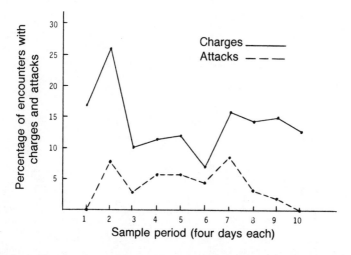

Figure A-15. Seasonal variation in the percentage incidence of charges and attacks during aggressive encounters between brown bears at McNeil Falls.

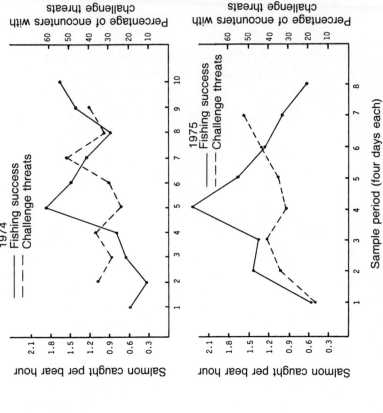

Figure A-17. Relation between the fishing success of brown bears at McNeil Falls and the percentage incidence of challenge threats during aggressive encounters between the bears.

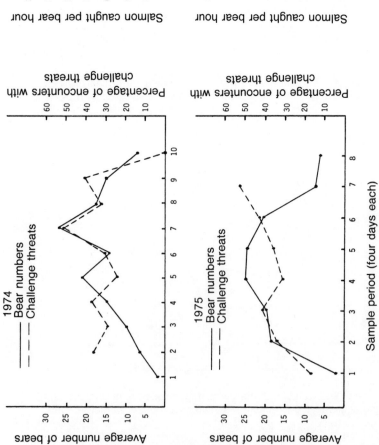

Figure A-16. Relation between the average number of bears present at McNeil Falls and the percentage incidence of challenge threats during aggressive encounters between bears at the falls.

her dominance over him. Recognition may go beyond such visual cues. For instance, there was an amazing encounter between Charlie Brown and Arlo, a large boar who was the only genuine threat to Charlie's alpha dominance. Charlie Brown was fishing at the number-one spot and Saddle, another large boar, fished about 30 feet downstream. Charlie glanced at Saddle occasionally but made no move to drive him away. Meanwhile, Arlo appeared on the bluffs above and behind Charlie and Saddle. I could see Arlo from our knoll, but there was no possibility that he was visible to Charlie Brown. Then suddenly Charlie became very uneasy. Several times he turned to leave but then stayed after glancing at Saddle. It was

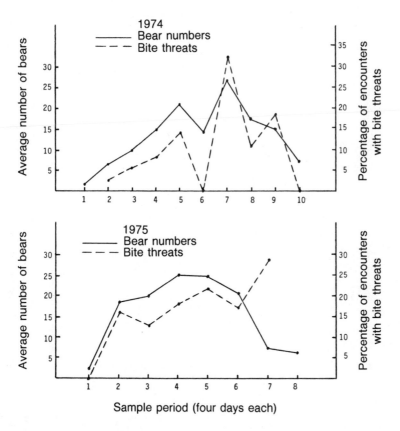

Figure A-18. Relation between the average number of bears fishing on McNeil Falls and the percentage incidence of bite threats during aggressive encounters between bears at the falls.

obvious that he wanted to leave but did not want to relinquish his spot to Saddle. Finally he turned and headed quickly up the bluff straight in Arlo's direction. When Charlie reached the top, he sighted Arlo and charged him immediately. Charlie had obviously detected Arlo's presence and the only means possible was by smell. This illustrates that bears are capable of being keenly aware of the identities and even remote presence of other bears.

My analysis of the predictability of brown bear communication was very simplistic. The method I used was that described by Altmann (1965). Each single behavioral event, or signal, had a probability of occurrence. I then determined the probability (or the uncertainty) of behavior if the preceding

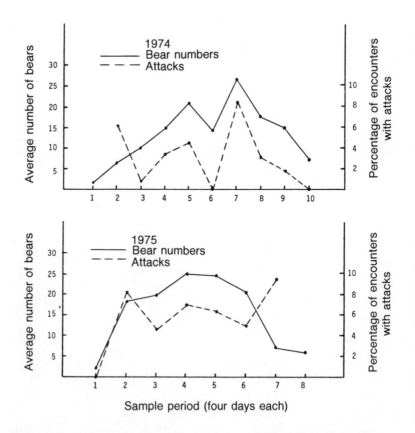

Figure A-19. Relation between the average number of bears fishing on McNeil Falls and the percentage incidence of attacks during aggressive encounters between bears at the falls.

TABLE A-13

Twenty-one discrete behaviors or signals that brown bears at McNeil Falls used during aggressive encounters with one another. Signals are listed in three major groups as they occur in three major types of encounters.

Signal number	Signal description	Encounter type
1	Recognition of dominance	Passive withdrawal
2	Withdraw	
3	Recognition of subordinate	Passive approach-withdrawal
4	Relaxed approach (followed by withdrawal of subordinate)	
5	Recognition of peer	Contesting encounter
6	Tense approach	
7	Stay put	
8	Bluff charge	
9	Intense challenge threat	
10	Low-level challenge threat	
11	Open-mouth threat	
12	Crouch	
13	Bite threat	
14	Lowered head	
15	Face away	
16	Back up	
17	Stare at	
18	Look away	
19	Attack	
20	Ears back	
21	Stealing approach	

behavior was known and taken into account. The observed decrease in uncertainty of behavior when the preceding behavior was considered is a measure of how much bear A was communicating to bear B about its intention. The uncertainty of behavior was then determined when two and three preceding behaviors were known. The decreasing uncertainty in a sequence of behaviors is a measure of the amount of information that the behaviors provided to each bear, or how much preceding behaviors controlled what each bear did next. Thus, decreasing uncertainty in a sequence of behaviors (fig. A-20) is a measure of how much the bears were communicating with one another concerning their intentions.

There would be no decrease in uncertainty if the bears

were not communicating with one another. This would mean that their behavior was entirely random. Even the most casual observation reveals that the bears' behaviors are not random. Clearly each bear's actions, or behaviors, influences the behavior of others. Figure A-20 illustrates the decrease in uncertainty or the amount of communication in sequences of brown bear behavior.

A comparison of uncertainty of brown bear and rhesus monkey behavior (fig. A-20) is especially useful. Rhesus monkeys are very social animals with a rigid social organization that is maintained by definite dominant and subordinate roles of the group members. As a result, their behavior is much more predictable than that of asocial brown bears. The latter have nothing to gain by accepting subordinate roles, and dominant bears enforce their dominance primarily for feeding privileges. Bears generally do whatever they can get away with in a given situation, and as situations, as well as each bear's motivations, are constantly changing, the result is that brown bear behavior is considerably less predictable than rhesus monkey behavior.

Correlations of social and environmental variables (dominance, fishing success, season, bear numbers) with measures of uncertainty were not possible because of the large amounts of data required to determine behavioral uncertainty. Thus, an ambitious objective of building a "model" of brown bear communication has not yet been accomplished.

Table A-14 summarizes the measures of uncertainty and *stereotypy.* Stereotypy has a range from zero to one, where

TABLE A-14

Summary of the uncertainty of brown bear communication and other related measures pertaining to the predictability of brown bear behavior (after Altmann, 1965)

Sequence order	Sample size	Joint uncertainty	Transition uncertainty	Stereotypy
0	21	4.392		
1	12,563	3.831		0.128
2	10,644	6.605	2.775	0.368
3	9,104	9.001	2.395	0.455
4	7,513	10.815	1.814	0.587

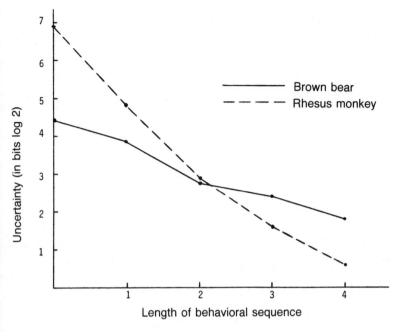

Figure A-20. Relation between behavioral sequence length and the uncertainty of behavioral events. Behaviors become more predictable (less uncertainty) as more preceding behaviors are considered. The rigid social organization of rhesus monkeys presumably makes their behavior more predictable than that of brown bears (after Altmann, 1965).

zero represents completely random behavior and one represents behavior that is completely predictable. This index of stereotypy for brown bears ranges from 0.128 to 0.587 for sequences of one to four behaviors, while the range for rhesus monkeys is 0.30 to 0.915 (Altmann, 1965). Clearly the behavior of the social rhesus is determined by the behavior of other monkeys, while brown bears have much more freedom in their actions.

The McNeil bears can be considered opportunistic in their behavior as well as their ecology. The hypothesis that the asocial McNeil bears modify their behavior in the social environment of the falls in order to obtain salmon more efficiently is at least partly valid. However, this question may be inappropriate. The bears are too opportunistic and asocial for me to draw definite conclusions on their behavioral ecology. They do whatever works best in a dynamic environment.

Bibliography

ALTMANN, S. A. 1965. Sociobiology of Rhesus Monkeys. II: Sto-
chastics of Social Communication. *Journal of Theoretical
Biology* 8:490–522.

———. 1967. Structure of Social Communication. In *Social
Communication Among Primates,* edited by S. A. Altmann, 325–62. Chicago: University of Chicago Press.

ANDREW, R. J. 1957. Influence of Hunger on Aggressive Behavior in Certain Buntings of the Genus *Emberiza. Physiological Zoology* 30:177–85.

ATWELL, T., D. L. BOONE, J. GUSTAFSON, and V. D. BERNS. 1980.
Brown Bear Summer Use of Alpine Habitat on the Kodiak
National Wildlife Refuge. In *Bears—Their Biology and
Management,* edited by C. L. Martinka and K. L. McAr-

thur, 297–305. The Bear Biology Association Conference ser. 3.

BACON, E. S., and G. M. BURGHARDT. 1976. Learning and Color Discrimination in the American Black Bear. In *Bears— Their Biology and Management,* edited by M. R. Pelton, J. W. Lentfer, and G. E. Folk, 27–36. IUCN Publication n.s. 40.

BALLARD, W. B., S. D. MILLER, and T. H. SPRAKER. 1982. Home Range, Daily Movements, and Reproductive Biology of Brown Bear in South-Central Alaska. *Canadian Field Naturalist* 96(1):1–5.

BARASH, D. P. 1974. Neighbor Recognition in Two "Solitary" Carnivores: The Raccoon (*Procyon lotor*) and the Red Fox (*Vulpes fulva*). *Science* 185:794–96.

BEKOFF, M. 1972. The Development of Social Interaction, Play, and Metacommunication in Mammals: An Ethological Perspective. *Quarterly Review of Biology* 47:412–34.

———. 1974. Social Play in Coyotes, Wolves, and Dogs. *Bio-Science* 24:225–30.

BERNS, V. D., G. C. ATWELL, and D. L. BOONE. 1980. Brown Bear Movements and Habitat Use at Karluk Lake, Kodiak Island. In *Bears—Their Biology and Management,* edited by C. L. Martinka and K. L. McArthur, 293–96. The Bear Biology Association Conference ser. 3.

BLAFFER-HRDY, S. 1977. Infanticide as a Primate Reproductive Strategy. *American Scientist* 65(1):40–49.

BOLWIG, N. 1964. Facial Expressions with Remarks on Parallel Development in Certain Carnivores. *Behaviour* 22:167–92.

CHATFIELD, C., and R. E. LEMON. 1970. Analyzing Sequences of Behavioral Events. *Journal of Theoretical Biology* 29:-427–55.

CLARK, W. K. 1957. Seasonal Food Habits of the Kodiak Bear. *Transactions of the North American Wildlife Conference* 22:145–51.

———. 1959. Kodiak Bear–Red Salmon Relationships at Karluk Lake, Alaska. *Transactions of the North American Wildlife Conference* 24:337–45.

COWAN, I. McT. 1972. The Status and Conservation of Bears in
the World—1970. In *Bears—Their Biology and Management,* edited by S. Herrero, 343–67. IUCN Publication n.s.
23.

CRAIGHEAD, JR., F. C. 1976. Grizzly Bear Ranges and Move-
ments as Determined by Radiotracking. In *Bears—Their
Biology and Management,* edited by M. R. Pelton, J. W.
Lentfer, and G. E. Folk, 97–109. IUCN Publication n.s. 40.

——, and J. J. CRAIGHEAD. 1972. Grizzly Bear Prehiberna-
tion and Denning Activities as Determined by Radiotracking. *Wildlife Monographs* no. 32.

CRAIGHEAD, J. J., F. C. CRAIGHEAD, JR., and J. S. SUMNER. 1976.
Reproductive Cycles and Rates in the Grizzly Bear, *Ursus
arctos horribilis,* of the Yellowstone Ecosystem. In *Bears
—Their Biology and Management,* edited by M. R. Pelton,
J. W. Lentfer, and G. E. Folk, 337–56. IUCN Publication
n.s. 40.

——, M. G. HORNOCKER, and F. C. CRAIGHEAD, JR. 1969.
Reproductive Biology of Young Female Grizzly Bears.
Journal of Reproduction and Fertility, suppl. 6:447–75.

CURRY-LINDAHL, K. 1972. The Brown Bear (*Ursus arctos*) in
Europe: Decline, Present Distribution, Biology, and Ecol-
ogy. In *Bears—Their Biology and Management,* edited by
S. Herrero, 74–80. IUCN Publication n.s. 23.

DEAN, F. C. 1976. Aspects of Grizzly Bear Population Ecology
in Mt. McKinley National Park. In *Bears—Their Biology
and Management,* edited by M. R. Pelton, J. W. Lentfer,
and G. E. Folk, 111–19. IUCN Publication n.s. 40.

EGBERT, A. L. 1978. The Social Behavior of Brown Bears at
McNeil River Alaska. Ph.D. diss., Utah State University,
Logan, Utah.

——, and A. W. STOKES. 1976. The Social Behavior of Brown
Bears on an Alaskan Salmon Stream. In *Bears—Their Biology and Management,* edited by M. R. Pelton, J. W. Lentfer, and G. E. Folk, 41–56. IUCN Publication n.s. 40.

ELGMORK, K. 1982. Caching Behavior of Brown Bear (*Ursus
arctos*). *Journal of Mammalogy* 63(4):607–12.

ERICKSON, A. W. 1964. A Mixed-Age Litter of Brown Bear
Cubs. *Journal of Mammalogy* 45(2):312–18.

————, and L. H. MILLER. 1963. Cub Adoption in the Brown Bear. *Journal of Mammalogy* 44(4):584–85.

————, H. W. MOSSMAN, W. A. TROYER, and R. J. HENSEL. 1968. The Breeding Biology of the Male Brown Bear. *Zoologica* 53(3):85–105.

ETKIN, W. 1964. Cooperation and Competition in Social Behavior. In *Social Behavior and Organization Among Vertebrates,* edited by W. Etkin, 1–34. Chicago and London: University of Chicago Press.

FOLK, JR., G. E., M. A. FOLK, and J. J. MINOR. 1972. Physiological Conditions of Three Species of Bears in Winter Dens. In *Bears—Their Biology and Management,* edited by S. Herrero, 107–24. IUCN Publication n.s. 23.

————, J. M. HUNT, and M. A. FOLK. 1980. Further Evidence for Hibernation of Bears. In *Bears—Their Biology and Management,* edited by C. L. Martinka and K. L. McArthur, 43–47. The Bear Biology Association Conference ser. 3.

————, A. LARSON, and M. A. FOLK. 1976. Physiology of Hibernating Bears. In *Bears—Their Biology and Management,* edited by M. R. Pelton and G. E. Folk, 373–80. IUCN Publication n.s. 40.

FOX, M. W. 1969. The Anatomy of Aggression and Its Ritualization in Canids. *Behaviour* 35:242–53.

————. 1971. A Comparative Study of the Development of Facial Expressions in Canids: Wolf, Coyote, and Foxes. *Behaviour* 36:49–73.

GARD, R. 1971. Brown Bear Predation on Sockeye Salmon at Karluk Lake, Alaska. *Journal of Wildlife Management* 35:193–204.

GEIST, V. 1974. On the Relation of Social Evolution and Ecology in Ungulates. *American Zoologist* 14(1):1–463.

GITTLEMAN, J. L., and P. H. HARVEY. 1982. Carnivore Home Range Size, Metabolic Needs and Ecology. *Behavioral Ecology and Sociobiology* 10:57–63.

GLENN, L. P. 1971. *Report on 1970 Brown Bear Studies.* Alaska Department of Fish and Game. Federal Aid in Wildlife Restoration, Project W-17-3 and W-17-4.

————. 1972. *Report on 1971 Brown Bear Studies.* Alaska De-

partment of Fish and Game. Federal Aid in Wildlife Restoration, Project W-17-3 and W-17-4.
———. 1973. *Report on 1972 Brown Bear Studies.* Alaska Department of Fish and Game. Federal Aid in Wildlife Restoration, Project W-17-4 and W-17-5.
———. 1975. *Report on 1974 Brown Bear Studies.* Alaska Department of Fish and Game. Federal Aid in Wildlife Restoration, Project W-17-6 and W-17-7.
———. 1980. Morphometric Characteristics of Brown Bears
on the Central Alaska Peninsula. In *Bears—Their Biology
and Management,* edited by C. L. Martinka and K. L.
McArthur, 313–19. The Bear Biology Association Conference ser. 3.
———, J. W. LENTFER, J. B. FARO, and L. H. MILLER. 1976.
Reproductive Biology of Female Brown Bears (*Ursus
arctos*), McNeil River, Alaska. In *Bears—Their Biology
and Management,* edited by M. R. Pelton, J. W. Lentfer,
and G. E. Folk, 381–90. IUCN Publication n.s. 40.
———, and L. H. MILLER. 1980. Seasonal Movements of an
Alaska Peninsula Brown Bear Population. In *Bears—Their
Biology and Management,* edited by C. L. Martinka and
K. L. McArthur, 307–12. The Bear Biology Association
Conference ser. 3.
HARRINGTON, C. R., A. H. MACPHERSON, and J. P. KELSALL.
1962. The Barren-Ground Grizzly Bear in Northern Can-
ada. *Arctic* 15:294–98.
HAZLETT, B. A., and W. H. BOSSERT. 1965. A Statistical Analysis
of the Aggressive Communication of Some Hermit Crabs.
Animal Behaviour 13:357–73.
HENRY, J. D., and S. M. HERRERO. 1974. Social Play in the
American Black Bear: Its Similarity to Canid Social Play
and an Examination of Its Identifying Characteristics.
American Zoologist 14:371–91.
HENSEL, R. J., W. A. TROYER, and A. W. ERICKSON. 1969. Repro-
duction in the Female Brown Bear. *Journal of Wildlife
Management* 33:357–65.
HERRERO, S. 1972. Aspects of Evolution and Adaptation in
American Black Bears (*Ursus americanus* Pallas) and

Brown and Grizzly Bears (*Ursus arctos* Linne). In *Bears—Their Biology and Management*, edited by S. Herrero, 221–31. IUCN Publication n.s. 23.

HOCKETT, C. F., and S. A. ALTMANN. 1968. A Note on Design Features. In *Animal Communication*, edited by T. A. Sebeok, 61–72. Bloomington: University of Indiana Press.

HORNOCKER, M. G. 1962. Population characteristics and social and reproductive behavior of the grizzly bear in Yellowstone National Park. Master's thesis, Missoula: Montana State University.

JOHNSON, L. F., and P. LeROUX. 1973. Age of Self-Sufficiency in Brown/Grizzly Bear in Alaska. *Journal of Wildlife Management* 37(1):122–23.

JONKEL, C. J., and I. McT. COWAN. 1971. The Black Bear in the Spruce Fir Forest. *Wildlife Monographs* 27:1–57.

JORDAN, R. H. 1976. Threat Behavior of the Black Bear (*Ursus americanus*). In *Bears—Their Biology and Management*, edited by M. R. Pelton, J. W. Lentfer, and G. E. Folk, 57–63. IUCN Publication n.s. 40.

KLEIMAN, D. G. 1967. Some Aspects of Social Behavior in the Canidae. *American Zoologist* 7:365–72.

———, and J. F. EISENBERG. 1973. Comparisons of Canid and Felid Social Systems from an Evolutionary Perspective. *Animal Behaviour* 21(4):637–59.

KLOPFER, P. H., and J. J. HATCH. 1968. Experimental Considerations. In *Animal Communication*, edited by T. A. Sebeok, 31–43. Bloomington: University of Indiana Press.

LENTFER, J. W., R. J. HENSEL, L. H. MILLER, L. P. GLENN, and V. D. BERNS. 1972. Remarks on Denning Habits of Alaska Brown Bears. In *Bears—Their Biology and Management*, edited by S. Herrero, 125–32. IUCN Publication n.s. 23.

LEYHAUSEN, P. 1965. The Communal Organization of Solitary Mammals. *Symposium of the Zoological Society of London* 14:249–63.

LINDERMANN, SPENCER. 1974. *Ground Tracking of Arctic Grizzly Bears.* Alaska Department of Fish and Game. Federal Aid in Wildlife Restoration, Project W-17-6.

LUQUE, M. H., and A. W. STOKES. 1976. Fishing Behavior of

Alaska Brown Bear. In *Bears—Their Biology and Management,* edited by M. R. Pelton, J. W. Lentfer, and G. E. Folk, 71–78. IUCN Publication n.s. 40.

MARLER, P. 1961. The Logical Analysis of Animal Communication. *Journal of Theoretical Biology* 1:295–317.

————. 1967. Animal Communication Signals. *Science* 157: 769–74.

MARTINKA, C. J. 1976. Ecological Role and Management of Grizzly Bears in Glacier National Park, Montana. In *Bears —Their Biology and Management,* edited by M. R. Pelton, J. W. Lentfer, and G. E. Folk, 147–56. IUCN Publication n.s. 40.

MILLER, S. D., and W. B. BALLARD. 1982. Homing of Transplanted Alaskan Brown Bear. *Journal of Wildlife Management* 46(4):869–76.

————, and D. C. MCALLISTER. 1982. *Big Game Studies: Volume VI. Black Bear and Brown Bear.* Alaska Power Authority Susitna Hydroelectric Project Environmental Study Phase I Final Report. Alaska Department of Fish and Game, Juneau.

MILLER, S. J., N. BARISCHELLO, and D. TAIT. 1982. *The Grizzly Bears of the Mackenzie Mountains Northwest Territories.* Northwest Territories Wildlife Series report 3. Yellowknife, Northwest Territories, Canada.

NELSON, R. A., H. W. WAHHER, and J. D. JONES. 1973. Metabolism of Bears Before, During, and After Winter Sleep. *American Journal of Physiology* 224:491–96.

PEARSON, A. M. 1976. Population Characteristics of the Arctic Mountain Grizzly Bear. In *Bears—Their Biology and Management,* edited by M. R. Pelton, J. W. Lentfer, and G. E. Folk, 247–60. IUCN Publication n.s. 40.

RAUSCH, R. L. 1963. Geographic Variation in Size in North American Brown Bears, *Ursus arctos* L., as Indicated by Condylobasal Length. *Canadian Journal of Zoology* 41:33–45.

REYNOLDS, H. V. 1976. *North Slope Grizzly Bear Studies.* Alaska Department of Fish and Game. Federal Aid in Wildlife Restoration, Project W-17-6 and W-17-7.

————, J. A. CURATOLO, and R. QUIMBY. 1976. Denning Ecology of Grizzly Bears in Northeastern Alaska. In *Bears—Their Biology and Management*, edited by M. R. Pelton, J. W. Lentfer, and G. E. Folk, 403–409. IUCN Publication n.s. 40.

ROGER, L. L. 1976. Effects of Mast and Berry Crop Failures on Survival, Growth, and Reproductive Success of Black Bears. *Transactions of the North American Wildlife Conference* 41:431–38.

SCHALLER, G. B. 1972. *The Serengeti Lion.* Chicago: University of Chicago Press.

SCHENKEL, R. 1967. Submission: Its Features and Function in the Wolf and Dog. *American Zoologist* 7:319–29.

SCOTT, J. P. 1967. The Evolution of Social Behavior in Dogs and Wolves. *American Zoologist* 7(2):373–81.

SEBEOK, T. A. 1962. Coding in the Evolution of Signaling Behavior. *Behavioral Science* 7:430–42.

————. 1965. *Animal Communication. Science* 147:1006–14.

SMITH, W. J. 1965. Message, Meaning, and Context in Ethology. *The American Naturalist* 99(908):405–09.

————. 1968. Message-Meaning Analyses. In *Animal Communication*, edited by T. A. Sebeok, 44–59. Bloomington: University of Indiana Press.

————. 1969. Messages of Vertebrate Communication. *Science* 165:145–50.

STEINBERG, J. B., and R. C. CONANT. 1974. An Informational Analysis of the Inter-male Behavior of the Grasshopper *Chortophaga viridifasciata. Behaviour* 22:617–27.

STONOROV, D. 1972. Protocol at the Annual Brown Bear Feast. *Natural History* 81:66–73, 90–94.

————, and A. W. Stokes. 1972. Social Behavior of the Alaska Brown Bear. In *Bears—Their Biology and Management*, edited by S. Herrero, 232–42. IUCN Publication n.s. 23.

TAIT, D. E. N. 1981. Abandonment as a Reproductive Tactic—The Example of Grizzly Bear. *American Naturalist* 115: 800–808.

TROYER, W. A. 1961. The Brown Bear Harvest in Relation to

Management on Kodiak Island. *Transactions of the North American Wildlife Conference* 26:460–68.

————, and R. J. Hensel. 1964a. Cannibalism in Brown Bears. *Animal Behaviour* 10:231.

————. 1964b. Structure and Distribution of a Kodiak Bear Population. *Journal of Wildlife Management* 28:769–72.

VROOM, G. W., S. HERRERO, and R. T. OGILVIE. 1980. The Ecology of Winter Den Sites of Grizzly Bears in Banff National Park, Alberta. In *Bears—Their Biology and Management*, edited by C. L. Martinka and K. L. McArthur, 321–30. The Bear Biology Association Conference ser. 3.

WILSON, E. O. 1975. *Sociobiology: The New Synthesis.* Cambridge, Mass., and London: Belknap Press of Harvard University Press.

WIMSATT, A. W. 1963. Delayed Implantation in the Ursidae with Particular Reference to the Black Bear. In *Delayed Implantation*, edited by E. C. Enders, 49–76. Chicago: University of Chicago Press.

Acknowledgments

It is a pleasure to thank Dr. Allen W. Stokes for selecting me to work on the Utah State University brown bear research project at McNeil River and for his guidance during my studies. His review of this manuscript was helpful and much appreciated.

My research was entirely funded by the National Science Foundation and Utah State University. I am most grateful for the support.

I am especially thankful to Derek Stonorov for conceiving the Utah State University research project and for organizing and funding it initially. Derek's early work was the basis for all the studies that followed.

Allan Egbert and Michael Luque helped me to learn the bear identities in the summer of 1973.

The Alaska Department of Fish and Game provided facilities in 1973 and allowed Jim Taggart and me to stay in the McNeil camp during 1974 and 1975. I am grateful for the access to McNeil Falls for this study.

My thanks to Jim Taggart are too many to mention: Thanks Jim.

Bill and Barbara deCreeft, owners and operators of Kachemak Air Service, not only flew us to McNeil each summer, but also provided us with mail service and radio communications through the summer. Barbara filled our grocery and supply lists for Bill to deliver. These services, which are daily routine for the deCreefts, can be fully appreciated only by those living in the Alaskan bush.

I give special thanks to Larry and Mo Aumiller for their friendship and invaluable assistance on my return visits to McNeil 1976 through 1984. Larry is the best thing that ever happened to the McNeil bears. His genuine care and love of the bears is a breath of fresh air. He has kept me informed and up to date on the annual activities at the falls. Larry's review of this manuscript was much appreciated.

Elizabeth Mills produced all the excellent drawings in the text. Libby's extended stays at McNeil gave her the insight to create her wonderful illustrations.

I should like to thank Dr. Donald A. Ingold for inspiring me to study animal behavior and ecology, and for his friendship and guidance in the early 1970s. His reviews of this manuscript over the years from its early stages to the final form was helpful and appreciated.

Index

Page references to illustrations are in **boldface** type.

239